THE
ART Of
RAGTIME

The collected Works of Scott Joplin by Vera Bodsky

P45 - The death of ragtime.

Facsimile of an ad composed and distributed
by John Stark, in 1916.

THE
~(ART OF)~
RAGTIME

Form and Meaning of an Original
Black American Art

WILLIAM J. SCHAFER
AND
JOHANNES RIEDEL

With assistance from
MICHAEL POLAD and RICHARD THOMPSON

A DA CAPO PAPERBACK

Library of Congress Cataloging in Publication Data

Schafer, William John, 1937-
  The art of ragtime.

  Reprint of the 1973 ed. published by Louisiana State
University Press, Baton Rouge.
  Bibliography: p.
  1. Ragtime music—History and criticism. 2. Afro-
American music—History and criticism. I. Riedel,
Johannes, writer on music, joint author. II. Title.
ML3556.S34 1977   781.5'72   76-51398
ISBN 0-306-80057-8

ISBN 0-306-80057-8

First Paperback Printing 1977

This Da Capo Press paperback edition of *The Art of Ragtime* is an
unabridged republication of the first edition published in Baton
Rouge, Louisiana, in 1973. It is reprinted by arrangement with
the Louisiana State University Press.

Published by Da Capo Press, Inc.
A Subsidiary of Plenum Publishing Corporation
227 West 17th Street
New York, N.Y. 10011

The following musical examples are reproduced by permission: Gladiolus Rag, Scott
Joplin's New Rag, and "Stoptime" Rag, all by Scott Joplin; and Trilby Rag, by Carey
Morgan (copyrights 1907, 1912, 1910, 1915 by Edward B. Marks Music Corporation,
copyrights renewed, all rights reserved, international copyrights secured).
  Excerpts from Scott Joplin's Maple Leaf Rag, Peacherine Rag, and Eugenia are from
The Collected Works of Scott Joplin (Copyright © 1971 by the New York Public Library)
and used by permission of the editor, Vera Brodsky Lawrence.
  Excerpts from Scott Joplin's *Treemonisha* are from *The Collected Works of Scott
Joplin* (Copyright © 1971 by the New York Public Library) and are used by permission
of the editor, Vera Brodsky Lawrence, and by permission of the Music Trust of Lottie
Joplin Thomas.
  Quotation from *The Life and Death of Tin Pan Alley*, by David Ewen (copyright 1964
by Funk & Wagnalls Publishing Company, Inc.) reproduced by permission of the publisher.

This Book Is for Two of
the Tutelary Spirits of Ragtime
James Hubert (Eubie) Blake and
Charles Edward Ives

Contents

Acknowledgments

So many people have helped us with advice, encouragement and vital materials for this study that it is difficult to express our thanks adequately to all. We owe everything, of course, to the legion of men and women—many now lost in the anonymity of history—who created and played ragtime. To our contemporaries who shared this work with us, we must give profoundest thanks.

The staff of Indiana University's Lilly Library made available the large Dr. Saul Starr collection of sheet music. We thank especially William Cagle, Assistant Rare Books Librarian; Miss Geneva Warner, Librarian for Reader Service; and Mrs. Constance Work, Reference Librarian.

Frank Gillis, Director of the Archives of Traditional Music, and David Baker, Assistant Professor of Music at Indiana University, provided advice, counsel, and materials. Also, Robert Gunderson, acting director of the American Studies program at Indiana University, we thank for sponsoring our work on campus.

Richard B. Allen, curator of the Archives of New Orleans Jazz at Tulane University, gave judicious and highly detailed criticism and additional information. Richard also brought our work to the attention of Lars Edegran, pianist and leader of the New Orleans Ragtime Orchestra, to whom thanks are also due for his reading and criticism.

Paul G. Kaatrud, a student in the music program of the University of Minnesota, we thank for his lengthy and painstaking work with the bibliography.

Workers who contributed many hours of small but vital chores to the research and collation of materials for this study, include Nina Archabal, Bertus F. Polman, Colleen T. Davidson, and Jean Strommer. Without their work, all the many loose ends would yet be untied.

Michael Polad and Richard Thompson are acknowledged for their meticulous transcriptions from phonograph records and for many long hours of consultation, argumentation, and discussion concerning all facets of the art of ragtime.

We owe especial thanks to the hardest workers in the field of ragtime: to William Russell, for generously contributing many rare items from his matchless collection of American music materials and for his advice and support; to Rudi Blesh, the Columbus who first charted the continent of ragtime, for his active encouragement and kind interest in our project; to Max Morath, who has clearly inherited Tony Jackson's mantle as "the greatest single-handed entertainer" in the ragtime tradition, for his inspiration-by-example and his interest in our writing.

Our appreciation also extends to the National Endowment for the Humanities, which helped sponsor the research and writing; to Berea College, for its sabbatical leave program; and to the University of Minnesota, for its active interest in ragtime as a significant branch of American music.

Introduction:
Tempo Di Rag

WHY STUDY RAGTIME?

Ragtime, the first black music of the United States to achieve wide commercial popularity, was a pervasive and profound influence on the shape of American music, changing the concept of the popular song and popular dance styles. It was disseminated and thoroughly appreciated in Europe, directly influencing such giants of modern music as Claude Debussy, Erik Satie, Igor Stravinsky, Darius Milhaud, and Paul Hindemith—just as it influenced a generation of American composers, beginning with Charles Ives. It inspired a new direction in the musical theater, both in America, through the work of Irving Berlin, Cole Porter, and other masters of the Broadway musical, and in Europe, through new theater forms by Bertolt Brecht and Kurt Weill, among many others.

Ragtime, as a written and published musical form, communicated both black folk styles of playing and black conceptions of art music. Whereas earlier forms of black music—work songs, plantation songs, spirituals, and minstrel tunes—existed essentially in performance, with only a sporadic tradition of transcription and publication (notably the works of Dan Emmett, Stephen Foster, and James A. Bland) to make them widely available, ragtime was conceived and executed as a written piano form. It was possible, in the ragtime years of 1895–1915, to hear ragtime performed by itinerant pianists, on piano rolls, in adaptations by minstrel troupes and casual instrumental ensembles, through the work of popular singers—and it was also possible to obtain full and accurate scores of classic ragtime. Ragtime effected a total musical revolution, the first great impact of black folk culture on the dominant white middle-class culture of America.

xi

Commentators on black music generally work backwards in regard to ragtime, beginning with later developments in black music — specifically jazz — and viewing ragtime as at best a precursor, an interesting fossil curiosity found on the road to a fully developed black art form. Scott Joplin and his peers, however, conceived ragtime as a complete and self-sufficient art music in itself. It was their careful, imaginative interpretation of the virile and fecund folk music tradition of the Negro in America. Ragtime was a fully developed piano form, with a unique structure and organization, and it established a lively tradition of composition and performance that spread across America in two brief decades. As an aesthetic force, ragtime communicated the astonishing intellectual and artistic abilities of the black man at a time of crisis and confusion in the racial history of the nation.

In addition to the impact of written piano ragtime, there occurred simultaneously the impact of the folk *style* of ragtime on popular music. The heavily syncopated, regularly rhythmic style of ragtime was a living folk tradition long before the publication of scored ragtime and the development of a classic ragtime tradition. In schematic form, it can be said that classic ragtime derived from traditions of minstrel music, through the popular rage for "coon songs" in the 1890s, through a similar fad for march-cakewalk music for dancing in the late nineties, on to classic ragtime as formulated by Scott Joplin and his peers in Missouri from 1900 to 1910, through popular adaptations of piano ragtime as instrumental music and in song forms, on to late adaptations of ragtime as dance music (the foxtrot and variants) from 1910 to 1920. The immense popularity of instrumental jazz and vocal blues then displaced ragtime as the central black popular music form.

Yet it is oversimplifying, in the fashion of most histories of jazz, to say either that jazz grew from ragtime or that jazz was a more sophisticated and more interesting development of ragtime. History is rarely so neat, rarely follows the metrical regularity of chronology or the symmetrical logic of commentators.

Just as the history of ragtime as a style antedates and postdates the history of ragtime as a popular written piano music, so the influence of ragtime concepts precedes and follows the public popularity of ragtime. Jazz is clearly something more than instrumental ragtime, and as clearly, piano ragtime is much different from jazz piano styles. It is vital to distinguish between forms of black music, to trace the contributions of each form and give it its due after a half-century of misconceptions and oversimplifications. If we are ever to understand and appreciate the wonderfully diverse and imaginative contribution of the black man to American culture, we must begin by seeing how individual artists worked with specific genres and how their work contributes to a total culture.

One basic reason to study ragtime now, some sixty years after its genesis and eminence, is to recognize the inspiration of the men who played and wrote it. The story of ragtime is a significant chapter in the history of twentieth-century American music, and it is long past time to give Scott Joplin and his co-workers the recognition they sought vainly in their lifetimes. Joplin was in every sense of the term a serious musician with lofty goals and complex musical insights. That he should die in isolation and neglect, misunderstood and ignored, is a major tragedy not just for the development of black American music but for all our culture. That he should die relatively young, at forty-nine, when he should have been at the peak of his powers, intensifies the tragic quality of his story. His career epitomizes in many ways the story of the black musician in America— ephemeral success followed by cold neglect and relegation to the status of an exploited and discarded popular entertainer. It was not only Joplin's large-scale works—*A Guest of Honor, The Ragtime Dance* and *Treemonisha*—which were ignored by the public; his best piano rags were also largely overlooked in the hubbub of the marketplace. For a few years Joplin's name was golden, and anything he wrote sold in respectable numbers. And certainly John Stark stubbornly opted for quality in his publications, backing Joplin, James Scott, and Joseph Lamb when the public fancy turned to novelty sensations. But some of Joplin's finest rags came late in his career and received scanty attention from a public apparently sated by the deluge of commercial ragtime. Experimental works like "Euphonic Sounds," "Magnetic Rag," or "Stoptime Rag," or the excellent concert waltz, "Bethena," never received the attention paid to "Maple Leaf Rag" and other early sensations.

A primary goal of this study is to restore an understanding of the best of ragtime. It is past one hundred years since Joplin was born, and there are indications of a sensitive and thorough revival of piano ragtime by young men and women, musicians born a half-century too late to live through the golden age of ragtime. They are demonstrating that ragtime is not a relic, a dead issue from ancient times; it is as alive as intelligent and careful performance can make it. This book is offered as a starting point for study and performance of the art of ragtime.

MATERIALS FOR THE STUDY OF RAGTIME

The beginning of any study of ragtime is the excellent social history, _They All Played Ragtime,_ by Rudi Blesh and Harriet Janis, which has stood as the standard reference work and "bible" of ragtime for twenty years. It contains a great wealth of social, musical, and biographical information on ragtime and its practitioners, including photographs, letters, interviews, scores, and a comprehensive listing of books, scores, piano rolls, and discs. Our debt to _They All Played Ragtime_ is monumental. It is impossible to acknowledge this book's all-pervasive influence, since it provides all central data for a study of ragtime. Anyone beginning to study ragtime must use _They All Played Ragtime_ as his point of departure.

Why, then, another study of ragtime? Because there is a need for a thorough examination of ragtime's form and structure and of its influence on white popular music and culture. Little has been written on the structural characteristics of ragtime, its existence as a unique musical formation; and much that has been written about the musical techniques and materials of ragtime is erroneous or superficial. This study undertakes to analyze exhaustively ragtime's aesthetic and musical contributions to black and white musical culture.

Other work on ragtime is insightful and of great use to the student. Guy Waterman has written analyses of ragtime structure: "Ragtime," in *Jazz*, ed. Nat Hentoff and Albert McCarthy (New York: Grove Press, 1961); and also "A Survey of Ragtime" and "Joplin's Late Rags," in *The Art of Jazz*, ed. Martin Williams (New York: Oxford University Press, 1959). A detailed examination of rhythmic foundations of ragtime is given in Frank Gillis, "Hot Rhythm in Ragtime," in *Music in the Americas*, ed. George List and Juan Orrego-Salas (Bloomington, Ind.: Indiana University Publications, 1967). Ann R. Danberg Charters has studied the pentatonic scale patterns and certain harmonic progressions in "Negro Folk Elements in Classic Ragtime," in *Ethnomusicology*, V (September, 1961), 174–83, and has a lengthy introduction to ragtime in her anthology *The Ragtime Songbook* (New York: Oak Publications, 1965). Elliott Shapiro included facsimile copies of selected sheet music covers in his article "Ragtime, U.S.A.," in Music Library Association *Notes*, VIII (June, 1951), 457–70. In *Ragtime Blues Guitarists* (New York: Oak Publications, 1970), a guitar instruction manual by Stefan Grossman, a few guitar rags are included; and Eileen Southern, *The Music of Black Americans: A History* (New York: W. W. Norton Co., 1971), Chapter 11, presents a survey of ragtime style and personalities. Several periodicals deal with ragtime exclusively—most useful are *The Ragtimer*, published by the Ragtime Society of Toronto, and *The Rag Times*, published by the Maple Leaf Club of Los Angeles. More articles of direct interest are listed in the bibliography, along with phonograph records and other materials.

The importance of ragtime in the rise of black music in America cannot be overstressed. Ragtime must be included comprehensively in any study of Afro-American music, and it must be examined as more than a sidelight or digression in the broad way of black music. Some questions which need to be answered about ragtime are: Why should a piano form occur at all so early in the history of popular black music? What role did the piano have as an "acculturating" force among black Americans? It is significant that Joplin considered his work to be art music and that he spent his career trying to demonstrate the "legitimate" qualities of ragtime, its rightful place as an art form and not an ephemeral entertainment curiosity. The piano itself was the king of instruments, as far as the middle-class American of the nineteenth century was concerned—representing a tradition of romantic keyboard virtuosi, a symbol of respectability, gentility, and economic security. To what degree did the drive toward white middle-class acceptance motivate Joplin? Because ragtime was a strongly pianistic music, conceived as a total exploitation of keyboard resources for the production of dance music, we need to know more about piano sales, promotion, and production relating to the emerging Negro at the end of the nineteenth century. Research is also lacking on the relationship between country folk forms in primitive ragtime style and the development of a written form. Undoubtedly much of this development from a rural to an urban form can no longer be traced, since the generation of pre-ragtime performers is long dead. But a thorough study of country blues, juke-band and play-party songs relating to ragtime would be exceptionally useful. Ragtime's direct comparison with early jazz is an open topic, also—especially the apparent division between blues and ragtime musicians in early ensembles, the distinction made between blues as "low-down" lower-class music and ragtime as the acceptable music of middle-class working musicians like Charles Love, Manuel Manetta, Armand Piron, and Lorenzo Tio, Jr., in New Orleans and of the New York musicians who disdained country blues forms. Another open and important area of research is investigation of original ragtime manuscripts (where they exist) and publishers' interpretations or "corrections": to what degree did the commercial publishers edit and rearrange the composers' original intentions?

Ragtime was, in the history of black music in America, a form precariously balanced between rural folk traditions and sophisticated urban musical forms. It bridged a gap between early wholly oral traditions and later scored versions of jazz and dance music, and it provided a clear example of a successful black art form. For ragtime achieved its goals in large part; and Joplin, Scott, and Lamb forged a large body of finished and self-consistent works of art and transmitted them to a large audience. This pattern was later recapitulated in the history of jazz, as musicians worked to assimilate and reorganize the folk materials of jazz to create a new art form — culminating in the works of jazz composers like Jelly Roll Morton, Joe Oliver, James P. Johnson, Duke Ellington, and their followers. The example of ragtime as an antecedent form directly influenced these composers. Thus any study of the formulation of the art of jazz must proceed from a knowledge of the art of ragtime.

One basic reason for any study of the art of ragtime is to encourage performance. If commentators on black music can move performing artists to include ragtime in their repertoires as an essential black musical accomplishment, then it will again exist as a living and vital cultural force. Such meticulous and comprehensive projects as *The Collected Works of Scott Joplin*, edited in two volumes by Vera Brodsky Lawrence, will help disseminate musical scores; and much more of this vital work must be done by musicologists and archivists. Beyond this, concert performers must be petitioned to include ragtime as a basic part of their repertoires of American music. Ragtime has suffered from the same disgraceful negligence as other contemporary music, and it is long past the time when practicing American musicians can ignore their heritage. The time has come when American concert audiences, students, and performing musicians should have the chance to hear classic ragtime played with the same love and care given to Bach, Chopin, or

Bartok; when ensembles should play ragtime instrumental transcriptions; when opera companies should stage Joplin's *Treemonisha,* the first ragtime opera and one of the earliest and most imaginative folk operas. America must acknowledge its rich artistic heritage, black and white, and hear itself singing.

Many performers have helped keep ragtime traditions alive. One of the most indefatigable laborers in the fields of ragtime is Max Morath — pianist, singer, racounteur — who has made innumerable appearances as a pianist and lecturer on the art. He has produced a remarkable series of programs covering all aspects of ragtime for educational television, constructed a brilliant one-man show which has played Broadway and toured the country, and he continues to travel as an ambassador for the music. Eubie Blake, an original ragtimer, is still very active after a phenomenal ninety years, still playing beautifully and completely belying his age. Younger pianists like Joshua Rifkin, William Bolcom, and Alan Mandel now work with ragtime as a serious musical form, presenting beautifully organized concerts and recordings of the music. Many other musicians in the United States and Canada — Trebor Tichenor, John Arpin, Dick Zimmerman, Bob Darch, Donald Ashwander, Thomas Shea, and many more — study and play ragtime; and active groups in Toronto, Los Angeles, St. Louis, and other cities offer extensive aid and comfort to the ragtimer. Rudi Blesh has worked for thirty years to spread the word about ragtime — through writing, recording, interviews, and lectures, seeing his pioneering book, *They All Played Ragtime,* through four editions in twenty years.

While it is important that these artists and amateurs of ragtime continue their work, it is also time that music schools, universities, and cultural institutions of America offer serious support for the study and performance of ragtime in all its forms. It is time for us to realize Scott Joplin's concept of ragtime as a noble, beautiful, and intricate art — an American art of the first rank.

Echoes From Etude:

HOW THE WRITERS AND CORRESPONDENTS FOR *Etude Magazine* VIEWED THE NEW MUSIC OF RAGTIME.

F.H.F. — "Rag time" is a term applied to the peculiar, broken, rhythmic features of the popular "coon song." It has a powerfully stimulating effect, setting the nerves and muscles tingling with excitement. Its esthetic element is the same as that in the monotonous, recurring rhythmic chant of barbarous races. Unfortunately, the words to which it is allied are usually decidedly vulgar, so that its present great favor is somewhat to be deplored.

(October, 1898)

M.E.P. — "Rag-time" is essentially a simple syncopation. The faculty for it must be acquired, much like a taste for caviar. The negroes of the South employed it in the banjo accompaniments to their songs, but not until the "midways" of our recent expositions stimulated general appreciation of Oriental rhythms did "rag-time" find supporters throughout the country. There are several varieties of this rhythm, the most common being those in which the regular beats of the melody alternate with those of the accompaniment, and vice versa. There are various degrees of skill in this process of distortion, and occasional chromatic progressions in the bass add greatly to the weirdness, if not to the beauty, of "rag-time." Another of its peculiarities is that its best exponents are generally execrable musicians.

(December, 1898)

W.R.B. — "Rag-time" originated in the South, where bands of colored musicians first played it. These bands are not usually organized, not uniformed, being volunteer affairs. The colored race is extremely imitative, and, all playing mostly "by ear," any mistake or peculiarity made by one band, which happens to take their fancy, is readily taken up by all the others.

This music got its name from the rough appearance of the bands, which are called rag-bands, and the music rag-music, or "rag-time" music.

The popularity of "rag-time" music is certainly not diminishing, and it remains to be seen what effect it will have on the American music of the future.

(February, 1900)

THE
ART Of
RAGTIME

What is Ragtime?

*We look to the future for the American composer, not, indeed, to the
Parkers and MacDowells of the present, who are taking over a foreign
art ready-made and are imitating it with more or less success and with
a complete absence of vital force, but to some one as yet unknown,
perhaps unborn, who will sing the songs of his own nation, his own
time, and his own character.—London Times, 1913*

Scott Joplin: b. November 24, 1868—d. April 1, 1917

*If one gets the feeling . . . of these shifts and lilting accents, it seems
to offer other basic things not done, or done very little, in music of
even beats and accents; at least, it seems so to me.—Charles Ives, 1922*

RAGTIME IS DEAD! LONG LIVE RAGTIME!

As with all forms of popular culture, myriad legends and
misconceptions exist about piano ragtime. The mythical (but
useful) Man on the Street, asked for an impromptu definition
of ragtime, would doubtless answer something like this: "Oh,
yeah—ricky-tick piano music, knocked out on an old out-of-
tune barroom upright, with thumbtacks in the hammers. You
know, that fast, jerky music they used to play for silent movies."
He would envision a mustached, white figure of the nineties,
with striped silk shirt, straw skimmer, arm garters, red vest or
suspenders. The name would conjure up nickel beer, swinging-
door saloons, brothels, steamboats, a massive apparatus of
sentimental nostalgia and pure hokum.

If this simple stereotype can be dismissed quickly, even more
learned or considered definitions of ragtime appear weak under
scrutiny. A few casual examples may suffice. *Webster's Seventh
Collegiate Dictionary* defines ragtime as "rhythm characterized
by strong syncopation in the melody with a regularly accented
accompaniment." This seems sound for a vest-pocket definition,

and most people would accept it as accurate enough. However, it is fundamentally misleading and might be mistaken for a thorough description. It relies on the single characteristic of syncopation as the key to ragtime. But is ragtime *always* syncopated? Is this even the basic characteristic of the style? A more learned definition partakes of the same misleading generalization: "The essence of the rag is its unremittent *pattern* which, though habitually syncopated, is never violent."[1] This attempts to be more exact, emphasizing "pattern" (or formal organization) and qualifying the remark on syncopation with "habitually," but it is still an open-ended statement.

A second problem in defining ragtime is the way most commentators view black music. Ragtime is usually considered quickly and casually, as an amusing but trivial progenitor of jazz, a music of little intrinsic interest aside from its role as a precursor of the more complex and important jazz. Even highly sympathetic and sensitive critics err here. For instance: "In itself, ragtime proved to be a kind of blind alley, but its contribution to jazz, and to form in jazz, is probably immeasurable."[2] Or, in one of the best succinct definitions, Gunther Schuller describes ragtime as "another form of American Negro music leading toward the full flowering of jazz."[3] While this viewpoint is not totally erroneous, its constant repetition has had the effect of devaluing ragtime or concentrating only on its contributions to jazz. It makes the history of ragtime lopsided—as if ragtime had been nothing more than an ancestor of jazz. It ignores other qualities and ingredients of ragtime, folk sources and accretions; and it leads toward viewing ragtime as a dead and feebleminded proto-jazz (which also contributes to poor performances of ragtime by jazz-oriented pianists).

A third fallacy, implied in the Man on the Street's view, is a moral judgment of ragtime which has persisted since its first

[1] Wilfrid Mellers, *Music in a New Found Land* (New York: Alfred A. Knopf, 1964), 277.
[2] Martin Williams, *The Jazz Tradition* (New York: New American Library, 1971), 26.
[3] Gunther Schuller, *Early Jazz* (New York: Oxford University Press, 1968), 34.

popularity—that it is "whorehouse music," or in more directly racist terms, "nigger music," that it is inherently inferior, barbaric, crude or grotesque. Whether this view stems from a moral judgment that syncopation is sinful ("Who put the sin in syncopation?") and somehow carries suggestions from its inception in sporting house districts and black ghettos, or that any black music is inferior to products of white culture (since it is the product of an inferior race)—this view is uniformly malignant and destructive. Its appearances are most often covert, but it is a perverting innuendo which must be quashed in any intelligent examination of ragtime.

If we are to understand ragtime, we must guard against these fallacies and stereotypes. Mainly, we must proceed not with generalizations but with specific examinations of ragtime, its sources and effects. We must distinguish between kinds of music grouped under the rubric of ragtime, differentiate between folk resources and developments of the popular music industry, examine elements of ragtime which have kept the music alive and well for three quarters of a century.

Ragtime is a black musical form developed and brought to maturation between 1890 and 1910. It is rooted in several musical traditions, all vital in the flow of folk and popular urban musical culture of the late nineteenth century. Basically it is a formation, an organization of folk melodies and musical techniques into a brief and fairly simple quadrille-like structure, written down and designed to be played *as written* on the piano. It is formational music, as distinct from improvisational music. In a sense, ragtime composers served as folk collectors or musicologists, collecting music in the air around them in the black communities and organizing it into brief suites or anthologies which they called piano rags. (This process is exemplified in the title of Scott Joplin's first published work, "Original Rags," which uses the plural form. Evidently the term "rag" was applied to simple black folk melodies, and Joplin was asserting that this was a collection of rag tunes of his own invention.)

The form, then, is a unified medley, sewing small musical elements into an extended composition. This is ragtime's first important characteristic: *it is a vehicle for transmitting black musical materials previously only used in simple song forms.*

The ragtime composers constructed a method for musical organization. But what materials were they organizing? Basically the sources of ragtime flow through two distinct channels: (1) "pure" folk musics—*i.e.,* black music created by nonprofessional musicians for self-entertainment, handed down and preserved by oral traditions; and (2) professional-commercial strains of minstrelsy and vaudeville. From early in the nineteenth century, various white arrangers had transmuted black folksong into products "presentable" for genteel audiences. Stephen Foster is the prime example of an observer living outside the black community drawing on black folk-community resources. The entire tradition of white (*i.e.,* blackface) minstrelsy also lived as a parasitic organism, albeit a highly effective one. Ragtime composers, then, drew from black sources either directly or at one remove. This distinction is a subtle but very necessary one.

The materials of ragtime were primarily brief melodies melded into a coherent pattern. But what was the pattern, and why were ragtime composers moved to construct it? The answer is crucial to an understanding of ragtime: *Ragtime is based on black dance music.* The little melodies collected and integrated by ragtime composers were primarily dance tunes; a piano rag is a keyboard dance suite, and the rhythmic impulse behind the music is one intended as accompaniment for dancing, for expressive physical motion. This fact, certainly clear in the era of ragtime's inception, has become blurred by subsequent stereotypes about the music. The Man on the Street imagines the ragtime pianist as a shadowy figure in the corner of a sleazy bar or brothel, beating out tinkly background music for communal sin, pre-electric Muzak. The use of piano rolls and nickelodeons created this stereotype, and there is no denying what ragtime became as it was commercially exploited. The point is that it was conceived as a highly functional music, as a formalized communal dance music.

This is supported by an example like Scott Joplin's *The Ragtime Dance,* a formally designed suite which appears in an abbreviated (4-minute) standard form and in an extended (20-minute) ballet version. It is a stylized suite of dance tunes illustrating a wide range of rhythm patterns and dance steps. In its unabbreviated form, *The Ragtime Dance* included a "caller" who announced the dances and dance figures for each segment; it was arranged, in fact, as a highly formalized ballet suite. This points back to ragtime's ancestry in the quadrille, a formal nineteenth-century dance notable for two characteristics also shared by ragtime: the adaptation of widely miscellaneous popular/folk song materials, and a great range of rhythmic and melodic flexibility. Joplin's highly imaginative adaptation of formal ballet attitudes to his ragtime style reveals at once the folk roots of the genre and his persistent intention of organizing his music as a complex art form. Joplin also used rag tunes throughout his opera *Treemonisha* the way he had used them in his piano rags, as dance music expressive of elegant motion. And many classic rags are designated as slow-drags, marches, two-steps, or cakewalks. The dance tradition which grew up with ragtime was double-stemmed. There were the traditions of genteel white ballroom dancing of the nineteenth century, drawing on the polka, schottische, two-step, jig; and there were the folk dance forms of black culture—cakewalks, buck dances, breakdowns.

These folk dance forms undoubtedly originated as playtime dances on the plantations (and may have transmitted tribal/communal dance rituals and forms from Africa), but they were widely disseminated and adapted through white minstrel shows. Repeatedly, in observing the growth of ragtime, we can see how black folk feelings and forms flow out of the black community, through white entertainment media, and back to black creative sensibilities before they are developed and widely accepted. White minstrelsy served a vital function in the nineteenth century by making black music "respectable" or palatable to white audiences, thus giving black musicians a chance to present their own work to an audience at least partially educated in the feeling of black music. Beyond that, the cruelties, ironies, and paradoxes of black-white relations confuse the scene—a recurrent theme in the story of ragtime.

The basic dance rhythm of ragtime is that of the two-step or cakewalk—a rather formal, if nonetheless exuberant, dance, a promenade or grand march form. This is not what we normally think of as popular dancing. Later forms—which grew up after ragtime—supplied a musical background or vehicle. The Grizzly Bear, Bunny Hug, Texas Tommy, and Turkey Trot are stages in an evolution toward the fast dances of the 1920's: the one-step, Charleston, Black Bottom, Lindy Hop, and other variants of Vernon and Irene Castle's one-step or foxtrot and of the eccentric dancing of vaudevillians like Bert Williams. The dances which Turpin, Joplin, Scott and other ragtime pioneers scored were social dances of some regularity and stylization. The cakewalk, for example, is essentially a grand promenade with improvisatory possibilities. Its rhythmic feeling is that of the march. This is consonant with developments in white genteel dancing, also; John Philip Sousa's "Washington Post March" was first used to introduce the two-step (and was so identified with it that the dance itself was often called "The Washington Post"). The use of $\frac{2}{4}$ march rhythms (sometimes even the $\frac{6}{8}$ of cavalry marches) in polkas and galops accelerated transmutations in dance forms, and grand promenades, marches, and medley dances (like the lancers) were very popular. When Jelly Roll Morton sang the epic of his "transformation" of old quadrille tunes into "Tiger Rag," he described one basic process of ragtime, although it is doubtful that the process worked as smoothly and consciously as Morton implied.

The dance feeling in ragtime cannot be overemphasized. It is clear that it was the single most vital impulse behind the creation of ragtime, and it is the source of the complex rhythmic pulse in the music. Ragtime composers consciously aimed to write a music which would inspire its hearers to dance, which could provide an interesting pattern for dancing. And clearly this was the basic use of ragtime — rhythmic piano sounds converted into motion. The fluidity and percussiveness of the piano keyboard were put to a complex task. The music provided a steady rhythmic pulse linked by exciting fluid phrases. The pioneer ragtime composers worked to undergird melodic folk tunes with strong rhythmic foundations, to assert both sides of the music simultaneously — lyrical beauty inseparably meshed with rhythmic vitality.

The question of syncopation arises at this point. If ragtime is essentially an extension and reprocessing through black imaginations of the march or quickstep ("the evidence points overwhelmingly to the march as the formal progenitor of ragtime"[4]), why has the popular definition always turned on the phenomenon of syncopation? This is basically a symptom of ragtime's initial impact on the white listener, its reception at the end of the nineteenth century. To a modern listener, familiar with half a century of jazz and its all-pervasive influence, ragtime does not seem highly syncopated or "hot." (Again, many jazz-oriented pianists impatiently insert jazz rhythms they expect to hear but which simply are not there in ragtime scores, creating a bastard jazz/ragtime form.) However, to a white listener in the 1890's, schooled in European rhythms or the bland popular arrangements of folk tunes, ragtime seemed massively syncopated, positively shocking in its broken rhythms and shifted accents. This is also a function of ragtime's regular marchlike bass line,

---

[4] *Ibid.,* 33. The identification of ragtime only with syncopation occurs quite early. An explanatory note attached to Ned Wayborn and Stanley Whiting's "Syncopated Sandy" of 1897 (billed as "May Irwin's Great 'Rag-Time' Song") is explicit:

The authors and publishers in presenting "Syncopated Sandy" to the public have succeeded in illustrating for the first time the absolute theory of the now famous "Rag-Time" music, which originated with the negroes and is characteristic of their people. The negroe [*sic*] in playing the piano, strikes the keys with the same time and measure that he taps the floor with his heels and toes in dancing, thereby obtaining a peculiarly accented time effect which he terms "Rag-Time."

"Rag-Time" is an exaggerated form of what is known in musical literature as Syncopation, illustrated thoroughly in "Syncopated Sandy."

which does accentuate the irregularity of treble syncopations.[5]
Thus, an immediate response to ragtime centered on the "new"
device of syncopation, and this tended to become the only cri-
terion for defining the ragtime feeling. Popular piano instruction
courses advised students that any music could be "ragged"
simply by shifting accents, by introducing syncopation. And one
of the stock devices of Tin Pan Alley rag songs was the ragged
allusion—a popular tune, hymn, march, introduced into a strain
but with ragtime syncopation and bass.

This is not, however, the process by which ragtime composers
created classic ragtime. Examination of a Joplin rag shows that
syncopation is sporadic and relatively restrained, not a ceaseless
device. Some strains may be free of syncopated measures.
Further, a simple test can be conducted: select a classic rag,
play a strain as written, then play it with syncopations omitted,
with all accents falling regularly on the beat. It will still sound
unmistakably like ragtime—less lively, perhaps, or oddly mis-
shapen, but ragtime nevertheless. Syncopation is not the *sine
qua non* of ragtime; it is simply one characteristic among many
which define the form. A smug coverall definition which asserts
that ragtime is simply "syncopated music" misses the fact of
varied rhythmic resources in ragtime, the many devices which
develop the rhythmic flow in the music. Exploring the range
of ragtime, we find devices like the break, stoptime, various
complex bass patterns beyond the usual march or oompah
bass line and many other methods of varying and contrasting
rhythmic patterns.[6] The very construction of the rag as a multi-

[5] One hallmark of ragtime is the polarity of left- and right-hand patterns, which when
organized into the multithematic march-trio structure of many rags inevitably suggest
the treble-bass parts of the standard band march. It can hardly be coincidental that the
golden ages of the brass band march, the cakewalk, and ragtime occurred nearly simultaneously in America.

[6] Jazz terminology is useful here, since these same musical devices appear as standard
practices in later jazz (and other black music forms). Brief definitions may be helpful:

break—an abrupt cessation of the basic rhythm and the bass line, with a single line
inserted into the hiatus, as a contrast to the regular bass-treble flow of sound.

stoptime—a broken rhythmic pattern of single-note figures separated by rests, accen-
tuating the sound through the repeated silences; used as a standard accompaniment
for eccentric and tap dances (see Joplin's "Stoptime Rag").

thematic form insures rhythmic variety. So, to designate syncopation as ragtime's only unique or distinctive characteristic is to miss entirely the shading and feeling behind the structure.

Related to this insistence on ragtime's supposed limitations or simplicity is the feeling that it is inherently a less expressive music than jazz (part of the "mere-precursor" syndrome). This attitude is clearly expressed by so acute a commentator as Wilfrid Mellers:

> Rag is the Negro's attempt at the buoyant optimism of the Sousa march and the brilliant elegance of the Gottschalk dance, and the mass feeling is depersonalized because personal feelings may be too much to bear. In this sense, rags are an *alternative* to the blues; and their use of the discipline of military music becomes equated with the disciplined non-humanity of a machine. This is literally true: for many rags were transferred to the pianola roll and, even if not played by a machine, should be played *like* a machine, with meticulous precision.[7]

Several fallacies are apparent in this definition. If rags are an "alternative" to the blues, does this mean they express totally different feelings, and how can such a statement be demonstrated? What of the pianists of the next generation (James P. Johnson, Willie the Lion Smith, Fats Waller) who amalgamated ragtime and blues styles? That rags were transferred to piano rolls and therefore are mechanical is obvious *ex post facto* reasoning. There is no reason to assume that since commercial manufacturers applied a mechanical recording method, the only way to record pianos accurately at that date, to ragtime it was because ragtime was inherently mechanical; this is like saying that since Caxton chose quite early to print Chaucer's work, it was because Chaucer was a cold, mechanical writer, well suited to the new medium of movable type. The phrase "should be played *like* a machine, with meticulous precision" seems to conceal a couple of misconceptions: (a) that precisely played music is automatically machine-like (Does this apply to per-

[7] Mellers, *Music in a New Found Land,* 278.

formances of Bach, Mozart?); and (b) that, by comparison with jazz or blues piano, ragtime is "precise" (Does this mean that jazz/blues styles are inherently sloppy or imprecise?).

This attitude is only a way of pointing up the expressive qualities of jazz and blues at the expense of ragtime. We contend that ragtime is a highly expressive music using many of the same resources of jazz and blues, that it is not emotionally limited or restrained. It is more accurate to say that it is a decorous music — i.e., it follows a well-defined form and obeys simple rules within that form. The whole question of expressiveness becomes a chimera, since there is no clear way of articulating what a music expresses. It is the same dangerous procedure as saying that Beethoven is more expressive (or emotional) than Scarlatti. Ultimately this kind of assertion only reflects a subjective preference or a wholesale generalization too large to be useful. Certainly it is clear that blues and jazz piano styles do things beyond the scope of ragtime; it is not at all clear that there is any basic superiority in doing these things.

An essential problem is that these critical errors arise in part from viewing ragtime exclusively as a *genre*. While there is a basic and simple form to piano rags, this is not the whole of their value. Ragtime is also a *style*. A fundamental rule in the history of black music seems to be that style precedes form; a form or genre develops to fill an emotional need or to accomodate a set of musical techniques. Ragtime style clearly existed before the first piano rags were written. It was the style of banjo virtuosi and string bands, minstrel shows and buck dancers. It was a folk style, a black mode that grew through the nineteenth century and ultimately coalesced in the complex works of Scott Joplin and his peers in the Midwest in the 1890's. That style, Ur-ragtime, existed before classic ragtime, coexisted with it, and continued to exist long after the heyday of the classic rag composers. It can be heard in recordings of black and white string bands, jug bands and country guitarists, well into the 1930's. As late as the 1960's, a fine country folk guitarist,

Elizabeth Cotton, recorded a little folk rag, "Washington Blues," and Mississippi John Hurt recalled a fine archaic version of J. Bodewalt Lampe's "Creole Belles." This "play-party" country ragtime style is of great age and hardiness. Classic ragtime — basically the work of three gifted men, Scott Joplin, James Scott, and Joseph Lamb — was the ultimate coherent organization of ragtime style, but it was by no means its only manifestation. Folk ragtime, classic ragtime, popular-commercial adaptations, and ragtime influences in jazz are different shapes of the same impulse, not separate entities or modes of music.

The flowering of ragtime between 1895 and 1915 was probably understood well by discerning listeners of the era. This has caused some confusion among later commentators, for early discussions of jazz often label it as "ragtime," since this is how people heard early jazz — as another version of instrumental ragtime. (The term *jazz* was a novelty word, a catch-phrase applied first as a libel on the Original Dixieland Jazz Band, then used to its advantage, when the public caught it and demanded to know what this "jass music" might be.) Early jazzmen understood that they played ragtime. The shading from instrumental transcriptions of classic rags, to popular ragtime songs, to head arrangements of folk tunes, to early jazz was a gradual process over a decade and a half; no one woke up one morning to exclaim, "Today, early jazz has been born out of classic ragtime by Tin Pan Alley, with Joe Frisco as midwife." Obviously, ragtime musicians intuitively understood what we may overlook — that cultural evolution is a slow and confusing process, as mysterious and inexorable as biological evolution. The musicians continued to create music from materials they knew firsthand — basically from music inspired by or stolen from ragtime.

If ragtime is a style, a method of organizing folk materials, as much as a form or genre, it is clearly not the same kind of style as jazz. Ragtime is not improvisatory music, not based on the principle of theme-and-variations which controls jazz

performance. It is closer in spirit to most traditional folk musics
—*i.e.,* ragtime tunes tend to be received and repeated as heard,
in a line of oral tradition.[8] What distinguishes ragtime from, say,
Appalachian balladry, in which old Scots-English folksongs
were passed from generation to generation without substantial
change, is that during the late 1890's a group of creative musicians attempted to organize and rework traditional black
materials in a new and revolutionary manner. The ragtime
pioneers took folk style as a point of departure and created
from it a permanent written form. There is a strong analogy
with the work of folk-oriented musicians in England at about
the same date. Composers like Ralph Vaughn Williams, Frederick Delius, and Gustav Holst worked in much the same way
as Turpin, Joplin, Scott, and Lamb. On the Continent, composers like Grieg and Dvořák — somewhat later, Bela Bartok —
also worked as collectors. They found folksongs or folksong
fragments and synthesized them, along with their own original
materials, into larger compositions, formal works which reflect
the spirit of folk music in an organized, architectonic fashion.
The ragtime pioneers in middle America, however, had a vastly
more difficult task, since they worked with music of a despised
minority in an atmosphere considerably more hostile to artistic
pretensions. No wonder that Joplin broke his heart, mind, and
body at his labor, that James Scott ended his career puzzled
and cynical, that Joseph Lamb retired from music and stowed
his manuscripts away for half a century. No wonder that,
flowering in a basically hostile and commercial culture, rag-

[8] One basic aspect of ragtime's folk basis is often overlooked or misunderstood by
commentators who deal with it solely as a jazz-related idiom. Like most folk-derived
dance music, ragtime is a static or nondevelopmental form—*i.e.,* it tends simply to state
and to juxtapose a series of musical themes, which are then repeated *exactly* as first
stated. It does not treat themes as bases for improvisation or as sources for complex
enlargement. The form tends to be brief, simple, and highly repetitive. Themes, once
stated, are repeated literally with little variation or embellishment. Many country
dance tunes are simply the same melody repeated over and over, *ad infinitum,* or until
the dancers tire. Ragtime drew on such varied medley forms as the quadrille, which at
least offered a series of contrasting tunes (sometimes with different tempos or rhythmic
patterns), which relieved the monotony of severe and unvaried repetition, and which
offered the dancers changes of pace, a series of dance-forms to follow.

time was transmuted into a vulgar and cheap password for snappy dance and inane lyrics. America's commerce-culture has always possessed an inverted Midas touch, a backwards alchemy, turning artistic gold into pure dross.

Ragtime, then, became a folk medium for transmitting the spirit and substance of black dance/folk tunes in the shape of a decorous and aesthetically interesting structure. This brings us, in another gyre, back to white minstrelsy, which did some of the same work in a less organized way. Viewed historically, ragtime seems to grow directly from the last traditions of the blackface minstrel shows. The legendary Ben Harney, sometimes credited with introducing piano ragtime (as distinct from string music and songs), went to Tony Pastor's theater to bring ragtime to New York. Pastor himself was a renowned minstrel of half a century's experience. Obviously these men viewed ragtime as a logical extension of the "coon songs" and minstrel novelty numbers which they had known over their long show business careers. This brings us in turn to the complex attitudes of white America toward the black man and his music. For the vehicle of white minstrelsy was as obvious an example of pervasive racism as is possible to find, and at the same time it was a means for bringing black music — and to at least a marginal extent, the black man's imagination and vitality — to white America. Tony Pastor himself, at the moment when classic ragtime was being born, summed up his view of his work in minstrelsy.

> "The intention of the originators of this kind of entertainment," said the veteran minstrel, as he warmed to the subject, "was to picture the negro of the South in all his simplicity, his happy-go-lucky way of living, his quaint humor and his inordinate love of music, both vocal and instrumental, in its crudest, plainest possible form. It was a decided novelty in the line of public amusement and rapidly became popular, not only in the Northern States, but also below Mason and Dixon's line, in the home of the American negro himself."[9]

[9]Tony Pastor, "The Beginning of Negro Minstrelsy," *Ev'ry Month* (September, 1898), 10–11.

The number and complexity of racist assumptions here are astonishing. They are fairly overt and obvious, as is the tone of condescension in the statement. Clearly, Pastor felt himself superior to "the negro of the South" and subscribed to beliefs in the black man's "happy-go-lucky way of living, his quaint humor and his inordinate love of music" and deliberately chose words like "crudest" and "novelty." The basic object of white minstrelsy was to present a caricature of the black man as a target for malicious humor.

Ernest Borneman has traced five stages in the evolution of the black stereotype in minstrelsy, culminating with actual black artists working in their own tradition. He sees in the history of minstrelsy a coalescing of earlier attitudes toward the black man, moving from a view of the black man as "a barbarous, comic and somewhat childish figure," to "an attitude of pity and compassion," to a conception of the black man as "a patriotic character," until minstrelsy itself emerged with "a further advance in social and political awareness which is reflected in the use of actual folk song material."[10] This complex and now largely lost social history culminates at the end of the century with an authentic black musical culture in ragtime composition. But ragtime carried with it, at least implicitly, this twisted heredity of white attitudes, misconceptions, superstitions, and fears. They exist as a dim shadow in the background.

However, the immediate paradox involved is that minstrelsy formed a medium of transmission for genuine black musical traditions. The minstrels sought strictly commercial products, but they were shrewd enough to use folk music of considerable quality and power. And there was a broad streak of presumably genuine sympathy for the black man in minstrelsy. Pastor speaks not with the violent racism of the rabid white supremacist but with the gentler tones of middle-class superiority and super-

[10] Ernest Borneman, *A Critic Looks at Jazz*, quoted in Rex Harris, *Jazz* (London: Pelican Books, 1952), 56.

ciliousness. At any rate, the simplistic assessment of black life that Pastor transmits is part of the deep and persistent mythology of the Old South which lay behind minstrelsy and which was transplanted into ragtime. The tradition of the "coon song" depicts the black man as a gross comic caricature — stupid, shiftless, superstitious, mysterious, and ultimately harmless. It is a partial antidote to the other ominous social tradition of the Klan and violent racism which depicted the black man as bestial and an impending threat hovering on the outskirts of orderly white society. In this respect at least white minstrelsy was not as destructive or corrosive as it might have been.

The point is that when black ragtime departed from the popular line of the "coon song" and the grotesque dances of the minstrel show, it carried with it a built-in freight of this racism and the concomitant myth of the Old South, so that even the work of serious black artists partakes of the idiotic paraphernalia and terminology of the minstrel show. Music publishers, capitalizing on the old love for "funny coons," tended to push ragtime as another manifestation of this imbecilic psychosis of racism. It is important not to confuse black satire on white attitudes, the quiet rebellion of irony, with the genuine tenets of white supremacy. One critic states it concisely: "Yet while rag is a composed music, an emulation of white techniques that seems to belie the instinctual character of American Negro music, it is also in an odd way a parody music — like the cakewalk from which it had descended. And we cannot be sure whether it parodies the white man's image of the Negro or the Negro himself."[11] It is important to recognize the reflexive irony in ragtime, especially in ragtime songs and titles. It is not an indication of subservience or self-loathing on the part of the composers but an instance of the defensive humor and sheer endurance to which the black artist was driven in his bondage.

On the positive side, ragtime inherited from minstrelsy a profound sense of showmanship and the exuberance of a suc-

[11] Mellers, *Music in a New Found Land,* 277.

cessful tradition of popular performance. Yet this is also a double-edged weapon. Joplin became famous overnight with "Maple Leaf Rag." He was then forced to carry the burden of popularity — the inevitable compulsion to continue with success — atop his already difficult ambitions toward serious composition and acceptance. Once stereotyped as a minstrel-style entertainer, it was difficult for the ragtime composer to demonstrate that his work was serious and significant beyond the reach of popular art.

These are the conditions under which ragtime was born, under which ragtime composers labored. Like all black artists, they worked in exile in their own land, and their efforts were persistently misunderstood, scorned, or perverted by the white culture which was exposed to them. Further, the handful of men working seriously with ragtime as a complex and aesthetically operative form were misunderstood or exploited even within their own culture:

> The tragedy for Joplin was that the Negro musicians with whom he was associated in New York rejected him even more completely than the white audience did. The young Negro composers like J. Rosamond Johnson, Tim Brymn, Chris Smith, and James Reese Europe were as uninterested in the richness of their musical tradition as the white composers were — unless they could make some money out of it. When the tasteless and degrading "coon songs" were popular — the most popular of them all was written by a Negro — the young Negro composers wrote "coon songs," when tangos were popular they wrote tangos, when blues were popular they wrote blues. In fact, their appreciation of the musical genius of Scott Joplin was even less enthusiastic than that of many white composers. They felt that ragtime music was "low class," and as members of an insecure middle class they seemed to be afraid to associate with the music in any more than a very superficial manner.[12]

Ragtime, heir to an ambiguous tradition of racism and exploitation, was stricken from its inception.

[12] Samuel B. Charters and Leonard Kunstadt, *Jazz: A History of the New York Scene* (Garden City, N.Y.: Doubleday and Co., 1962), 45-46.

However, this might be said of any important artistic idea or movement grounded in popular culture. In every case, the great pitfall, the great enemy of quality and intelligence in popular art, is not social or political oppression but commercial exploitation. The commercialization of ragtime is a parallel to its finest achievements, and we must take into account the perversions and purely commercial mutations of the form as well as the handful of masterpieces written outside the bounds of commercial interests. The story of ragtime is, in large measure, the story of honest artists transcending the restrictions of their culture — both the miseries of the black community and the temptations of the larger white society. What is important to emphasize and to see clearly is the magnitude of the achievements of ragtime, despite the forces set against it. That it ever came into being is miracle enough, but that it went on to change the whole shape and meaning of American popular music transcends the miraculous. For it is justifiable to say that American music was never the same after the explosive impact of ragtime at the turn of the century.

The most immediate effect of the "ragtime revolution" was to bring attention to black musicians, either as serious artists or as capable and inventive entertainers. Black musicians had seized control of the image of the black man in popular music, as white minstrelsy died upon their emergence. After all, what they offered was the real thing, not a mime or imitation. So, whites who were attracted to minstrelsy because it fed their ideas of a strange and fascinating image of the black man were now further fascinated by the black man appearing on his own, no longer a puppet but a three-dimensional and indisputably living man. For more than a century, the Negro had been America's homegrown exotic, a local curiosity. No wonder black entertainers at least briefly continued the traditions of exoticism and caricature they inherited from white minstrelsy. This was their meal ticket, a goose which laid golden eggs for a century. But very quickly, with the emergence of such gifted all-round entertainers as Bert Williams, this image shifted to a much more positive and human one. And a pervasive figure, a ubiquitous character in the show business landscape, was the ragtime pianist, a new black man playing a new black music for America. It is again miraculous that white Americans were able to respond so quickly and positively to this revolution.[13]

The constant expression of ambivalence in white attitudes emerges as clearly in ragtime as anywhere in the culture of the era. Race relations were at a point of crisis at the end of Reconstruction. The nation had opted for the "solution" of reconciliation with the South by forfeiting black rights (through the adoption of innumerable Jim Crow laws)—and the black population was offered as hostage or scapegoat, to form a buffer in the movement toward pacifying and accepting the conquered South. The mythology of Dixieland grew up, a self-consciously nostalgic regionalism recalling antebellum days, the golden age before the wounds of war ruptured the Union, when peace was maintained at the price of slavery. The repression of black people at the end of the nineteenth century was a concession to militant racism, a return to conditions before the war, as if the North were willing to say, "See, we don't like niggers any better than you, so let's keep them in their places and sing ourselves to sleep with an old darky lullabye."

Part of the mythology was inherited willy-nilly by black musicians of the era. Ragtime and related rag songs and dance

[13]One of the earliest comprehensive discussions of the history of minstrelsy and its connections with ragtime, Charles Reginald Sherlock, "From Breakdown to Rag-Time," *Cosmopolitan,* XLI (October, 1901), 639, makes some concise observations on the dance-dramatic elements of the new music and the black man's new role in minstrelsy:

In the back streets of most Southern cities the eccentric evolutions of the buck- and wing-dancers have been known for years. Even the rag-time, that decidedly unique phenomenon of harmonies, is a child of the stage. As for the cake-walk, it had been a waiters' diversion in hundreds of hotels long before it was subjected to the glare of the footlights, and introduced into ballrooms to relieve the monotony of the Virginia reel. . . . in the end the American negro has come into his own. And that he reads his title clear is proved by his determination to share the rewards of minstrelsy with his white imitators. The Georgia Minstrels were the most notable of the early organizations in which genuine black men replaced the usual white performers, and in these latter days the company of real "coons" and "yaller gals" and "pickaninnies" with its cake-walks and characteristic rag-time songs has almost a monopoly of the negro minstrelsy field. The real negro is on the stage himself in full feather, for the first time in his history the professional disputant of the white actor in the same line.

forms were self-consciously exotic or grotesque. The tradition of minstrelsy, especially the "coon songs" in vogue in the nineties, was based on the proposition that black people were alien, exotic, esoteric, mysterious. Hence the demand for expression of this feeling in popular music, the blending of other exotica with rag songs — "Indian intermezzos," orientalia, Hawaiian songs.[14] Ragtime became our own "primitive" music (a feeling often still expressed in later jazz, as in Ellington's "jungle music" for the elaborate reviews at the Cotton Club). The implication of this trend (a double vision combining the old Noble Savage philanthropic condescension toward the blacks with a nostalgia for the Old South in all its unreconstructed glory) is that black culture is at best a species of "uncivilized" or "instinctual" activities. Many serious black musicians of the time — Will Marion Cook, James Reese Europe, W. H. Tyers — worked hard to erase this image, rebelling against the stereotype of the black musician as a menial entertainer. Although economic and social pressures forced these men to work at least in part as commercial tunesmiths or jobbing musicians, they strove to be accepted on white society's highest terms. In part, the same impulse toward respectability and acceptance motivated Scott Joplin and the early ragtime masters, who were consciously turning simple folk materials into polished and controlled art.

The last problem of ragtime is this one of art: the complex formula for musical expression called ragtime is more than a product of social and historical forces; it is also a conscious aesthetic construction. We return to questions of definition, of limiting and explaining what this style and genre were, what they became. A basic force behind all genres and modes of

[14]The impulse to pull together "sure-fire" elements of popular music into novelty songs led to weird and hilarious efforts toward portmanteau music in the early ragtime years. Every trend was followed and every conceivable combination of ingredients tried in the search for new and better songs, leading to such grotesque absurdities as "The Oriental Coon," by Edward Rogers (1899), "The Spanish Coon," by George A. Nichols (1904), and perhaps the ultimate in synthesis, "Arrah-Wanna: An Irish-Indian Intermezzo," by Theodore Morse (1907).

black music is the principle of eclecticism — the ability to absorb, rework, and develop every musical material and influence, to be protean, taking on any shape yet remaining substantially the same in feeling or spirit. An initial problem with any attempt to describe black music is the temptation to limit and restrict. The music itself expresses a voracious creativity and imagination, while musical history or criticism tries to be exclusive and categorical.

Criticism like Rudi Blesh's *Shining Trumpets,* for instance, fails because it sets up absolute standards that are contradicted by hundreds of examples from the music itself.[15] The "norms" of black music tend to be inclusive and flexible, and black music is the product of black musicians (or "black-trained" white musicians) trying to communicate special feelings to a black audience. Every phase of black music has tended to be at once traditional and revolutionary, drawing on old and continuing feelings but putting them into new and startling shapes. Every phase has created its own rules and decorum, but in every case there has been a direct communication with an active audience — a group which used the music for communion and self-expression, through participation (usually through dancing). It is important that we see ragtime as a significant part of this development of black cultural traditions. Ragtime was the vanguard for the musical/cultural revolution of the American Negro in this century.

A recent comprehensive critical work, Ben Sidran's *Black Talk,* reveals a basic flaw in its inability to deal with ragtime as a legitimate aspect of black music. In Sidran's view, ragtime is only "a perversion of commercial and white-oriented music, embellished with various harmonic flourishes." Because ragtime's characteristics fail to fit his basic thesis, which describes black music as basically oral in conception and tradition, he cannot allow it in his complex scheme. Therefore, it is dismissed peremptorily as "watered-down" rhythmically. Because rag-

[15] Rudi Blesh, *Shining Trumpets* (New York: Alfred A. Knopf, 1946).

time was, according to Sidran, "basically a piano music, conforming to the nonvocal properties of the instrument and lacked the great rhythmic drive that generally characterizes black music,"[16] he throws it out of the canon. This kind of procrustean methodology ultimately tells us more about the critic, his limitations and preconceptions, than it does about the music itself. Any theorizing about black music which has to omit or disregard a major thrust toward a black art form like ragtime cannot be very strong. It is not enough to wish away history in the interest of neatly symmetrical logic.

To dispel myths and misunderstandings about ragtime, to at least crack the old image of the honkytonk piano and clattering pianola, we must look at the men, music, and times from which ragtime flowed. It is not easy, after seventy-five years, to grasp the feelings of an era, but through the still-living medium of the music itself we may approach it. If we listen to classic rags, and even to the commerical songs derived from them, we may hear what it felt like to be a black artist, a black musician, struggling to live and feel and think clearly in the America of 1900.

[16] Ben Sidran, *Black Talk* (New York: Holt, Rinehart and Winston, 1971), 27.

⤌ II ⤍

The Impact of Ragtime

There are sincere and sensitive musicians who hold that "ragtime" is decadent and deplore its popularity as an evil sign of the times. They see in it all the worst characteristics of the modern American (many of them, perhaps, caught from the despised negro race). — London Times, 1913

It would seem that the cultivation of Negro music is an important step — one of the most important steps — in the development of American music. — Current Opinion, 1913

Some regard [ragtime] as a national evil second only to the drug habit, while others think it is perfectly legitimate and may be found to be the basis of a national school of composition. — The Musical Monitor, 1919

O spiritual, work-song, ragtime, blues, jazz —
consorts of
the march, quadrille, polka, and waltz!
— Melvin B. Tolson, Harlem Gallery, *1965*

Ragtime arose directly from the traditions of white minstrelsy — traditions overtly racist in character and manifestation. Sheet-music covers from 1895 to 1915 reveal in visual form the virulence and grotesqueness of this warped vision of the black man. In cartoon form, the black man (or woman) is guyed, with enormous lips and eyes, an exaggerated "savage" or primitive aspect, grotesquely flashy clothing, all the marks of decadence described in standard racist folklore and propaganda.[1] In the

[1] Sheet-music covers of the era make a fascinating study of the social/cultural values of the middle class, the consumers at whom the mass-produced music was aimed. For instance, the success of Kerry Mills's cakewalk series engendered a whole spate of imitations, which even copied the cover design rather slavishly. There is a clear and distinct "cakewalk design" which can be followed from cover to cover, usually a line drawing of a bucolic scene on a plantation, with cartoon-style blacks frolicking behind stylized semi-art-nouveau poster lettering. Other instances of trends and fashions in

lyrics, racist jokes and epithets abound. The Negro is the constant butt of crude and simpleminded jokes, a total stereotype. The choicest jibes are rudimentary and consist basically in reiterating fears and hostilities of white society. One song sums it up in chorus (and title) by linking "a watermelon, razor, chicken, and a coon." In translation this might read: "Gluttony, murder, thievery, and stupidity." Clearly the persistent slander and ribaldry mask very deep fears, fears in turn generated by guilt and anxiety. The black man is depicted as lazy, stupid, and helpless (yet simultaneously sly, murderous, and powerful). The black woman is shown as sexually desirable, promiscuous, presumptuous, and also cleverly malicious. Although such lyrics might be dismissed easily as another illustration of the general neurosis of American culture, the fact remains that along with this verbal idiocy there arose a strain of vital and clear black music of great nobility and power.

The insidious aspect of the tradition of the "coon song" and the minstrels' object of satire is that the music purported to be by and about black people, when in fact minstrelsy was a prolonged charade in which white people acted the roles of blacks — roles they projected onto the black personality. Thus they broadcast stereotypes and gross caricatures in the person of "black" people. This acting out of racist dramas is at once subtler and more effective as slander than expository polemics or fictions could ever be. It is a constant example held before people. In the hinterlands, where Negroes were rare, the minstrels must have been totally convincing as representations of these strange, exotic people. So, when black artists themselves produced a music which caught and held public attention, they had to fight a pervasive and corrosive tradition of racism already imposed on them.

An example of the white-imposed stereotype is Ernest

---

the illustrations emphasize how fierce the competition in the music trade was, where every kind of trick and nuance was used to sell copies. For a more extensive discussion of the sheet-music covers, see Appendix I.

Hogan's "All Coons Look Alike to Me," the great smash hit
and a typical sample of the "coon song" craze of the 1890's.
The unfortunate paradox of this example is that Hogan was a
black songwriter of some real merit. The chorus expounds what
is clearly a white attitude (all black people look alike and therefore are alike, all inferior, lacking individuality or distinctive
human souls); but it puts the sentiment in the mouth of a black
persona. The song, then, is doubly damning, for it makes "black"
people say exactly what a white racist would want them to
admit:

> All coons look alike to me,
> I've got another beau, you see,
> And he's just as good to me
> As you, nig! ever tried to be.
>
> He spends his money free,
> I know we can't agree,
> So I don't like you no how,
> All coons look alike to me.

The black woman purportedly singing this satisfies complex
demands of the devious racist mind. She is promiscuous, going
from one "beau" to another; she is stupid (only a stupid person
could not identify members of her own race); she is avaricious,
looking only for a free-spender; and she says precisely what all
racists want to hear, that there really are no differences between
black individuals, that they lack the nobility and intelligence of
real human beings.

Again, it is simple in the 1970's to dismiss this as an anti-
quated sickness, an example of outgrown feelings; yet the same
clichés and superstitions follow us today, and it is possible to
find covert references to such ideas in supposedly serious discussions of the problems of racism and identity. At any rate,
such is the mental world into which ragtime was born, the folly
which ragtime composers had to endure as a price of survival.
What is significant is that ragtime itself helped quell such
prejudices and gross caricatures of black reality.

The "coon song" craze was primarily a manifestation of white vaudeville trends. As early as 1893, the white vaudevillian May Irwin was using this material in her act, and she became firmly identified with a series of "coon songs" during their vogue. A white minstrel composer, Ben Harney, used what a publisher called "Negro Rag Tunes," markedly less offensive than most of the material. His songs have a genuine folk feeling and were probably simply collected from black singers and transcribed by Harney for his act. Such tunes as "Mr. Johnson, Turn Me Loose" and "You've Been a Good Old Wagon" avoid the directly inflammatory or derisive images of May Irwin's hits, such as "All Coons Look Alike to Me." During the commercial exploitation of the "coon song" fad, both black and white writers contributed equally malicious and stereotyped verses. It is difficult to choose between black Ernest Hogan's "All Coons Look Alike to Me" and white Dave Reed, Jr.'s "Leader of de Company B" or (for less vicious examples) between white Barney Fagan's "My Gal is a High Born Lady" and black Bert Williams' "Dora Dean." It is possible to plead that black composers wrote under the gun of dire economic and social necessity, but this hardly excuses the equal virulence of black stereotypes in their songs. It is impossible at this late date fully to understand the complex mental and social world of the period, the confusion and misunderstandings shared by white and black alike.

The racist elements in ragtime songs were a vehicle for commercial exploitation, an extension of "sure-fire" routines of minstrelsy and vaudeville. That they furthered social oppression is true, but this was only a by-product of their intent; first and foremost, they sold sheet music and music hall tickets. The attitude conveyed, like many racist stances, is ambivalent: the "inferior" darky's life is pictured as Edenic and enviable, a Land-of-Cockaigne existence, while simultaneously it is caricatured and debased. The black man, in this view, is truly the "white man's burden"—he sings and plays all day while the white man works and grinds compulsively in his constipated puritan way. This is a source of both irritation and superiority expressed ultimately as contempt for the lazy, shiftless darky.

One late "coon song" explicitly acknowledges the artificiality of this myth and compresses a whole series of racist and ethnocentric clichés into one expression; this is the Williams Brothers' "Niggerism" (1899):

> If you go to a theatre,
> A minstrel show to see;
> On the stage are darkies,
> As happy as can be,
> A coon he loves to sing and dance,
> Until he is out of breath,
> All you've got to do is jolly him 'long,
> And he'll work himself to death.
>
> Now dat is what you call niggeris'm,
> An it taint no white folks is'm,
> Taint no Dutch or Irish is'm,
> So it must be niggeris'm
> An if it taint, please tell poor Ephram what it am.

The picture here is interesting mainly because it converts the folk mythology of the white man's burden into an overt ideology and because it accepts totally the illusion of the minstrel show.

But behind this contempt is a sneaking envy, a wistful longing to be able to relax and be free, like the mythical levee lounger with his watermelon and banjo. Nevertheless, white minstrelsy and commercial songwriters depended almost solely on black folk sources for material. In this slough of sickness and perversion a curious backhanded compliment is submerged, a tribute to the vitality and interest of black music and its creators.

In terms of chronology, ragtime arose as an identifiable genre by the end of the 1890's. Folk rags and ragtime styles existed much earlier—in banjo styles, in song forms, and in folk piano styles. In the first half of the 1890's the popular music market was bombarded by a succession of "Ethiopian oddities," "darky songs," "coon songs," and "plantation songs." These all clearly showed the mark of the minstrel tradition, but they were produced as individual songs, out of the context of the comedy and dance routines of minstrelsy. They became staples of musical revues and music hall acts beyond the confines of the minstrel shows themselves. The "coon song" craze was a huge popular success, and it momentarily revitalized the blackface impersonation as a staple popular musical routine. Nostalgia for the minstrel show died hard—sturdy remnants of it motivated Al Jolson's success and even inspired the long-lived Amos 'n' Andy radio series. By 1895, a new vogue was in swing, the "characteristic march and two-step" or "patrol" based on black folk themes. This was quickly identified with the dance music known as the cakewalk, and suddenly there was a flurry of cakewalk music—essentially marches for piano, but with a lilting insistence borrowed from brief, syncopated source tunes. As early as 1892, D. Emerson published a banjo-piano instrumental transcription entitled "Kullud Koons' Kake Walk (See Appendix II)." From 1897 to 1900 the cakewalk was an international fad, only supplanted by the emergence of piano ragtime itself, as the Missouri ragtimers published their work. When W. H. Krell's "Mississippi Rag," Turpin's "Harlem Rag," and Joplin's "Original Rags" were published (among the earliest compositions actually called rags) there was a solid ground of interest in black song forms and in piano adaptations of these forms.

It is, in part, only a matter of terminology. The term "rag" must originally have designated a short folk tune, possibly a little song of derision. These small ditties were collected into larger compositions. This manner of constructing a medley, of synthesizing diverse and probably familiar tunes is shown clearly in Ben Jerome's "A Bunch of Rags" (1898). The score indicates the titles of tunes incorporated: "I Guess That Will Hold You for Awhile," "Hesitate, Mr. Nigger, Hesitate," "I Don't Like That Face You Wear," "I Wonder What Is That Coon's Game," "No Coon Can Come Too Black for Me," "Dat Yaller Gal By My Side," "She's a Spectable Married Cullud Lady," "Keep Your Eye on Your Friend Mr. Johnson" and "The Wedding of the Chinee and the Coon." This is all noxious "coon song" material, and it seems to be arranged with a "program," as a suite, suggesting a miniaturized version of a musical revue or operetta, reduced to piano score.

Another example of the process of suite composition comes in the two ragtime medleys by Blind Boone, the black piano prodigy from Missouri who led a long and illustrious career as a touring pianist, playing everything from classics through folk and popular songs of the day. His only ragtime compositions — "Boone's Rag Medley No. 1" and "Rag Medley No. II" — are suites of folk and rag song material. "Boone's Rag Medley No. 1" is subtitled "Strains from the Alley" (urban material) and indicates at least some of the lyrics to the tunes: "I got a chicken on my back," "Oh, no Babe!," "Make me a pallet on the floor," "I certainly does love dat yellow man" and "Dat nigger got lucky at last." The "Rag Medley No. II" is subtitled "Strains from Flat Branch" (rural material) and includes "Carrie's gone to Kansas City," "I'm Alabama bound," "So they say" and "Oh! honey ain't you sorry." The suites, which Boone wrote down *ca.* 1910, are clearly syntheses of various materials he collected on his travels through the Midwest. It is representative of the way the itinerant ragtime "professors" must have accumulated and organized their materials.

Scott Joplin's first published ragtime work was "Original Rags," with the plural indicating the same process of synthesis of themes. It is another step toward creation of a form, since these are "original" rags, i.e., tunes invented by the composer. After this the term "rag" comes quickly to indicate the larger structure, a unified whole; so the form changed from an un-integrated to an integrated and coherent composition in a few short years.

An interesting process of synthesis and creation was under way at the end of the 1890's. The most successful writer of cakewalks was Kerry Mills, a skillful and prolific hack composer capable of writing in any popular idiom and of instantly capitalizing on any fad. His "At a Georgia Campmeeting" (1897) is permanently identified with the word "cakewalk," and it is a good example of Mills's shrewd inventiveness. It is subtitled "A characteristic march which can be used effectively as a two-step, polka or cakewalk" and is part of a series — "Kerry Mills' Two Step Marches." This points directly to the march antecedents of ragtime and indicates a bridge between the old two-step danced to Sousa's "Washington Post March" and the emerging styles of black-derived dance, now called (in omnibus fashion) the cakewalk. Mills's composition is successful because it so thoroughly synthesizes musical materials: a regular piano march structure of several strains, with repeats, bridges, and trio effects combined with an old folk tune ("Our Boys Will Shine Tonight") guaranteed to evoke a complex Civil War/Old South/Minstrel nostalgia. All of this — using rhythms reminiscent of minstrel dances like the grand walk-around, with a percussive, banjo-like sonority. It would be hard to construct a better model for popular success. Mills's other cakewalk/march compositions are equally facile and melodic ("Whistlin' Rufus" is the only example much heard today).

The cakewalk fad was fueled by music provided largely by white composers. Besides Mills's series of tunes, Abe Holzmann wrote "Smoky Mokes," "Hunky Dory," "Bunch O' Blackberries," and other highly successful and infectious pieces. The composer-arranger J. Bodewalt Lampe contributed "Creole Belles" in 1900, at the end of the fad. The cakewalk was a natural for instrumental transcription and adaptation, and Sousa's band made a hit with Arthur Pryor's arrangements of these and other cakewalk tunes, taking the music all across America and Europe.

By 1900 the ragtime craze reached a peak. That is, the term "ragtime" was in vogue and widely applied (and misapplied). It was enough of a fad term to merit Robert S. Roberts and Gene Jefferson writing a song to detail its ubiquity — "I'm Certainly Living a Ragtime Life" (1900). However, it was not necessarily accepted as an accurate or meaningful label. James Scott's first compositions were still designated as marches or two-steps, in the old manner, and not until 1906 did he publish anything specifically called a rag. Joplin's "Maple Leaf Rag," a pinnacle of success in classic ragtime, came in 1899, although the balance of his writing was done later. And by 1899, S. Brainard and Sons, of Chicago, could publish *Brainard's Ragtime Collection* ("Being a Collection of Characteristic Two-Steps, Cake Walks, Plantation Dances, Etc."), which is almost wholly composed of white compositions from the tradition of minstrelsy, with a dominant mode of Old South evocation — titles like "Mississippi Rag" and "Cake-Walk Patrol" (both by W. H. Krell), "Florida Cracker" (Ellis Brooks), and "On a Southern Plantation" (Walter E. Petry). While not really a ragtime anthology, it capitalized on the name and vogue, and it does reveal some of ragtime's immediate sources.

As the traditions of white minstrelsy were displaced by a new synthesis of old folk tunes into instrumental structures, the music was reshaped and humanized, with racist lyrics and feelings of the old "coon songs" dropped or modified; and black folk musicians moved into a phase of popular music hitherto the province of hack composers working to meet the voracious demands of commercial minstrelsy and vaudeville. When Joplin's "Maple Leaf Rag" was a smash hit and made an unknown and modest Missouri man famous, a complex revolution in music was at least partially accomplished. Suddenly there was a demand for piano music of real folk feeling and quality, beyond the range of the pseudo-folk music produced as a matter of course for minstrelsy. It is significant that classic ragtime arose in Missouri, out of homemade music by largely untrained black men. The music they created is larger and more vital than the restricted products of the New York commercial music trade, and their example kindled a hinterlands rebellion. Composers all over the Midwest ground out "ragtime" compositions. Ragtime was a down-home music, produced on what was then part of the frontier. Only Joseph Lamb represents the city (and *not* the commercial music industry) as a classic ragtime writer, and his ambition was always to write as well as the black Missourians whose music he knew so thoroughly.

Along with the burden of racist traditions, ragtime also had to face demands of the commercial music market, at this time becoming a major cultural force, as new media of musical recording and transmission sprang up. This age begot Tin Pan Alley — coincident with the perfection of the player piano mechanism and the mass manufacture of the phonograph. There was an active amateur music movement, resulting in the wide sale of parlor pianos, music lessons, sheet music, a drive toward acquiring proof of "culture" for the newly settled middle class. It is not accidental that an instrumental music for piano should become widely popular. Ragtime was a pleasant alternative to Czerny exercises and the parlor classics, a relief to thousands of small boys and girls driven to daily practice, a boon to the semiskilled housewife looking for something interesting to whet her appetite. Because it did not pose staggering technical demands, ragtime appealed; here at last was a music relatively easy to grasp which was also eminently listenable. Thus, a market for ragtime existed and was satisfied.

The business of music publication at the turn of the century is an interesting study in shifting cultural/economic values. Hundreds of sheet-music publishers existed, many simply individual songwriters, music-store owners or other small-time entrepreneurs trying to break into the big time. They were scattered across the country in every city, large or small. While New York was indisputably the musical capitol of the nation, it was still possible to exist as a local musician, publisher, teacher, to compose and print sheet music for piano. Thus, the publisher's marks on ragtime scores are from every corner of the nation. Only a few, like John Stark, who published Joplin, Scott, and Lamb, were tenacious enough and honest enough to stick with ragtime through thick and thin. Most folded up silently, after an unsuccessful search for the right fad or fantasy to catch the "broad, flapping American ear," as Thoreau had called it. The appetite of the big publishers was whetted by grass-roots interest in ragtime. They often bought up and re-published promising works originally printed by small local publishers. A glance at a collection of ragtime sheet music from *ca.* 1900 shows two seemingly contradictory things: (1) the diversity of ragtime music, from many composers scattered over the country, and (2) the unity of the ragtime movement, the sense of a common trend being followed. This is sympto-matic of the popular music industry then, as now: once a fashion was established, a hit marketed, the rest of the industry moved to duplicate it as closely and as quickly as possible. The logic of the music business has always seemed to be "If one 'Maple Leaf Rag' is good and interesting, then let us have ten, a hundred, a thousand like it!"

The immediate effect of ragtime's popularity was to fuel the mass production of rags, ragtime songs, anything to capitalize on the trend. Hence, along with the work of sensitive and gifted musicians like Joplin and Scott, writing music they were born to create, there was an avalanche of pseudo-ragtime rubbish. This is easily dismissed today as clichéd, inept, and shoddy work, but in 1900, Joplin was competing with a formidable battery of publisher-underwritten hack writers, scavengers living off his inspiration. All the effects of the ragtime craze, however, were not bad. It did disseminate good ragtime along with the dross, and it did stimulate wide interest in the real thing. It took an acute sensibility like Joseph Lamb's or Brun Campbell's to pick Joplin's solid gold from the mountains of gilt, but they did manage to seize inspiration themselves from the work of the true ragtime geniuses.

These two examples — Lamb and Campbell — point to another trend of great import: the cross-cultural meeting of blacks and whites in the common interest of ragtime. While classic ragtime was clearly the creation of black men working in a rich folk tradition of black music, there was also a solid parallel tradition of white interests and capabilities. This emerges first in the de-cline of white minstrelsy, when veterans of the minstrel circuits first introduced folk rags to white audiences. Ben Harney is credited with introducing piano rags to New York, and he was essentially a minstrel entertainer doing what he had always done—interpreting black music for white people. But this was significantly different from the "coon songs" with their racist lyrics. In a sense, black music was now allowed to speak for itself, through the piano keyboard, regardless of the color of the player.

This is a key point. Again, we have a warped perspective on black music after a half-century of exposure to jazz. In 1900, black music was almost solely conceived of as rudimentary and quaint folksongs—spirituals, worksongs, "plantation songs" interesting mainly as remnants of the old slave culture and the black man's heritage of suffering. Audiences had been exposed to the music of choirs from Hampton Institute and Fisk University, knew simple arrangements of spirituals and adaptations of plantation songs (like Stephen Foster's). The stereotyped image was of a humble and untrained black man singing with natural or instinctual technique. One of ragtime's major contributions was to emphasize the black musician's ability to conceive and score a formalized instrumental music, quite an abstract form. There was an immediate shift in public recognition when the genuine complexity and sophistication of the piano form began to be understood.

When the Clef Club of New York, organized by skilled black composer-arrangers James Reese Europe and William H. Tyers, gave a concert in 1913, white reviewers were struck by the accomplishments of the music and musicians. It was clear that there were black musicians creative enough and competent enough to arrange and play music of a high order of complexity and interest. If the ragtime fad had not generally submerged the work of serious composers like Joplin and Scott so quickly, this might have been observed much earlier. However, if music critics and reviewers missed the immediate serious import of ragtime, musicians themselves did not. There were hundreds of immediate converts to ragtime, musicians committed to it—

both pianists and orchestral musicians. (Many older jazz musicians recorded in the traditional jazz revival of the 1940's still remembered and played classic rags, often still owned orchestrations.) The influence of ragtime on musicians was even more powerful than on the public imagination.

Some immediate questions occur: Why should an instrumental music without instant overt appeal through lyrics become popular at all? Part of the answer, to reiterate, is ragtime's association with the vaudeville tradition of "coon songs" and novelties like "Mr. Johnson, Turn Me Loose" or "You've Been a Good Old Wagon" of Ben Harney, which existed in parallel with the rise of ragtime. Undoubtedly audiences associated instrumental rags with songs they had known for a decade. Second, ragtime continued the minstrel tradition of black instrumental virtuosity; the long-standing image of the phenomenal banjo-picker was now transferred in part to an image of the agile and fascinating "jig-piano" player. A strong strain of this virtuoso feeling runs through ragtime. It is partly "show-biz razzle-dazzle," partly a basic feeling in the music, an attempt to create a complex and difficult form which is still highly expressive. This shows up early in pieces like Tom Turpin's "A Ragtime Nightmare" (1900) or Joplin's "The Cascades" (1904), later in showpieces by eastern ragtimers like Luckey Roberts and Eubie Blake. Jelly Roll Morton spoke of the ragtimers' habit of including "signature" pieces in their programs and of reserving especially brilliant and difficult numbers for ragtime contests. He demonstrated such pieces as Tony Jackson's breakneck "Naked Dance" and his own dazzling "Fingerbuster," as well as eccentric and imaginative novelties like "The Animule Ball." Some crowd-pleasers which might be used by ragtimers to demonstrate their technical skills are Jay Roberts' "Entertainers Rag" (1910), Robert Hampton's "Cataract Rag" (1914), and Joplin's "Euphonic Sounds" (1909). A third attraction of ragtime was its novelty, especially to listeners unacquainted with vaudeville and minstrel performances. The dissemination of sheet music and piano rolls suddenly put thousands of Americans in direct contact with black music for the first time, especially outside the South. A whole new world of music opened up, a music not too far from the spirit of Sousa's marches and the light dances of the day but with enough alien or exotic material to stimulate the imagination. Ragtime suddenly removed the walls from musical experience for many Americans.

It is no exaggeration to say that the modern music industry rose to full power on the tide of the ragtime revolution, an important point in the history of America's popular culture. It is true that the figure of the Negro loomed large in the popular imagination through works like *Uncle Tom's Cabin* (especially in its innumerable roadshow dramatic versions) and through folk-derived literary pieces like Joel Chandler Harris' stories. But this image had always been a passive and "external" one—the black man seen through white eyes, interpreted by white sensibilities, and produced for white consumption only. It portrayed a folksy oppressed black man, an object of pity and charity, basically a helpless victim of hard fate. With the advent of ragtime, a new and positive image of the black artist was available, largely through his own herculean efforts. Ragtime implicitly proclaimed that black artists stood on their own feet, met life's demands, and triumphed.

In contrast to the predictable moralizing about ragtime's wickedness, its low origins, there was also an intelligent and enthusiastic recognition of ragtime's originality, complexity, and manifold possibilities. Quite early in the century, white observers were intrigued by ragtime as a portent of a new age of black culture. One of the most detailed early examinations of black popular music gives a lucid insight into the impact of ragtime:

> Some authoritative colored men have traced the origin of the first "rag-time" melodies directly to the common working-songs and boisterous merrymaking of their own people; and in spite of white imitators and Broadway manufacturers of popular songs, no one can invent such attractive "rag-time" as that written by colored men (who are only just beginning to be adequately paid for their own

ideas); also ignorant colored people sing and play this kind of music naturally and instinctively in a way peculiar to themselves, and difficult, at first, to the average American. All this would help to prove the Negro's influence, at least, on the music of this country.[2]

After the initial impact of ragtime, white critics were deeply impressed by the form's art and vitality, enough so that one writer tried to combat a tendency toward overenthusiastic generalization: " . . . some critics have gone to the extreme of believing that in America the Negroes are the only native people natively musical."[3]

From about 1910 to 1925, considerable controversy developed over ragtime and (later) jazz. Part of the argument was simply confusion and animosity generated by any new and misunderstood popular phenomena—reactions of trend-watchers, custodians of the cultural establishment, and puritans of various stamps. But several strands of argument were important questions about the direction of American culture, especially questions about musical creativity and originality. Two camps developed: those who saw in ragtime and jazz a glimpse of the "music of the future" (*i.e.,* a new source of ideas and materials for American composers seeking an authentic native idiom), and those who saw ragtime and jazz as barbaric and corrupting expressions of a socially debased and genetically inferior people. These might be represented as avant-garde and conservative poles, but this is not precise. Nor is it altogether accurate to say that they represent tolerance versus racism. There were some tangled conceptions of taste and musical expression involved, attitudes essentially of the nineteenth century, in both camps. Basically the controversy is an extension of the long debate over the course of American music, nativist versus cosmopolitan, that began early in the nineteenth century.

There is a persistent strand of what might be termed "aesthetic

[2] Natalie Curtis, "The Negro's Contribution to the Music of America: The Larger Opportunity for the Colored Man of Today," *Craftsman,* XXIII (March 15, 1913), 661.

[3] *Outlook,* CIV (March 21, 1914), 611.

Darwinism" invoked by both pro-ragtime and anti-ragtime critics. This is the frequently expressed notion that there is something fundamentally "primitive" or "savage" in black music, an element appealing to the bestial in the listener and provoking him to wickedness, lewdness, or at best indecorousness. One early critic bases a lengthy jeremiad on the idea that ragtime rhythms are essentially barbaric and cause an hysterical reaction in the listener. Calling the ragtime craze a "new Tarantism," he says ". . . ragtime is rather a school than a rhythm. It denotes a species of music almost invariably associated with particular dances of a lascivious or merely ridiculous kind. . . ."[4] He goes on to use variants of this charge, noting that ragtime is a popular fad like various dance fads of the nineteenth century, only worse: "The *Valse Lente* might and doubtless did, drive people to conjugal infidelity, but ragtime, I verily believe, drives them to mania. . . ."[5] Finally, a form of racism emerges clearly when he describes ragtime songs as showing "precisely the kind of 'vitality' associated with Revivalism, and especially the type of Revivalism peculiar to the negro! What need have we of further witnesses? For of all hysteria that particular semireligious hysteria is nearer to madness than any other."[6] This is a stuffy upper-class British view of religious nonconformism and the "lesser breeds without the law" rolled into one diatribe, but it is fairly representative of the most violent attacks on the new Negro music.

Yet even early sympathetic descriptions of this new music could resort to decidedly peculiar "explanations" of the psychophysical reactions to ragtime. One early comment on syncopation as a musical device, and on the effects of ragtime, uses an odd bit of anthropology as apologetics: "Present rag-time is a ligno-musical stimulant. The ordinary music-listener wants to hear something musical that sets the head to nodding and the

---

[4] Francis Toye, "Ragtime: The New Tarantism," *English Review*, XIII (March, 1913), 654.
[5] *Ibid.*, 656.
[6] *Ibid.*, 657.

foot to stamping; something which he can grasp and comprehend with his present rhythmic sense, somewhat as he does a cane, because of his Simian descent."[7] Whether accepted tolerantly or derided, the idea of ragtime's "primitive" genesis with a "primitive" people clung to the music and obscured the aesthetics of the form for a full generation.

The ragtime controversy centered around democratic ideas of art and society. Pro-ragtime polemicists viewed the advent of a black-derived musical form of genuine substance and stature as a portent of greater things to come, a new wave of truly democratic culture. Anti-ragtime critics saw it as a symbol of decadence, a symptom of mass rule and mass culture, the overthrow of aristocratically dictated western art. The issue of race was sometimes overtly introduced, but most often it was a covert element in the argument, only glancingly acknowledged.

One of the most volatile anti-ragtime writers was Ivan Narodny, writing in 1913, who inaccurately described ragtime as a purely urban music: "It exalts the noise, rush and vulgarity of the street. It suggests repulsive dance-halls and restaurants. There is no trace of any racial idiom in a ragtime composition. It leaves rather images of artificiality in the mind." He proposed a "scientific" analysis of ragtime and its effects on audiences—a rough poll, as it turns out—and concluded by lodging the old antiexpressive charge against the music: ". . . I have found no genuine emotion in a ragtime composition." Since he mentions no specific works, it is hard to grasp what ragtime—commercial songs, instrumental versions, classic piano rags—he attacks. But he spoke directly to the future-of-American-music debate in his last sentences: "Like an American short story, drama or news article, it is altogether artificial, and without life and soul. It has no value in itself as a foundation of any future American music. . . ."[8]

While Narodny's essay is a hollow diatribe, it suggests the

---

[7] C. Crozat Converse, "Rag-Time Music," *Etude*, XVII (June, 1899), 185.

[8] Ivan Narodny, "The Birth Processes of Ragtime," *Musical America*, XVII (March 29, 1913), 27.

reactions of conservative musicians to ragtime, and there is an odd backhanded tribute to ragtime's impact here, especially to its unmistakable American qualities; however, the author saw nothing good in any of the distinctive features of modern American urban culture.

One of the strongest arguments for ragtime as the basis for a new American music was made by Hiram K. Moderwell, in 1915, when he described it as "the folk-music of the American city" and called it "the one true American music." He based his argument on ragtime's complexity and vitality, making sophisticated observations for so early a date (Scott Joplin was still alive, if in decline; James Scott was writing vigorously; Joseph Lamb was writing his best rags):

> It has carried the complexities of the rhythmic subdivision of the measure to a point never before reached in the history of music. It has established subtle conflicting rhythms to a degree never before attempted in any popular music or folk-music, and rarely enough in art-music. It has shown a definite and natural evolution — always a proof of vitality in a musical idea. It has gone far beyond most other popular music in the freedom of inner voices (yes, I mean polyphony) and of harmonic modulation. And it has proved its adaptability to the expression of many distinct moods.

And Moderwell recognized the connection of ragtime with dancing, even if he trod perilously near the "primitive-music" notion in his expression: "This ragtime appeals to the primitive love of the dance — a special sort of dance in which the rhythms of the arms and shoulders conflict with the rhythm of the feet. . . . " Moderwell's critique is well-organized and intelligent, if theoretical.[9]

A reaction to Moderwell's argument brought in obvious elitist ideas to refute the "new American music" concept: "The fundamental idea seems to be that if you can pervert the taste of ten million persons in these United States — no matter how inferior they are as a class — into liking a thing, you may

---

[9] Hiram K. Moderwell, "Ragtime," *The New Republic*, IV (October 16, 1915), 285–86.

then, with the fervor of a religious zealot, call the thing American
and insist that it is necessarily the fullest expression of the life
of the people."[10]

Moderwell's counter-retort seized directly on the elitist
assumptions: "The correspondent feels that the taste for ragtime is a depraved taste and that the class which entertains it is
an inferior class. Of course he is assuming that he is the superior."[11] Similar battle lines were drawn around ragtime and jazz
during the 1920's, with a strong liberal movement trying to
legitimize popular culture as an important and "respectable"
social phenomenon. Sympathy for black social and political
conditions was inevitably generated, and the racial issue became
a central topic. Thus, by a sidelong and indirect route, the argument shifted from aesthetics of popular music to social implications of the music. By the 1930's jazz was fashionable enough to
be the object of careful study and cultist enthusiasms. But the
first battles over ragtime prepared the way for a serious interest
in black music.

One strand of controversy over ragtime and jazz was an involuted and theoretical discussion over the "American music of
the future," largely stimulated by Anton Dvořák's visit to
America in the 1890's. Dvořák's famous advice to American
composers to cultivate their own garden—to use folksong
materials, especially black folk musics—had generated much
critical heat, little light, and little appreciable creativity among
working composers.[12] Dvořák himself had created the symphony
From the New World and the *"Nigger" Quartet* to show how
indigenous American materials could be sewn into a fabric of
late-nineteenth-century romantic music. American composers
had shown few signs of following his examples; however,
wide interest in the new black popular musics stirred academicians to evaluate the meaning and impact of ragtime and early
jazz. Unfortunately, few composers and critics involved took

[10] James Cloyd Bowman, "Anti-Ragtime," *New Republic,* IV (November 6, 1915), 19.
[11] Hiram K. Moderwell, reply to Bowman's letter, *ibid.,* 19.
[12] Anton Dvořák, "Music in America," *Harper's,* XC (February, 1895), 429–34.

the challenge seriously; most of them offhandedly dismissed ragtime and jazz as cheap, corrupt mass entertainment.

By 1920, Joplin had died of despair in neglect, even though a few early observers had admired his music. The period of classic ragtime was over, even if James Scott worked on for a few years and some secondary ragtimers (Charles Thompson, Henry Lodge) continued to compose and play in the idiom. The academicians nearsightedly sought a "major American composer" with a "program" of dignified and identifiable music on black themes. By 1920, Charles Ives had withdrawn from active composition, embittered by twenty years of neglect and scorn. The conservative musical establishment of the era blundered along in a paper war about the future of American music and the use of folk materials, when in fact the music they prescribed had already been written and rejected or relegated to the outer dark of "popular culture." Yet controversy rolled along for years, producing only a few thin puffs of smoke, a few dry columns in a journal or musical trade paper.[13] Some creative work appeared as a result of Dvořák's edict. Daniel Gregory Mason, a thorough conservative and enemy of popular music, wrote a *String Quartet on Negro Themes* in 1919, a stolid and orthodox conservatory piece, lacking the logic, imagination, and drive either of Ives's chamber works or of classic ragtime. In Europe, Debussy, Satie, Stravinksy, Milhaud, Ravel, and others were early impressed by ragtime and jazz and tried to incorporate them into their new music of the twentieth century, as some American composers did later. But despite an almost utopian interest in the "music of the future" among American musical commentators, the sad, ironic truth is that they failed to see it when it flourished around them.

One music critic summed up the shortsightedness and pedantic vagueness of the whole theoretical debate over the "new music" and black folk traditions: "Those who have endeavored

---

[13]Typical of the debate, and in part summarizing it, is Harry Farjeon, "Rag-Time," *Musical Times*, LV (September, 1924), 795–97.

to follow the kindly advice of Doctor Dvořák and make the folk-music of the negro the basis of their compositions have failed to conquer the public because that public declined to embrace slave music when dressed in the unbecoming robes of Teutonic tone poems. The arts do not descend upon the people, but rise from them."[14] But no one, in the brief period of ragtime's vigorous popularity, was willing to study it or even consider it seriously, as Joplin so desperately wished. Ragtime remained with the people who had created it, outside the gates of the cultural academy.

Ragtime had in a few years evolved from a folk form unknown outside black folk culture in the South and Midwest. Shaped and organized by first-rate musical sensibilities, it had been adopted by keen commercial arrangers and had made a deep and lasting impact on the American mind. In this sense, at least, ragtime was a harbinger or precursor of the revolutionary new black musics—jazz and the blues—about to reach the general public. The rhythms and feeling of ragtime were disseminated and adapted by the whole music industry. Sousa's band and Arthur Pryor's band made popular recordings of cakewalks and ragtime marches. Instrumental virtuosi like Vess Ossman and Fred Van Eps made banjo transcriptions of ragtime equally popular. Irving Berlin, at the beginning of his career, wrote ragtime songs and firmly identified ragtime with ensemble styles through his evergreen "Alexander's Ragtime Band." By the second decade of the century, the general public was pre-pared for the advent of the ragtime-derived instrumental dance music first known as "jass." The Castles had, with James Reese Europe's musical backing, popularized the new one-step, a dance designed for a new ragtime style, a faster, more effer-vescent music than the classic piano ragtime of the Midwest. Ragtime was evolving again.

When the first New Orleans ragtime band musicians came north—Freddie Keppard and That Creole Band, Tom Brown's

[14]W. J. Henderson, "Ragtime, Jazz, and High Art," *Scribner's*, LXXVII (February, 1925), 204.

Band from Dixieland, the Original Dixieland Jazz Band—the public was at least in part oriented toward their "new" music. One of the Original Dixieland Jazz Band's first hit records in 1918 was "Original Dixie Jass Band One-Step," an unacknowledged adaptation of Joe Jordan's "That Teasin' Rag" (1909). This was in the vein of the Castle-Europe one-step music (such as Europe's "Castle House Rag") which New York had heard for several years, so it was no wonder that audiences immediately responded to the exotic and barbarous sonorities and hysterical rhythms of the band. It has often been charged that "jazz killed ragtime," that the new popular craze obliterated interest in the old piano form. Actually, years of intensive commerical production of formula-constructed pseudo-ragtime killed the early interest in classic ragtime. Almost from the moment of classic ragtime's inception, commercial exploitation had glutted the market with cheap imitations. In effect, the wide popularity of jazz following the Original Dixieland Jazz Band's "discovery" was a "ragtime revival" of some proportions. It developed and extended the style of flashy and exuberant eastern ragtime exemplified by Eubie Blake and Luckey Roberts and the instrumental work of James Reese Europe—immediate inspirations for James P. Johnson, Fats Waller, and Willie the Lion Smith, giants of "stride" or "shout'" or "rent-party" piano styles of the next generation.

Ragtime reached across America in the form of sheet music, piano rolls, and itinerant pianists traveling in show business. Both classic ragtime and its spawn of popular and commercial imitations had a wide hearing in the first decade of the century. It can be said of ragtime what Beethoven once claimed for his music: "Once you hear my music truly, you will never know sorrow again." Ragtime style became, for a generation of musicians and listeners, the basic style for all popular music. It reached by musical and cultural osmosis into all the basic forms of American music. While the age of classic ragtime writing was brief, spanning no more than the two decades from 1895 to 1915, its influence and example flowed through the veins and arteries of American musical life for a generation following. America moved to a ragtime pulse after 1900, and the old ragtime song was prophetic—we *were* "leading a ragtime life." Every kind of popular and folk music absorbed valuable materials from ragtime, from primitive country music forms on through slickly manufactured musical comedies. The first campaign in the black music revolution of the twentieth century was clearly carried by ragtime. Its continued existence testifies to this triumph.

~◄ III ►~

Classic Ragtime

"All of those fellers is dead. They all passed and in fact it's very hard to find a blues player or a ragtime player living now who lived in the days of Joplin or Turpin or Louis Chauvin." — Charles Love, 1965

Ragtime was the Negro's music, but it was the white man who made it popular. — Brun Campbell, ca. 1950

What is ragtime? What is jazz? And whence and whither? Ragtime is no longer mentioned. "Jazz" has lost its original meaning. — W. J. Henderson, 1925

THREE BRIEF LIVES

Scott Joplin (1868–1917). Born in Texarkana, Texas, Joplin was largely self-taught. He traveled as an itinerant pianist, arriving in the St. Louis–Sedalia area in 1885. His first published songs, "A Picture of Her Face" and "Please Say You Will" (1895), were conventional popular waltzes. Working with ragtime pioneers like Tom Turpin, Otis Saunders, Arthur Marshall, and Louis Chauvin, he published his first ragtime work, "Original Rags," in 1899 (through Carl Hoffman of Kansas City). His "Maple Leaf Rag" (1899) became classic ragtime's first enormous hit. Joplin worked steadily from 1900 to 1910 on a brilliant series of varied and ingenious rags. He also wrote and staged a ballet, *The Ragtime Dance* (1902), and an opera, *A Guest of Honor* (1903); the latter has been lost. He aspired to wider recognition for ragtime, which he championed as a serious music in *The School of Ragtime* (1908), an instruction-exercise book; and he invested years of struggle into the composition and production of his folk opera, *Treemonisha* (1911). In 1906, Joplin moved to New York to be at the center of the music publishing world. His frustrating labor over *Treemonisha* and his lack of recognition in New York combined to break his

47

health, and he suffered a nervous breakdown and collapse some-
time after 1911. In his final years he made a number of "Connorized" piano-roll recordings of his rags and composed a few rags,
but by 1916 he was institutionalized, and early in 1917 he died,
largely forgotten by the entertainment world.

James Scott (1886–1938). Born in Neosho, Missouri, Scott
was also basically self-taught. He moved to Carthage, Kansas,
around 1900. His first compositions, "A Summer Breeze"
and "The Fascinator" (1903) and "On the Pike" (1904), were
in the early march-cakewalk mode. Beginning in 1906, after
Scott had met and worked with Joplin and the St. Louis–Sedalia
ragtimers, his works were titled as rags and published by John
Stark and Sons. Scott worked steadily from 1906 to 1920, and
his compositions are remarkably consistent in quality and
inventiveness. His rags attained immediate recognition and
popularity, ranking with Joplin's work. Pieces like "Frog Legs
Rag" (1906), "Sunburst Rag" (1909), "Grace and Beauty"
(1910), "The Ragtime Oriole" (1911), and "Climax Rag"
(1914) were widely played and transcribed for ensembles.
Although he ceased ragtime composition early in the twenties,
he continued to work as an arranger, bandleader, and theater
musician in Kansas City. When he died, twenty years after
ragtime's vogue, Scott's name was still remembered by those
familiar with the music as the greatest ragtime writer to follow
Joplin.

Joseph Lamb (1887–1960). Born in Montclair, New Jersey,
Lamb grew up distant from the ragtime milieu of the Midwest.
He was self-taught as a pianist and composer. With an early
interest in popular music, Lamb met Scott Joplin in 1907 and
was aided by him in his first publication (with John Stark and
Sons), "Sensation" (1908), which carried Joplin's name as
arranger. Lamb's natural gift for ragtime composition produced
a series of fine, widely popular rags from 1909 to 1919, including "Ethiopia Rag" (1909), "American Beauty Rag"
(1913), "The Ragtime Nightingale" (1915), and "Top Liner

Rag" (1916). When the ragtime vogue passed, Lamb retired from active composition to work in the import business. A quiet and modest man, his identity was lost for thirty years, when most musicians and commentators assumed—from the assured brilliance of his work—that he was a black midwestern contemporary of Joplin. Lamb was rediscovered and recorded in the years before his death, and he composed or completed several unpublished rags, among them the excellent "Blue Grass Rag" and "Cottontail Rag" (1959). Lamb came from his long retirement still able to play and think in the idiom of classic ragtime, demonstrating why he has long been accepted as the third member of classic ragtime's magnificent trinity.

RAGTIME'S DOMINANT TRIAD: JOPLIN, SCOTT, AND LAMB

Classic ragtime can be defined very simply as the piano rags of Scott Joplin, James Scott, Joseph Lamb, and their immediate collaborators, students, and followers. The term *classic* was promoted vigorously by John Stark, who published the main work of these composers, to offset the widely held conception of ragtime as a low-class and shoddy musical product. These three composers collected the materials of early folk ragtime, codified the style of a generation of folk players, and defined the structure of the classic rag.

Composers like Arthur Marshall, Artie Matthews, Henry Lodge, J. Russel Robinson, Charles L. Johnson, George Botsford, and Percy Wenrich all wrote several enduring works, among dozens of efforts, but none of these men assembled a body of work as impressively self-consistent as that of each of the big three. This indicates the difficulty in working creatively within the confines of a constricted, jewel-like musical form. The gift of exploring and mapping a microcosmic musical world is rare—Schumann, Chopin, and Bartok come to mind as men of genius who seemed able endlessly to develop the resources of the keyboard in limited small-scale compositions. Other great composers like Bach, Mozart, and Beethoven constantly strained at the conventions and worked to expand them.

Joplin, by the end of his career, had moved toward larger compositions, away from the piano rag. He had toyed with operatic and balletic works earlier, as if his talent were bursting the seams of the little form he perfected. Even within the conventions of his own ragtime form, he moved to enlarge or develop the boundaries, in works like "Euphonic Sounds" or *The Ragtime Dance* where he seems to violate or ignore the strictures he set up in his classic rags. His collapse and early death prevented him from ever succeeding fully at escaping the bonds of piano ragtime, although his opera *Treemonisha* is finished and shows lucidly how Joplin could assemble and integrate materials from many nineteenth-century folk traditions into a large, carefully organized composition. The folk opera, as Joplin conceived and executed it in *Treemonisha,* is a form that has still not been coherently developed, despite the later work of George Gershwin, Marc Blitzstein, and others. Joplin's death deprived us of another original black musical form which nothing — not even the comprehensive geniuses of James P. Johnson or Duke Ellington — has been able to reconstruct. Johnson's *Jasimine* and Ellington's various forays into operatic/oratorio forms are much different in concept and direction from Joplin's genuinely naïve and folk-oriented opera.

In the piano works of Joplin, Scott, and Lamb, a complete anthology of the devices and formulas of ragtime can be catalogued. In the short version of Joplin's *The Ragtime Dance,* the six strains form a dance suite illustrating the diversity and flexibility of Joplin's style. The first three strains are in the mold of many Joplin rags, but the last three strains break away and shift into highly intricate rhythmic exercises — complex syncopations and stoptime effects evoking clog and eccentric dancers, etc., or the traditional buck-and-wing and breakdown dances from which ragtime evolved. Joplin further developed this use of sounds and silences in intricate rhythmic formations in "Stoptime Rag," the entire structure of which is built on stoptime breaks and choruses. Rags demonstrating a highly polished lyrical flow, in contrast to these jagged rhythms, include Joplin's "The Entertainer," "The Chrysanthemum," and his remarkable "Bethena" ragtime waltz; Scott's "Grace and Beauty"; Lamb's "The Ragtime Nightingale" and "American Beauty Rag." These works partake of the nineteenth-century genteel traditions of romantic music as much as they draw from ragtime's black folk sources. The range of classic ragtime's inventive resources is displayed in Joplin's astonishing "Euphonic Sounds," which suggests possibilities for developing the harmonic frontiers of the form. The possibility for genuine development of musical materials within the strict ragtime form is explored in Joplin's last completed rag, "Magnetic Rag." His ragtime studies included in *The School of Ragtime* show in miniature the conventions of ragtime rhythms and melodies that he developed in the context of his rags.

From 1899, when Joplin's first rag appeared in print, through the early 1920's, when Scott finally gave up publishing his work, these three men marked the pinnacle of quality and imagination in ragtime. The work of all three is distinguished by a consistency of style and creativity not shown by any other ragtime composer. Essentially all three men were as much collectors as composers, assembling and synthesizing the works of itinerant ragtime stylists who were too unskilled, or too indifferent, to write down their own creations. Brun Campbell described the process of compilation/composition precisely: "Ragtime was a pool of many men's ideas, and the one who could put it down on paper was considered the rightful composer, even if he did not originate the tune."[1] Basically Joplin, Scott, and Lamb simply gave a permanent form to an already mature and vigorous folk art — and to do this required great imagination and aesthetic insight.

Scott Joplin was the central figure of ragtime, universally acknowledged as the genius of the genre. From his work flowed

[1] S. Brun Campbell, "The Ragtime Kid (An Autobiography)," *Jazz Report*, VI (1967), 12.

the inspiration which moved his followers to commit themselves to creating beautifully shaped piano pieces in the mode scornfully labeled "ragtime" by an uncomprehending public. Joplin devoted his life to creating a true art from the miscellaneous materials of folk inspiration. He died believing himself a failure in this heroic mission. Joplin worked with Tom Turpin, Scott Hayden, Louis Chauvin, Arthur Marshall, and Otis Saunders—all accomplished pianists who invented their own music, or who borrowed it from anonymous earlier sources or a legion of faceless folk musicians traveling through. By 1897, "ragtime" was a label for black folk music widely accepted in the commerical entertainment world; and the school of folk pianists in Sedalia and St. Louis, Missouri, adopted the label to exploit their music commercially. (Joplin always felt that "ragtime" was a scurrilous term invented to discredit black music and musicians, and he only grudgingly accepted it in the titles of his compositions— many of which, it may be noted, are not actually called rags.) As piano/instrumental music widely called ragtime began to appear on the market, Joplin wrote down and published the music of his environment. He immediately became the focal center of the ragtime movement.

Gifted as a boy, Joplin seems to have been driven all his life by an impulse to create a music which would be recognized as art—a music which by its own stature would convince the "respectable" (white) world that a black man could invent an original and unique musical form worthy of acceptance across the world. The central, maddening irony of Joplin's life was the fact that this music was never to be accepted on his (or its own) terms. Joplin dreamed of writing a music which would be accepted with the piano works of Chopin, Schumann, and Liszt but which would reveal the mind and soul of the black man; instead, he was hailed as a master of "jig piano" and treated as a curiosity of the show business world. While Joplin conceived his music as beautiful and lyrical (the titles reveal this clearly: "Euphonic Sounds," "The Chrysanthemum," "Heliotrope Bouquet," or as Scott put it, "Grace and Beauty"), the public heard it as raucous and lively only. Joplin imagined his music in terms of a stately quadrille, but the age demanded a buck-and-wing.[2]

Joplin and the Sedalia pianists were the first generation of midwestern ragtime. Very soon, as rags were published and disseminated, a group of younger men appeared, seeking out Joplin himself. Among them were Brun Campbell, whose ambitions were to master ragtime as a performer; James Scott from Missouri who wrote in Joplin's vein and sought help with his developing music; and Joseph Lamb, a city boy from the East who was drawn to this new black music and who studied with Joplin in New York to perfect his compositions. By 1910, a clear "Joplin School" of classic ragtime was in flower, pro-ducing music in the mold defined by "Original Rags," "Maple Leaf Rag," "Swipsey Cakewalk," and other early Joplin rags. This is the mainstream of classic ragtime and can be described by reference to Joplin's personal musical imagination.

Simultaneously two other movements developed: another, younger group of black midwestern ragtime writers, including Artie Matthews, Robert Hampton, Charles Thompson, and others; and a group of white composers oriented toward a com-mercial popular music market, including Percy Wenrich, Charles L. Johnson, George Botsford, Henry Lodge, and J. Russel Robinson. By 1910 these two subsidiary branches of ragtime were in full bloom. Affected by both the second generation midwesterners and the commercially oriented easterners was another group of young black pianist-composers—native easterners like Eubie Blake and Luckey Roberts. Their work—influenced by the examples of such successful black artists in the commercial publishing world as Robert Cole and Rosamund Johnson, William H. Tyers, Ernest Hogan, and James Reese

[2] Joplin's consistent use of gentle flower- and plant-titles is an intriguing clue to his sensibility. His titles form a kind of musical portraiture or landscape of the South, a distinctly American version of the romantic tendency to use descriptive titles. Joplin's titles identify scenery in persistently concrete terms, going a step further than European romantics like Robert Schumann, who visualized piano compositions as generalized landscape or nature pieces.

Europe — peaked shortly afterwards, between 1910 and 1915, when ragtime became a widely accepted social-dance craze. With the eastern ragtimers the classic ragtime style evolved into a sophisticated dance music acceptable as light entertainment, a long way from its down-home conception in the back streets of Sedalia. The problem for all these serious workers in the garden of ragtime was that the mass public had very early accepted the term *ragtime* as a portmanteau synonym for any kind of lively popular music. Ragtime, like most popular art, was in danger of being swallowed by its own expanded reputation.

What differentiates classic ragtime — especially work by Joplin, Scott, and Lamb themselves — from the purely commercial or imitative products of this era? Put very simply, the answer is quality. But it is important to look at this generalization in detail. What does quality mean in terms of the canon of ragtime? How do specific works by the big three demonstrate imagination and aesthetic development? What techniques and structures do their works incorporate? What defines the "Joplin ragtime" in itself?

First of all, two elusive but vital aesthetic traits are consistently present in the rags of Joplin, Scott, and Lamb: the combination of imagination and craftsmanship. All their rags are worked out with an internal logic which is the ultimate definition of art. Joplin's first task was to create from a widely known folk *style* an actual *genre* of scored music. (This is roughly analogous to the manner in which Bela Bartok and Zoltan Kodaly collected and organized Hungarian folk music.) To do this, he had to invent and perfect a set of conventions of structure and form.

CLASSIC RAGTIME: TYPES OF STRUCTURE
THE BOOM-CHICK BASS — SYNCOPATION AND FORM

The formula for the piano rag as it developed in Joplin's works and among his hundreds of imitators was, as noted, usually a disposition of three to five themes in sixteen-bar strains often organized with repeats. This may be varied, either simplified or complicated. The rag falls always into two sections. The first section consists of the first two strains, their repetition, and a return to an unrepeated statement of the first strain: AA BB A. This return of the A strain is very characteristic for the first section of the rag. It makes it a direct relative of the many popular dance forms of the time—the polka, the schottische, the various single strains of the multistrained quadrille—all of which use the return (*da capo*) device.

The rag usually opens with a bright and memorable strain, followed by a similar theme, leading to a trio of a more marked rhythmic character, with the structure concluded by a lyrical strain which parallels the rhythmic developments of the earlier themes. The aim of the structure is rising—to mount from one theme to another in a stair-step manner, going from one peak of rhythmic and melodic brilliance to another and ending on a note of triumph or exhilaration. Each strain is likely to be divided into two 8-bar segments which are essentially alike, so the rhythmic-melodic unit of ragtime is usually only eight bars of $^2/_4$ measure, or sometimes as little as four bars. This means, obviously, that themes must be very brief and tightly pointed, just a few figures pulled together. They are linked directly to other brief figures to form a whole strain, which is then itself linked directly to another strain. The thrust, then, in ragtime composition must be toward the invention of very clear and sharp melodic figures; the whole process of organization becomes one of uniting a series of small conventionalized figures, not too different from Bach's methods in *The Well-Tempered Clavier*. Only rarely do composers deviate from the sixteen-bar strain or work conceptually with larger or more elastic units (see Joplin's late "Magnetic Rag" or Robert Hampton's "Cataract Rag" for ways of expanding and contrasting the sixteen-bar limitations). Basically the ragtime composer worked to develop three or four small melodic statements into coherent sixteen-bar statements, then to organize them into a continuous and logical composition of three or four such self-contained strains—a more arduous task than it may at first seem.

If we take Joplin's "Maple Leaf Rag" as archetypal, we can
see how it creatively incorporates and organizes these conventions of ragtime. "Maple Leaf Rag" begins directly, without
introduction, but the first eight bars of the A strain offer an
introductory feeling, almost a bugle-call motif:

MAPLE LEAF RAG   *Scott Joplin*
 A strain, ms. 1–8

The upward run from bass through treble leads into the second
eight-bar unit, a brilliant treble theme over a pressing, marchlike four-beat bass:

MAPLE LEAF RAG   *Scott Joplin*
 A strain, ms. 9–16

So the A strain breaks up into four-bar units, then can be assembled into two larger eight-bar units, actually forming an introduction-theme statement.

The second (B) strain is more vigorously rhythmic, with a syncopated theme derived from the first four-bar unit:

MAPLE LEAF RAG   *Scott Joplin*
B strain, ms. 1–4

This is reiterated and slightly varied through the strain.

The third (C) strain, after a recapitulation of A, is the trio, another brilliant theme developed from the first four bars:

MAPLE LEAF RAG   *Scott Joplin*
C strain, ms. 1–4

This is lyrical and fluid, in contrast to the broken rhythms and marchlike insistence of the first two strains, and it uses an upswung bass rather than the march bass of the A strain or the characteristic oompah bass of the B strain.

The C strain flows directly into the songlike fourth (D) strain, which uses much longer melodic lines than any of the preceding strains. Nevertheless, the basic melodic line is contained in the first eight bars, then restated:

MAPLE LEAF RAG   *Scott Joplin*
D strain, ms. 1–8

This supple and singing theme is the climax of the structure's rising impulse.

The bass lines throughout are either a marchlike four-beat or the oompah accents on one and three, following approximately the line a brass bass plays in a march. The second strain uses an effect like organ-point, and in the third strain Joplin places rising bass figures against the agile syncopations in the treble. In the fourth strain, the bass shows through a few holes in the melody line, but it is basically the oompah left hand of march-time.

The listener is apt to remember "Maple Leaf Rag" for the introductory eight bars of the first strain and for the song-chorus of the last strain. Joplin's most intense creative energies went into the tuckets in the treble and their echoes in the bass which open the first strain, and his second and third strains serve as exciting bridges to carry us into the exultation of the last eight-bar theme. Throughout "Maple Leaf Rag" the listener should note devices which recur: one theme echoing or mirroring another, patterns of call and response between the treble and bass, cunningly disposed suspensions of the bass to accentuate the treble and vice versa, a consistency of brightness and lyricism in each theme or subtheme. There is no way of breaking the melodic flow down into strictly conventionalized units, as in the blues or in most popular songs. Inside the bounds of the sixteen-bar strain, Joplin allows himself great imaginative freedom; he can build the melody in any way he wishes. His main impulse seems to be to keep the composition flowing, to drive the march-like rhythmic pulse ahead by any means, and within the regularity of this four-beat matrix to create as many subtle rhythmic variations as possible, to generate rhythmic tension through dozens of small polyrhythmic motions.

The overall structure of the rags allows two classifications: (1) the *linear* rag and (2) the *rounded* rag. A linear rag consists of the presentation of up to four new strains within the bisectional rag structure, one following another and its corresponding repetitions. Joplin's "Maple Leaf Rag" is such a linear rag. It consists of the AA BB A / CC DD-strain structure. In contrast, in a rounded rag the first section of the rag is followed by one or two new strains and the return-quote of either its first or second strain or the first strain of the second section. Scott Joplin's "Felicity Rag" illustrates the first case: AA BB A / CC Bridge AA; Joplin's "The Chrysanthemum" shows the second case: Intro AA BB A/CC DD C. A great many variants of these two types of rag can be found in the works of Joplin, Scott, and Lamb. There is a standard harmonic progression found in many first strains of rags, especially earlier rags, *ca.* 1900. This appears in the first four measures of "Maple Leaf Rag": //C/G7/C/G7// (simplified). This also occurs in Joplin's "The Cascades," "The Favorite," and "The Sycamore"; it appears in Scott's "Frog Legs Rag" and "The Ragtime Betty"; in Joseph Lamb's "Patricia Rag" and "Contentment Rag." It can also be traced in many other works. A stunning example of Joplin's craftsmanship is present in his "Maple Leaf Rag." In the fourth and fifth measures of the bass part of the D strain he uses the characteristic ascending halftone progression, $a - B^b$, of the first and third measures of the A strain—*i.e.,* he employs a rounding out technique in conjunction with a nonrounded, linear rag.

The second section of the typical rag is made up of one or two new strains, or of either of the two strains of the first section in combination with a new strain. This structural flexibility is in contrast with the stiff, hierarchical use of the *da capo* form in the first section. Another contrast with the first section is the key of the subdominant, in which the second section is written. The rag approaches in this way the key relationships which exist between the first section of a traditional march and its corresponding trio section. Very often the rag concludes with this new key. Marches will always return to the original key. Rags are not developmental in the sense of the sonata allegro or concerto forms or the form of the symphonic poem (*i.e.*, in the sense of nineteenth-century art music) in that they must take a "round trip" away from a given key to a new key and back to the original key. The only connection between the rag and the sonata form is that the first section of the rag uses the *da capo* form which is also the form of the third movement of many sonatas or symphonies: minuet-trio-minuet or scherzo-trio-scherzo.[3]

The ragtime composer simply is not concerned with the problem of development of musical themes; the theme is set down intact, in its finished form, and it is linked to various related themes. But there is rarely an attempt made to develop the theme or to create variations on it. Nor is there an attempt to treat it canonically, to use a theme for a rigorous exercise in part-composition. Like the two-step march, like the formal waltz, like most of the popular dance and song forms of the late nineteenth century, the piano rag is meant to be accepted as a finished and self-enclosed showcase for melodic and rhythmic invention.

---

[3] A literary analogy may clarify the bisectional structure of the rag: it is analogous to the bisectional form of the Italian sonnet, which consists of fourteen lines, divided into eight and six (octave and sestet); in the Italian sonnet, the octave is always constructed with the same rhyme scheme (ABBA ABBA), while the sestet may be organized in many different ways (CDCDCD, CDE CDE, CCD CCD, etc.). The rag is built on the same principle, with the opening (A-B) section following a consistent pattern, while the second section may be constructed in many different ways.

Some rags, linear or rounded, are also *motto* rags. In a motto rag the composer uses a memorable figure or motive at the beginning of all or most of the strains. The upbeat figure at the beginning of all strains of Joplin's "Maple Leaf Rag" makes this a motto rag:

MAPLE LEAF RAG   *Scott Joplin*
(beginnings of each strain [upbeats])
A strain

B strain

C strain

D strain

All strains of Lamb's "Sensation" begin with a motto of two, three, or four notes which is derived from the initial arabesque-like motive of the A strain:

SENSATION   *Joseph F. Lamb*
(motto of each strain)
A strain

B strain

C strain

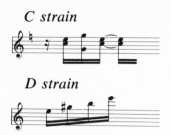

D strain

This use of the motto allows the composer to tighten the otherwise loose medley-like structure of the rag. The motto device is not an all-round device firmly in use like the *da capo* structure of the first section of each classic rag. It is not necessarily a device borrowed from classical music, but is rather in accordance with the innate playfulness of black music.

In many rags, as in much jazz and dance music, rhythmic and dynamic activities increase in the final strain. The music is "coming home," as jazz musicians put it. The ostinato bass progressions of the D strain in Lamb's "Patricia Rag" show such an increased accumulation of rhythmic activities. Lamb's "Champagne Rag" also "comes home" in the final strain.

Some rags belong to the category of *contrapuntal* rags. A contrapuntal rag contains a very linear melody in the right hand, counterbalanced by a melodic line which is shaped by the uppermost notes of the chords or octaves of the left-hand part. Lamb's "Contentment Rag" is a beautiful example of this kind of contrapuntal polarity, as is Joplin's pioneering "Euphonic Sounds."

Some rags are explicitly labeled as medleys — *e.g.*, the works of Blind Boone: "Boone's Rag Medley No. 1" and "Rag Medley No. II." A medley, like a rag, has a multisectional structure. In both the medley and the rag various themes and strains exist side by side. In both, the musical material is not developed but rather combined by chance. In both, all strains are of equal importance, and a true democratic relationship exists. Little interaction between the various strains is evident. In both, each strain stays intact, unchanged, undeveloped. Both are characteristic musical expressions of servants and slaves, black and

white, produced for the growing market of urban mass audiences. Although widely used by Schubert in his piano compositions, by Weber and Meyerbeer in their opera overtures, and
by John Cage in his chance music, adherents of classical music
often disdain the medley technique as musical refuse or trash.

Ragtime pieces have many connections with urban, popular,
and folk musics. There is the duple meter, the slow tempos, the
oompah accompaniment, and moderate syncopation of the
cakewalk. There is also the march, with its bisectional organization of march and trio, the transfer of the trio sound to the
piano, and the nonsyncopated motion of uninterrupted fast
notes (see "Bohemia Rag" by Lamb).

Rhythmic and melodic patterns of the polka, schottische, and
quadrille can also be found. Traces of polka rhythm are present
in the B strain of Joplin's "Peacherine Rag":

PEACHERINE RAG   *Scott Joplin*
 B strain, ms. 1–3

POLKA PATTERN
 B strain

Likewise, the B strain of Clarence Wiley's "Carbarlick Acid,"
a two-step cakewalk (1903), shows similar dependencies on the
polka. The C strain of Joplin's "Eugenia" is similar to the B
strain of a schottische:

EUGENIA   *Scott Joplin*
 C strain, ms. 1–3

SCHOTTISCHE PATTERN
B strain

The first four measures of the D strain of Tom Turpin's "St. Louis Rag" also show connections with the polka. The dotted sixteenth-note rhythm of Lamb's "Cleopatra Rag" is in sympathy with the same dotted procedure of the "Lancers Quadrille":

CLEOPATRA RAG   *Joseph F. Lamb*
A strain, ms. 1–2

LANCERS QUADRILLE
final strain pattern

The trio strain of Joplin's concert rag, "The Sycamore," has sounds of a cakewalk melody (see Kerry Mills's "Whistlin' Rufus").

The flexibility of rags has been treated at length, but rags are stiff and flexible at the same time. They adhere to a strict beat which permeates the entire piece, a metronomic unit which allows no tempo or mood modifications, alterations, or developments. Rigidity is present in the incessant counting of time pulsations in the continuo accompaniment and its melodic syncopated counterpart. And it is present in the strict adherence to the principle of symmetrical structure, as far as the large form of the rag and its basic component, the single strain, are concerned. Each strain is subdivided into two periods of eight, each period into two phrases of four measures each. Phrases and periods are filled out by relatively simple harmonies which lead to half- or authentic cadences. As in any conventionalized genre, superficial characteristics may at first seem overpowering. Each rag looks like any other rag; each rag sounds like any other rag, always the same syncopated beat, always the same player-piano-like sound, always the same *perpetuum-mobile*-like effect; each rag seems to be another personification of "primitive," "naive," "innocent," formal procedures in music.

It is impossible to look at American music without considering this concept of "innocence" for a moment. One of the most persistent myths before the beginning of the twentieth century was that America was the land of the innocent, the good, the free, the simple, the unadorned, the pure; while old Europe was viewed as a land of complexity — over-adorned, corrupted, hopelessly enchained. Europeans were bound to old concepts, old customs and traditions. In American music this innocent freedom from European concepts appears in the "wrong" progressions of parallel fifths and octaves in William Billings' patriotic anthems and fuging tunes; in Lowell Mason's simple, corny, and butchered arrangements of selections from the works of famous European composers. Later, this use of "wrong" musical devices and concepts appears in the works of Charles Ives, Carl Ruggles, Henry Cowell, and others, as a self-conscious musical philosophy. Innocence was also reflected in the adoration of anything foreign in music over anything native. The fact that a pilgrimage to Bayreuth may be of greater significance for many Americans even today than a pilgrimage to, say, New Orleans suggests that this idea is still alive.

The aspect of innocence that appears in ragtime relates to harmonic practices. Ragtime composers used a stereotyped form of dance-hall music, then filled this form with very sophisticated melody-continuo relationships within each strain, so that many rags begin in one key and end in the key of the trio section. This contrasts with compositional practices in such popular dance forms as the cakewalk, march, schottische, waltz, polka, gavotte, and with classical forms derived from the dance, such as the minuet or scherzo. The titles are a further clue: "classical" composers provide informative titles, indicating the form or the emotional aim of the music; ragtime composers often use titles drawn from the trivia of their immediate environments, referring to the animal or plant life of a state or region. Only an "innocent" composer could write a "Chrysanthemum," a "Gladiolus," a "Sunflower" composition or use such colloquial terms as "Dynamite" or "Easy Winners." Only an "innocent" composer like Joseph Lamb would attempt to describe "American Beauty" through highly suggestive sexual images in its bass part: (a) widely spread leaps, in combination with (b) chromatic stepwise progressions; (c) sixteenth-note progressions in contrary motion to the right hand (coitus); and (d) shifts of register of the right hand against a widely ranged descent in octaves of the bass line:

AMERICAN BEAUTY   *Joseph F. Lamb*
  A strain, ms. 1–2

  B strain, ms. 2–3

  C strain, ms. 8

D strain, ms. 1–2

Ragtime music was written for the piano. It is a major American contribution to world piano music, black America's contribution to white piano music. It helped to round off and establish once and for all America's characteristic piano sound —a loud, orchestral, aggressive, swinging keyboard sound which can outsound the noise of crowds gathered to be entertained. It might have had ancestors in the orchestrally emancipated piano music of Franz Liszt and his American pupils. It received its real American percussiveness through the Afro-American beat of black folk ragtime.

The tension in ragtime arises from a polarity between two basic ingredients: a *basso continuo,* a continuous bass—or as it is called by jazz musicians, a boom-chick bass—in the left hand, and its melodic, syncopated counterpart in the right hand. The boom-chick bass distributes the sound between heavy and light impulses within a duple-meter rag. Octaves produce the heavy sounds; chords produce the light sounds. The sound sequence reads: heavy, light/heavy, light. In notation, a boom-chick bass looks as follows:

CREOLE BELLES   *J. Bodewalt Lampe*
  C strain, ms. 1

Ragtime composers observe this sequence most often. Sometimes it is changed. The first four measures of Joplin's "Maple Leaf Rag" show an octave, chord, chord, octave organization.

The second and fourth measures of his "Gladiolus Rag" present three octaves followed by one chord:

GLADIOLUS RAG   *Scott Joplin*
  A strain, ms. 2

SCOTT JOPLIN'S NEW RAG   *Scott Joplin*
  C strain, ms. 1

The first four measures of the C strain of "Scott Joplin's New Rag" have the octave, chord, octave, octave organization. The feeling of the *continuo* quality of the boom-chick bass is not changed by these subtle shifts of heavy and light sounds.

For variety's sake the ragtime composer also uses other bass devices. In the last eight measures of the A strain of "Maple Leaf Rag," each measure has four equally heavy chords. They are almost always the same chords. This establishes a four-beat feeling which contrasts convincingly with the boom-chick measures to follow. In measures 5–7 of the C strain of Lamb's "Ethiopia Rag," left and right hands exchange their roles. The right hand, with its four-beat chord pattern (!) is the timekeeper, while the left hand executes the syncopated sequential counterparts. The first four measures of the same strain of this rag have another device: the boom-chick bass is abandoned, while both voices supplement each other in the form of a dialogue. One voice sustains a chord while the other voice plays a distinct melody, and vice versa:

Joseph F. Lamb

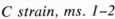

C strain, ms. 1–2

Still another device is at hand when in measures 5–7 of the first strain of Joplin's "Euphonic Sounds" the chords of the left hand only double the melody of the right-hand part.

In the "hot" rhythm of the melodic syncopated counterparts, certain basic rhythmic motives are used. Frank Gillis lists some of them for us:[4]

RHYTHMIC MOTIVES

a.   *b.*   *c.*   *d.*

In addition to a variety of shifting accents these patterns are repeated, varied, and extended in many different ways within the inflexible frame of the corresponding phrases or periods of the strain. The strict observation of the phrase, period, strain structure is necessary to control, to dam up the overflow and playfulness of rhythmic syncopated energies. Within the phrase and period structure the composers show great imagination and sophistication in handling, combining, contrasting, extending the various motivic-rhythmic techniques as they are applied and combined within the phrases and periods of the composition.

The introduction and the first strain of Joplin's "The Enter-

[4] Frank Gillis, "Hot Rhythm in Piano Ragtime," in George List and Juan Orrego-Salas (eds.), *Music in the Americas* (Bloomington, Ind.: Indiana University Publications, 1967), 91–104.

tainer" consist of three basic rhythmic patterns which are repeated and extended. The first pattern appears first in the introduction and then in the first strain. It is the most important motive of the entire strain. It is given in five slightly different versions. The second and third motive form a very strident rhythmic contrast to the first motive, and they remain untouched.

THE ENTERTAINER   *Scott Joplin*
The three rhythmic motives

a.  ♫♫♫ ♫♫ *(Introductory ms. and ms. 15)*

  a_1  ♫♫♫ ♫♫♫ *(ms. 14)*

  a_2  ♫ | ♫♫♫ ♫♫♫ *(ms. 12–13)*

  a_3  ♫♫ | ♫♫♫ ♫♫ | ♩ ♪ *(ms. 2–4 and 10–12)*

  a_4  ♫ | ♫♫♫ ♫♫♫ | ♩ ♪ *(ms. 7–8)*

b.  ♫ | ♫♫ ♩ *(ms. 1, 5, 9, with pickup beat)*

c.  ♩ ♫♫ | ♩ ♪ *(ms. 1–2, 5–6, and 9–10)*

This chart shows that the three motives of the introduction and the A strain are combined in various complex ways. The motive proper appears in the introduction and in the next-to-last measure. Motives a_3, a_2, a_1, and a follow in successive order (measures 12–15). Two motives may occur in one measure (measures 1, 2, 9, 10 of the A strain). Three motives appear in these same measures. Motives may often be displaced across the barlines (see motive b in measures 4–5, motive c in measures 5–6, motive a_4 in measures 6–7). Some motives may span across more than one measure (motive a_3 in measures 2–4, motive a_4 in measures 6–8). Variants of the first motive also make up the essential rhythmic material of the B strain. The introduction and the A and B strains of "The Entertainer" form a very closely knit rhythmic structure.

The C strain of Joplin's "Gladiolus Rag" has at least six different rhythmic patterns, all connected with each other. A minimal economy of motivic patterns is present in the second strain of "Scott Joplin's New Rag" which uses only two motives.

If we turn from a general survey of classic ragtime as represented in miscellaneous works by the three masters of the genre to a specific look at each composer's contributions, we can see further the great variety of means and achievements within the form. Scott Joplin, James Scott, and Joseph Lamb each had a highly individual style of his own; each had a distinct vocabulary within the idiom of ragtime.

JOPLIN'S RAGTIME:
STRUCTURE – FORM – MELODIC BEAUTY
POLARITIES BETWEEN LEFT AND RIGHT HANDS

The scheme of "Maple Leaf Rag," "Gladiolus Rag," "The Strenuous Life," "Kismet Rag," and "The Cascades" is that of the linear rag: AA BB A / CC DD. "The Strenuous Life" and "The Cascades" have an introduction, and in "The Strenuous Life" there is an additional introduction to the C strain. "Scott Joplin's New Rag," "The Chrysanthemum," and "Felicity Rag" show some interesting applications of the rounded rag pattern. "Scott Joplin's New Rag" – Intro AA BB AA / CC Intro D A Coda (D) – inserts the introduction between the repeated C strain and the D strain. The latter is given only once, but to make up for it D material is included in the final coda. His "The Chrysanthemum" – Intro AA BB A / CC DD C – uses the rounded rag form by referring back to the third strain in the second section. "Felicity Rag" – Intro AA BB / CC Transition AA – excludes a repetition of the first strain at the end of the first section and a second strain in the second section.

The structure is complicated slightly in a rag like "The Entertainer," using scheme Intro AA BB A / CC Bridge DD, with a repeat of the first strain before the trio and only a partial recapitulation of the whole. And in so unusual a work as the short version of *The Ragtime Dance,* a miniaturized dance suite intended for ballet presentation, Joplin used a larger kind of linear structure: Intro AA BB CC D E F, with the last three strains in intricately syncopated stoptime and unrepeated. The piano rag presents the same problem of invention and compression as the march; the composer must be able to create brilliant melodic units and impose them on rhythmic patterns which keep the music flowing, and everything must be as tight and direct as possible. The three or four themes of a Joplin rag are likely to be similar in rhythmic flow and melodic shape yet distinct enough to form contrasts within the structure.

Joplin's nostalgic "The Entertainer" offers a striking example. The entire rhythmic output of the first strain is generated through three basic patterns which are distinguished by two different dynamic levels, piano (p) and forte (f). The head motive of the second strain is derived from the introduction and the second pattern of the first strain. It reverses the dynamic levels first to f and then to $p-f$ for the first eight, p for the last eight measures. The initial motive of both trio strains leans again on the second pattern of the first strain. The different key and the use of melodic sequences form, however, an interesting contrast. The composer built this rag with an inner logic, a beautiful sense of continuity, elaboration, and balance.

Joplin's rags are miniatures in musical form. It is easy to see that the composer often used the same motivic elaborations in different rags. The first strain of his "Gladiolus Rag" uses the same techniques of repetition as the first strain of "Maple Leaf Rag," in addition to the same impressionistic use of four-beat chord successions. Because of their diminutive form and scope, they depend on melodic and rhythmic beauty.

Rhythmic beauty may be shaped sometimes by a lack of syncopated action in the right hand. Joplin's "The Chrysanthemum" shows a syncopated rhythm only in its D strain, this delightful medley consisting actually of an A impromptu, a B march, a C cakewalk, and a D rag. (Its subtitle, "An Afro-American Intermezzo," points to this medley or suite construction.) Sometimes the same rhythmic figures in the bass are developed. An early work like "Original Rags" (1899) and a late one like "Magnetic Rag" (1914) are much alike in this respect. "Original Rags" is built on a series of bright, banjo-like tunes, very simply organized and displayed. "Magnetic Rag" uses much more introspective tunes, tinged with minor interludes, while the bass rhythms continually suggest blues motives or "walking basses" (and, in fact, the "Connorized" piano roll reputedly cut by Joplin himself contains interpolated passages of "walking bass").

The occasional three-note chromatic bass pattern of the first strain of "Gladiolus Rag" becomes a four- to seven-note chromatic bass pattern in the second strain, to grow into a twelve-note bass pattern in the third strain:

GLADIOLUS RAG   *Scott Joplin*
A strain, ms. 2

B strain, ms. 8

C strain, ms. 6–8

Melodic beauty is sometimes obtained by a sophisticated use of motivic repetition. In the first strain of "Maple Leaf Rag," Joplin first repeats a motive of two measures (twice), then a motive of one measure (twice), then a motive of half a measure (four times), only to complete the entire strain with a repetition of a motive of four measures (twice). The same device is used in the first strain of "Gladiolus Rag."

A whole network of tense polarities is present between the boom-chick continuo of the left hand and the syncopated right hand and between the rhythmic-melodic patterns, as such, of the right hand alone. Joplin gives some tremendous melodic rhythmic polarities in the first five measures of the right hand of the D strain in his "Maple Leaf Rag":

MAPLE LEAF RAG   *Scott Joplin*

Each of the five measures has a different rhythmic pattern. Each forms a contrast with the following pattern. These ever-changing rhythmic patterns of the right hand are set off against a two-measure unit in the left hand of octave, chord, chord, octave and octave, chord, octave, octave — modified boom-chick combinations. The fifth and sixth measure unit repeats the octave-chord groupings of the fourth measure:

1.   2.
octave, chord, chord, octave   octave, chord, octave, octave

3.   4.
octave, chord, chord, octave   octave, chord, octave, octave

The secret of Joplin's ragtime is the subtle balance of polarities, continuity, and repetition of melody and rhythm, much the same combination of energy and lyricism as in the marches of his contemporary, John Philip Sousa. The sense of continuity and unity within a rag is probably, in the end, inexplicable. No amount of analysis can determine, for example, why "Maple Leaf Rag" became a brilliant and enduring success, while "The Chrysanthemum" or "Paragon Rag" remain obscure. Nor does a piano rag yield to the same sort of analysis which can be applied to a composition in, for example, sonata form.

The ragtime composer simply was not concerned with the problem of sonata-like development of musical themes. He was concerned with motivic-rhythmic elaborations and forms as they occur in American popular and African folk music. African 2-to-4 time makes its appearance in the duple time of the typical rag. The metronome-like beat of African percussion instruments is transferred to the piano. A great variety of rhythmic bass patterns is developed. These create a polyrhythmic feeling. Polyrhythmic structure is one of the most outstanding features of African music.

Part of the aesthetic effect of classic ragtime is created by Joplin's personal style, the individual and idiosyncratic touches he applied to the idioms of folk ragtime. Joplin's musical voice and personality were so powerful and self-assured that his followers immediately identified his version of ragtime as the essential thing itself. There is, however, a consistent characteristic subtlety and delicacy of touch in Joplin's work absent in the rags of lesser composers who could hear and imitate the gross mannerisms and devices of ragtime, but who lacked a discriminating ear for the gentler flourishes of pure Joplin captured inside the rhythms.

Scott's Ragtime:
Originality — Melodic Simplicity
Descriptive Music — Structure

The composer most akin to Scott Joplin in spirit and in ability is James Scott. Scott came closest to capturing Joplin's sensitive handling of Missouri folk materials, and in Scott's best work there are the same gentle touches and the same subtle quadrille-like dance feeling. "Grace and Beauty" and "The Ragtime Oriole"—two very different compositions—show Scott's melodic invention at its best, a clearer, simpler lyricism than Joplin's. Scott's rags often sound like Joplin slightly aerated and simplified, as Handel sometimes seems a sleeker, more architectonic version of Bach. A quasi-Handelian impres-

sion is caused, for instance, by the reiterated selection of un-
syncopated diatonic tone-steps for the initial motive of the A
strain of "The Great Scott Rag" or the reiterated use of tones
of the b flat major triad for the head motive of the A strain of
"The Ragtime Betty," and for the quasi-baroque, concerto-like
exchange of the same triadic materials between the right and
left hand parts of the B strain of the same rag.

Where Joplin creates a lacework of sound, filling in every
space with lyrical embroidery, Scott concentrates on large,
simple motives which are self-contained and effective. The
drive in Joplin's composition seems to be to create unity by
linking every passage, while Scott's rags depend more on the
continuity of a theme or a lyrical flow, so that each section seems
a logical extension or a mirror image of the preceding one.

Scott often uses sweeping ascending and descending melodic
lines of extensive range, which give his rags drive and continuity. While the A strain of his "Hilarity Rag" swoops down
like a burst of hilarious laughter in a line of two and a half
octaves, the B strain through its climbing line of three octaves
presents this in mirror image:

HILARITY RAG   *James Scott*
   A strain, ms. 1–3

In the introduction and A strain of "The Ragtime Oriole,"
Scott musically describes various flight patterns of the bird.

An ascending and descending motion from *a'* flat to *a''* flat in measures 1–4, an ascending motive from *c'* to *c'''* in measures 5–7, its descending counterpart from *c'''* to *e* flat in measures 7–8, and another descent from *f'''* to *c'* in measures 11–12 are all examples of this flight imagery:

RAGTIME ORIOLE   *James Scott*

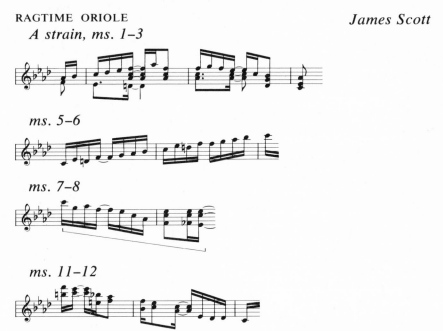

The entire trio (C) strain is a schoolbook example of contrary motion. Scott's melodic invention is at its best a clearer and simpler lyricism than Joplin's. His is a preference for four-note tetrachordal, chromatic patterns as they appear in strains of "Troubadour Rag," "The Ragtime Oriole," "Kansas City Rag," "Sunburst Rag," and "The Great Scott Rag," to mention a few.

Joplin often works by sharp contrasts, throwing a jagged, syncopated theme back-to-back with a simple and straightforward marchlike strain (compare B and C strains of "Paragon Rag," for instance), while Scott seems to strive for comparison of themes, trying to show us how much one melody echoes another. There is no basic contrast in sound or style between the four strains of his "Troubadour Rag." All four strains of "The Ragtime Oriole" indulge in similar musico-descriptive devices. His charm and directness are close to the pianistic genre piece of the romantic era. His descriptive salon pieces, "The Great Scott Rag," "The Ragtime Betty," and "The Ragtime Oriole" show an interesting combination of white salon and black folk ragtime music.

Scott's structure tends to reflect this simplicity of lyrical intention. He most often uses the straight linear rag structure. The structure of "The Ragtime Betty" and of "Troubadour Rag" is AA BB A / CC DD, while "Hilarity Rag" is even simpler: AA BB / CC DD, omitting the single A restatement in the first section of the rag. The structure of "Frog Legs Rag" and "Grace and Beauty" is AA BB A / Bridge CC DD, while "The Ragtime Oriole" is much more complex: AA BB A / Bridge CC DD *da capo* A. The final *da capo* statement of the A strain makes this birdcall rag a rounded rag. The *da capo* device is also used in "Kansas City Rag": Intro AA BB / CC *da capo* B. This particular rag is actually AA A_1A_1 / BB A_1, like a simple folk dance, since the B strain is only a variant, a transformation of the A strain. In "Sunburst Rag" and "The Great Scott Rag," the rounded rag structure is Intro AA BB A / Intro CC B and Intro AA BB CC B, respectively. In both cases, the B strain is transposed back to the original key of the rag.

Scott inter-relates the various strains of his rags in a still tighter fashion. The last four measures of the A and B strains of his "Troubadour Rag" quote the same music both in the left and right hands, while the last five measures of the C and D strains show the same chord progression in the left hand. The D strain of his "Hilarity Rag" works very pronouncedly with the descending motive of the C strain. And "The Ragtime Oriole" depends on straightforward exposition of the three strains, each one built on "oriole" motives, small singing birdcall figures. The effect is one of openness and unornamented charm, an impression of artlessness typical of Scott. The very simplicity of the linear structure also suggests a kind of musical development; we are directed to the birdcall motives themselves and the way Scott cunningly varies them. This rag was recorded and popularized in a banjo transcription by the brilliant Fred Van Eps, and its folk-style openness lends itself very well to this treatment. Scott's rags communicate an impression of charm and directness closer to folk styles than to a finished art form.

When Joplin used a linear construction, as in "The Cascades" (Intro AA BB / Bridge CC DD), it was in Scott's mode, to present a series of similar themes or developing ideas. "The Cascades" purports to represent or describe the ornamental watercourse built for the 1904 St. Louis Exposition; and the rippling, rumbling motives demand a consecutive presentation, like the course of a rapids straight down a stream. But most of Joplin's rags are more intricately conceived, while Scott's music works best in precisely this linear presentation. Scott's melodies have a clear, crystalline, dance-like rhythm, for the most part; and where he uses complex rhythmic exchanges between bass and treble (as in "Climax Rag's" first two strains, or "Victory Rag's" first two strains), he is never as adroit as Joplin in "Euphonic Sounds" or *The Ragtime Dance*.

Yet there are things in Scott's music apparently beyond Joplin's talents. The sense of integrity in a piece like "The Ragtime Oriole" is very strong; there seems to be a kind of melodic treatment which is absent from Joplin's rags. Scott displays a sense of the *organic* possibilities of simple themes, using them elastically; while Joplin's themes are carefully finished, each one built, polished, and set aside as the composer moves on to another. The four themes of "Grace and Beauty" seem to originate from a sustained mood or idea, while the themes of many Joplin rags seem less consistent and, in fact, are often deliberately contrasted. Scott often returned to his second theme as a final theme, sometimes modulating to return, as in "Kansas City Rag":

(key of C)   (key of F)   (key of C)
Intro AA BB / CC Modulating Bridge BB.

This form is rare in Joplin's rags, but Scott used three strains as a rule. Three strains are used similarly by Joseph Lamb in "Cleopatra Rag," "Reindeer Rag," and "The Ragtime Nightingale." Scott's music works by a sustained combination of closely related themes, while Joplin's is often strongest for its contrasts and abrupt shifts of feeling.

The craftsmanship of James Scott's ragtime is as remarkable as Joplin's, even if his work is not as varied or as experimental. Obviously, Scott shared with Joplin a belief in the dignity and value of his music, the idea that this music labeled "ragtime" was an art music developing under a wholly new aesthetic. Since Scott worked with Joplin, studied his compositions, and delved into the same regional folk background, it is not remarkable that their rags should be so similar. Yet while Scott has existed in Joplin's shadow, he is clearly a composer of great genius, a talent as large as Joplin's.

LAMB'S RAGTIME:
QUOTATIONS — BASS LINES — SYNTHESIS OF RAGTIME AND OTHER DANCE FORMS

The most remarkable appearance is that of the third member of classic ragtime's triumvirate — Joseph Lamb of New Jersey, a young white man totally removed from the sources of midwestern folk ragtime. Lamb's success arose from study and absorption of a music almost completely alien to him, a triumph of careful imitation and intuitive understanding. It shows how much a musical genius can shape itself to the demands of a new creative force. For years — the forty-odd years of his retirement from the music world — most musicians and musicologists had assumed that Joe Lamb was a black midwesterner of the Joplin-Scott circle, so thoroughly did he assimilate and develop the principles and spirit of the "Joplin ragtime."

In his "Sensation," written with Joplin's supervision and assistance, Lamb transposes literally the first measure and a half of Joplin's "Maple Leaf Rag" from a flat to c major. However, the upbeat pattern of "Maple Leaf Rag" is changed to a downbeat beginning. Lamb's famous "American Beauty Rag" shows remote similarities with Joplin's "Maple Leaf Rag" in that the initial motive of the B strain is a melodic inversion of the initial motive of the A strain, and in that the upbeat pattern in the bass is repeated by an upbeat pattern in the right hand. The first two measures of the bass part of "Patricia Rag" are closely related to the same measures in "Maple Leaf Rag." The first four notes in the right hand of Joplin's "Gladiolus Rag" are identical with the first four notes of Lamb's "Patricia Rag."

Lamb does not quote only Joplin but himself also. Thus the first strains of his "Cleopatra Rag," "Champagne Rag," and "Reindeer Rag" show the same motivic material:

CLEOPATRA RAG   *Joseph F. Lamb*

CHAMPAGNE RAG (*transposed*)

REINDEER RAG

Furthermore, the B strain of "Champagne Rag" is similar to the D strain of "Patricia Rag." The first strains of "Ethiopia Rag" and "Bohemia Rag" are related to the trio strain of "Reindeer Rag":

ETHIOPIA RAG (*transposed*)   *Joseph F. Lamb*

BOHEMIA RAG (*transposed*)

REINDEER RAG

The motive of the C strain of "Ethiopia Rag" leans on the initial motive of the B strain of "Sensation":

ETHIOPIA RAG (*transposed*)   *Joseph F. Lamb*

SENSATION

Like James Scott, Lamb was a disciple of Scott Joplin, learning through the examples of Joplin's published rags and through direct study and discussion with Joplin. As with James Scott, Joplin read and played Lamb's prentice compositions and helped him score them. Again, as with Scott, this critical collaboration stamped Joe Lamb's music for the rest of his career as a ragtime composer. Lamb's rags, like Scott's, are closely modeled on Joplin's magnificent precedents, but they are still individualistic. There is a "Lamb style" as clearly as a "Scott style" and a "Joplin style."

In the "Lamb style," the treatment of the bass parts is a notable point. Many chords of the B strain of his "Sensation" use the same harmony—*i.e.,* while they are almost motionless, the bass line of the D strain experiences a tremendous melodic curve. The bass part in his "Patricia Rag" has various qualities: a four-note pattern is used in all four strains; ten of sixteen measures in the D strain use this octave pattern; the first bass phrase in the B strain lasts for three, while the second extends to five measures.

SENSATION *Joseph F. Lamb*

B strain, ms. 1–5, bass

D strain, ms. 1–10

PATRICIA RAG *Joseph F. Lamb*

A strain, ms. 1

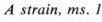

B strain, ms. 3–4

C strain, ms. 4–5

D strain, ms. 1

Joplin seems to have had the greatest attribute of the artist-teacher — the ability to direct an apprentice (and even to collaborate with him) without destroying his individuality. Lamb and Scott absorbed Joplin's organizational principles and his zeal for ragtime as an art music without becoming slavish imitators. Most important, both Lamb and Scott exhibit independent melodic concepts; they both phrase and develop the lyrical content of their rags much differently from Joplin and from each other. Even if classic ragtime is dominated by Joplin's guiding genius, he was right in insisting that it was a living and fecund genre capable of growth and evolution if attended by men of genius. The varied works of Lamb and Scott substantiate Joplin's belief.

Lamb uses the same approach to structure as Joplin and Scott. Most of his rags follow the pattern of the linear rag. Thus his "Ethiopia Rag" is organized AA BB A / CC DD, like some of Scott's linear rags or Joplin's earliest work. An unusual linear rag is Lamb's "Contentment Rag," which is structured according to an AA BB A / C C_1C_1 pattern. The C_1 strain, a variant of C, stresses the linear form of the rag. Here, the beat of ragtime is completely abandoned. It is superceded by a sound derived from band music. "Reindeer Rag" and "Cleopatra Rag" belong to the rounded rag type, built according to a scheme of Intro AA BB A / CC B_1B_1 or Intro AA BB A / Intro CC B. "Champagne Rag" is also a rounded rag. In its Intro AA BB A / CC D A_1 D A_1 structure, the D strain stands out because of its rhythmic push in unison sounds in both left and right hands. "Patricia Rag" is a linear rag organized AA BB A / Intro CC DD. Materials of the first two measures of the A strain both in the left and right hands are rounded out in all four strains. The arabesque-like figure of the right hand (the same as in Debussy's "La fille du cheveu de lin") is quoted literally in the eighth measure of the B strain. The initial measures of the introduction to the C trio and the C and D strains show the figure in a varied form.

Some of Lamb's rags are motto rags. All strains of his "Sensation" belong to the motto rag type, since all strains begin with an upbeat bass pattern. So does "American Beauty Rag." Some of Lamb's rags are "coming home" rags, in that the last strain or next-to-last strain is stressed. In "Patricia Rag," the octave bass progression of the left hand in the D strain makes this strain the unquestionable climax of the composition. "Champagne Rag" is also a "coming home" rag because of the importance of the D strain. "Contentment Rag" belongs to the rarer type of contrapuntal rags in that two melodic lines occur at the same time, one in the right hand and one in the left hand, throughout the entire rag.

Like Scott, Lamb wrote very lively and completely organized rags; their thrust was not toward technical or emotional complexity but toward lyrical flow, transparent vitality, and constant motion. Rags like "Cottontail Rag," "Reindeer Rag," and "The Ragtime Nightingale" show a powerful consistency of lyrical and rhythmic invention. Lamb's work is fully worthy of Scott or Joplin, and his rags are as "Negroid" and as individualized as anything written in ragtime.

An exuberant, clear melodic line marks Lamb's work as clearly as Scott's. In his "Sensation," Lamb obtained this melodic flow in all four strains by means of melodic sequences:

SENSATION   *Joseph F. Lamb*

A strain, ms. 1–4

B strain, ms. 1–2

In the trio of his "Ethiopia Rag," the melodic line is shared by the right and left hands. The bass part shows no syncopation, but it has its own melodic line, while the right hand remains frozen on a sustained chord, and vice versa:

ETHIOPIA RAG   *Joseph F. Lamb*
   C strain, ms. 1–2

In the second half of the first period of this strain, the right hand hammers out a slowly descending chordal repetition pattern, while the left hand surges upwards in sequential waves of parallel octaves. A persistent dotted rhythm is applied to the A and B strains of "Cleopatra Rag," creating a flavor of European popular melodism (a la Paul Linke). A similar impression is obtained with the sixteenth-note patterns (staccato) of the A strain of "Reindeer Rag." The much slower rhythmic values of the B and C strains of this same rag create a very convincing contrast of a march or two-step. Sometimes only a little figure, a small melodic twist, gives the melody personality, charm, and grace. This is evident in the nostalgic *jodler*-like interval of the seventh in the third and fourth measures of his "Ethiopia Rag":

ETHIOPIA RAG   *Joseph F. Lamb*

Lamb was able to use striking melody lines very deftly, and his ear for simple folk-derived tunes was acute. "The Ragtime Nightingale" uses a theme by Ethelbert Nevin, a nineteenth-century sentimental composer once almost as well known as

Stephen Foster, and transforms the theme and James Scott's idea of bird motives (see "The Ragtime Oriole") into ragtime. The themes of his work sound as "authentic" as any of the folk materials of Joplin and Scott. Even though Lamb was removed by distance and culture from the Missouri folk sources of the original ragtime, he was still clearly able to "think ragtime," to invent and transform materials into the ragtime style. Lamb's rags all reveal his ability to assemble and synthesize very original and distinctive themes in the tight structure of the Joplin style.

His "Excelsior Rag" presents in all its strains a combination of cakewalk and ragtime rhythms and patterns. His "Champagne Rag" shows a combination of march and two-step in the A, B, and D strains, while only the C strain is "pure" ragtime. Actually, the A and B strains exhibit a songlike quality. "Cleopatra Rag" reveals a synthesis of march-schottische-rag-schottische strains. By means of contrasting staccato with legato strains, a suitelike character is established in "Reindeer Rag." Suggestive description of Bohemian music in his "Bohemia Rag" is present through: (1) the transfer of a general band sound to the piano; (2) the omnipresence of the boom-chick bass accompaniment, typical of the Czech-originated polka; (3) a happy sound which comes out of the right hand part of the A strain by providing it with third doublings; (4) a relative lack of syncopation throughout the rag; (5) the ♫♫ rhythm; (6) the ♫♫♫ rhythm in the B strain; (7) the marchlike ♫♫ rhythm in the trio strain. Description of American music is shown through the turbulent rhythmic complexity of all strains of his "American Beauty Rag."

Lamb's contributions to classic ragtime came in his productive years from 1909 through 1916, and again at the end of his life, in the 1950's, when he returned to writing and finished many early works. His career was marked by the fact that he was outside the mainstream of folk ragtime and that he retired voluntarily from the hubbub of the commercial music world. Yet despite his distance from ragtime's sources, despite his own quiet, shy nature, Joe Lamb made a deep and permanent mark on the genre of ragtime. His rags will stand with Joplin's and Scott's as representative of the best of classic ragtime as long as people still play and hear the music.

THE END OF THE ERA

Lamb and Scott worked from about 1910 through the second decade of the century, producing an eruption of ragtime that proved Joplin's assertions about his music: that it was powerfully imaginative, that it could be written correctly and conceived in a broad variety of manners, that it was worthy of careful study. By the time of his early death in 1917, Joplin had at least had the satisfaction of seeing his best students carrying on his founding principles of musical craftsmanship. Even if the ragtime vogue was over and Tin Pan Alley glutted with reams of poor imitation ragtime, there was a solid and extensive body of truly excellent music whose one fountainhead was Joplin. Joplin felt that arranging and publishing folk rags as clear, playable scores would give the black composer his rightful place in the world. It is miraculous that he was able to transmit a music essentially of the ear to the charted dots and lines of a piano score without losing its rhythmic and lyrical subtleties.

Joplin, it is clear from his statements about ragtime and from the titles of his works, felt his music to be a beautiful and graceful form for the piano, not a raucous or rowdy music fit only for back rooms and bagnios. There is a serenity in many rags which is reflected in Joplin's flower titles — "The Chrysanthemum," "Heliotrope Bouquet," "Fig Leaf Rag," "Rose Leaf Rag," "Sunflower Slow Drag" — and in other title choices such as "Euphonic Sounds" and "Paragon Rag." Scott's title, "Grace and Beauty," captures this feeling for the music exactly. There is in ragtime an ambivalence, a wavering between a limpid nineteenth-century elegance and an explosive vigor. The other half of the ragtime feeling comes out in titles like "Dynamite Rag," "Something Doing," "Red Pepper — A Spicy Rag,"

"Efficiency Rag." Joplin, in his best work, strove to balance the bucolic grace against the rude exuberance of the form. But it is apparent from Joplin's repeated instructions to play his music slowly and correctly, to treat it with dignity and care, that he envisioned performances as "classical," as elegant and precise.

The problem that both listeners and performers faced at the turn of the century was that ragtime was poised between two traditions — that of nineteenth-century sentimental parlor music and that of rough, black, country folk-dance styles. The white would-be ragtime pianist had a background in one tradition but not in the other; while the black performer, coming to a rather difficult and exactingly precise score, would hear the outline of the folk style in it but not see the decorous modifications Joplin had imposed. This is not to say that ragtime was simply a bastard form, a pastiche of folk materials undigested or chaotic. The very process of careful organization and synthesis of musical materials and styles had made it quite difficult in comparison with other popular piano music of the era. Joplin put severe demands on his players, asking a kind of care and exactitude rare even among professional and semiprofessional entertainers in theaters and vaudeville.

Further complications in the tangled history of ragtime occurred later, when jazz-oriented pianists returned to ragtime. They brought to it a sense of rhythm and consistency of tempo which is vital to good ragtime performance; however, they also brought a sense of jazz as "ear music," in which the pianist uses improvisatory decorations, in which the score is altered by the pianist's sense of "swing." Most jazz pianists become impatient with ragtime's apparent four-square stance, its stiffness in comparison with the jazz-piano style evolved through the twenties and thirties; and they tend to swing the ragtime score, to insert syncopations where the score calls for non-syncopated rhythms. This causes an immediate confusion of the basic ragtime rhythms and motion, adding syncopation to syncopation, using slight rhythmic hesitations or misplaced accents to achieve what they believe to be a jazz feeling. But ragtime is not jazz, not even a kind of primitive or archaic jazz; and the imposition of jazz style onto ragtime does not produce ragtime but another jazz performance based on ragtime materials. In a sense these jazz-oriented ragtime players are retrogressing, returning to a folk style which Joplin sought to regularize and polish in his written scores. The usual tendency, as Guy Waterman has pointed out,[5] is to alter the bass line of a rag, to substitute a "stride" or jazz bass line with broken rhythms for the predictable marchlike regular lines of the rag. But no matter how agile the performer, this imposition of jazz atop ragtime does not produce the kind of graceful but energetic music envisioned by Joplin and his followers. Joplin's goal was not just to make ragtime "respectable" and acceptable to genteel sensibilities but to make it an exact and monumental art.

Other classic rags reveal the same sort of organization as Joplin's. Many also communicate the same feelings of joy and exhilaration through dance rhythms and lyrical song lines. Only a handful of composers, however, were able to use the ragtime conventions without reducing them to repetitive clichés. The *manner* of ragtime is not difficult to imitate—the internal spirit, the elusive distinctiveness of the best rags, is harder to reduce to a formula. Clearly Scott Joplin was the supreme master of the genre, the man most responsible for communicating the folk styles of Louis Chauvin, Tom Turpin, Scott Hayden, and the other semilegendary Missouri players to a wide audience. But those genuinely gifted and sincere followers who played the rags of Joplin, Scott, and Lamb and learned the form through them also had important contributions to make to the school of ragtime, even if their works are sometimes viewed only as footnotes or addenda to the brief era of classic ragtime. One of the strongest proofs of ragtime's powerful hold on the popular imagination was the production of fine rags by dozens of musicians across the country. Ragtime moved from the grass

[5] Guy Waterman, "Ragtime," in Nat Hentoff and Albert McCarthy (eds.), *Jazz* (New York: Grove Press, 1961), 47–48.

roots of the first folk players to publication and distribution by the music industry and back across the nation to a new generation of composer-players far removed from the back streets of Sedalia. The echoes of "Maple Leaf Rag" were heard in a hundred thousand parlors, and they come back to us after three quarters of a century in the dusty pages of all the old rags inspired by Scott Joplin's pioneering efforts. If imitation is the sincerest form of flattery, then Joplin must have been flattered indeed by the hundreds of imitators who produced ragtime in his mold.

~⟨ IV ⟩~

Ragtime's Second Line:
Lesser Luminaries

You can't tell an American composer's "art-song" from any mediocre art-song the world over. (Permit me to pass over the few notable exceptions.) You can distinguish American ragtime from the popular music of any nation and any age.—Hiram K. Moderwell, 1915

So, anyhow, after I was in Memphis, safe and sound on the shores of Memphis, Tennessee, I decided to go to this Beale Street I had heard a lot of talk about. I first enquired was there any piano players in the city and they told me that absolutely the best in the whole state of Tennessee was there. I asked them had they heard about Tony Jackson, Alfred Carroll, Albert Wilson, or Winding Boy, and they said they had never heard of them guys.—Jelly Roll Morton, 1938

The second generation of ragmen who followed the Joplin clan were midwesterners who not only had better musical education but had the time to assimilate the original rag concept and to bring it into line with the more advanced ideas of their time.—David A. Jason, 1968

IN THE WAKE OF CLASSIC RAGTIME

The secondary composers working with ragtime can be fit into three categories: (1) commercial songwriters who used ragtime opportunistically but who were gifted enough to create aesthetically respectable works (*e.g.,* Charles N. Daniels, Kerry Mills, Egbert Van Alstyne, and the Von Tilzer brothers); (2) young composers working on the fringes of Tin Pan Alley, whose basic feelings and preferences were for ragtime and who used it as the basis for their popular compositions (*e.g.,* George Botsford, Charles L. Johnson, Henry Lodge, Percy Wenrich); (3) pianist-composers working directly in imitation of the classic ragtimers, whose primary work was the creation of genuine piano ragtime, as opposed to songs and novelties in a

ragtime vein (*e.g.,* Artie Matthews, Charles Thompson, J. Russel Robinson, Paul Pratt, Eubie Blake, Joe Jordan, Luckey
Roberts). These are, of course, artificial distinctions, since
listeners of the era would have felt that all popular music was
"ragtime"; few people, even inside the music business, shared
Scott Joplin's missionary belief in ragtime as an art form.

A solid tradition of ragtime flourished both inside and outside
the commercial music-publishing world. It was possible to be a
hit songwriter and still write respectable piano rags following
Joplin's patterns. And it was equally possible to eschew Tin
Pan Alley's temptations and go a lonely way, like Joplin, Scott,
and Lamb, in working on ragtime as a highly complex and
polished piano music. A few gifted souls managed to trim a
course between these extremes, like Percy Wenrich, born with
ragtime in his Missouri bones, who was also very successful in
working within the conventions of the popular song ("When You
Wore a Tulip," "Moonlight Bay"). A few others wrote rags
popular enough to keep them going and often only a slight cut
in quality below the best work of the classic writers. Charles L.
Johnson's work (both under his own name and under the pseudonym Raymond Birch) is extremely impressive as a collection
of rags, as is the work of Henry Lodge and J. Russel Robinson.
Others, like Eubie Blake, worked schizophrenically — with one
side of their lives heavily involved in the demands of commercial
composition and another, private portion of their existence
committed to pure ragtime. Still others were content to write a
few brilliant, totally original rags, then to retire from competition
in the music world. Artie Matthews and Charles Thompson of
St. Louis are prime examples of this dedication to unadulterated
ragtime ideals.

The body of respectable ragtime by composers of less genius
than Joplin, Scott, and Lamb is larger than the body of work by
the big three, and it is possible to compile an anthology of their
work which is as vital and interesting as (and more varied than)
the works of Joplin, Scott, and Lamb. The collective impression
of this secondary ragtime is of a twentieth-century Fitzwilliam

Virginal Book, an astonishingly varied and vital cross-section
of black folk materials and keyboard techniques at the turn of
the century. Each of these composers has a personal approach to
ragtime, an idiosyncratic manner; and each contributes unique
technical and structural devices to ragtime. Their work taken
together provides an excellent study of the boundaries and
characteristics of ragtime as it evolved from 1900 to 1915.
Some composers surpass the classic composers in particular
areas: Charles L. Johnson's and Henry Lodge's rags are more
rhythmically explosive and vital than those of any of the big
three (see Johnson's "Dill Pickles" or "Powder Rag," Lodge's
"Temptation Rag" or "Red Pepper"); Artie Matthews explored
the uses of Latin rhythms and blues-derived bass lines in his
series of "Pastime Rags," going well beyond anything in Joplin,
Scott, or Lamb; Luckey Roberts and Eubie Blake wrote rags
more complex and demanding than anything of the midwestern
school.

Again, it must be stressed that the ears of 1910-1915 were
not attuned to the fine differences in quality and conception
between rags. Ragtime was ragtime, all pretty much alike to
the average listener. Thus it is important to look across the
broad body of work which was available to the listener (and
the pianist) of the time. The secondary ragtime composers
fulfilled a vital function in the history of ragtime by maintaining a
high level of imaginative and technical quality for so large a
body of work. There is no reason to condescend to composers
like Artie Matthews, Eubie Blake, George Botsford. Their
work holds up well when measured against the best, and many
of their rags were better known and more widely played than
any of the later works of Joplin or Scott. Their work is sometimes more characteristic of the era than the purer work of the
classic composers, who worked in relative seclusion and without overt influences by the commercial music world. The fact
that John Stark, himself a radical purist in ragtime tastes, published Joplin, Scott, and Lamb is significant. Stark, one of the
most interesting personalities of ragtime, was as demanding in

aesthetic principles as any of his writers. He required the highest quality in the ragtime he printed, and his early association with Joplin had given him lofty standards. He was well acquainted with the music, and his son, E. J. Stark, wrote reasonably good rags himself and made many of the orchestral transcriptions the firm printed. In effect, Stark set and maintained musical standards for classic ragtime. Lesser composers, working for a variety of miscellaneous large publishing houses, were rarely importuned to improve their works, to bring them up to any preconceived levels of quality. The opposite was probably true — the voracious appetite of commerce pressured them to produce more, not better, works. In view of this inexorable demand, it is amazing that these men — working generally in isolation from each other, outside any such mainstream of musical interchange as the first-generation men of Sedalia and St. Louis had known — were able to write ragtime of consistency, imagination, and variety.

This is partially because ragtime as a solid folk style had preceded its establishment as a written genre. Certainly many ragtime composers knew what were loosely referred to as "jig piano" or "shout piano" styles before they read a ragtime score. Eubie Blake has recalled that ragtime style, syncopations, were in the air in the black community before he knew what "ragtime" meant:

> I didn't hear ragtime until a little later, but I heard syncopation in the Negro bands coming back from funerals and, of course, in the shouting in the church.
> That was all right, it seems, but not at home. I'm in there ragging hell out of *Traumerei* on the organ and my mother opened the door and laid down the law, "Take that ragtime out of my house." That was the first time I ever heard the word.[1]

And the folk style persisted even after the beginnings of the avalanche of scored works. Charles Thompson published only one of his many rags in his long active career as a pianist, though he carried the "scores" to others in his head and played them

[1] Rudi Blesh, *Combo: USA* (Philadelphia: Chilton Book Co., 1971), 190.

over the years. This was the common practice of most itinerant black folk players. They felt a persistent reluctance to publish musical scores, since this gave away the secrets of a personalized folk style to any reader. Other musicians could steal the painstakingly evolved individual touches of a player's music. This long-standing attitude was echoed in Freddie Keppard's refusal to record with his Creole Band for Victor (before the pioneering Original Dixieland Jazz Band!) because then people "could steal my stuff." Folk players musically literate enough to score their improvisatory playing were rarely motivated to do so; publishers simply didn't pay well enough. However, the stupendous commercial success of ragtime and ragtime songs helped change this attitude.

Joplin, and Joplin's whole concept of ragtime as an articulated art music, profoundly changed the ragtime world. As the ragtime boom started and accelerated with the phenomenal success of "Maple Leaf Rag," it was clear that ragtime was a goldmine, an untapped lode of fully developed folk materials. Most of Joplin's circle in Sedalia either did not want to write their works down or could not. Louis Chauvin, probably the most gifted and inventive pianist of the group (including Joplin), simply lacked motivation for the gruelling task of notation and revision. Like most folk musicians, he believed in his improvisatory genius; there was always more music waiting inside his head, and a sheet of paper with all those little black dots was unnecessary. One of Joplin's tasks was his collaboration with Chauvin, with Scott Hayden, Arthur Marshall, and other folk players; in this role he accomplished several things. He preserved their "ear" music in a comprehensible form, and he absorbed for himself a variety of styles and devices. Joplin's drive was to write this music down and conquer it on paper. (Contemporary witnesses generally agree that Joplin was an adequate but not spectacular pianist.) A few other folk players saw the wisdom or necessity of publishing—Jelly Roll Morton began very early in his career to write and publish his works, out of mixed motives of avarice, pride, and musical logic. Like

Joplin, Jelly Roll was driven by the demon of "legitimate" composition and worked all his life to find means of expressing on paper his own complex improvisational style.

Joplin, then, established a musical convention and discovered a commercial attraction. The second generation ragtimers were not as directly in contact with such creative folk artists as Tom Turpin, Louis Chauvin, or Ben Harney, but they had the examples of printed works by Joplin, Turpin, Scott, and others to serve as the same kind of inspiration. They benefited from the experimentation and conventionalization that Joplin and Scott had performed. In essence, the second generation men received the outlines of ragtime codified; their job was to find materials to fit into the rag form, in some ways a more strenuous task.

This is a paradoxical situation: Joplin and his peers had folk inspiration aplenty but no form into which to cast it, while the later men had a perfectly well-defined form and no direct folk inspiration for resources. However, enough of the genuine black folk impulse existed (even if in bastardized vaudeville versions) to keep composers active. A further impetus to composition was the continued tradition of the folk player himself, who might or might not be a skilled note reader. Brun Campbell, for example, went to Joplin not to study composition but to absorb the style itself. He became an accomplished interpreter of ragtime, but he was never primarily a composer in Joplin's demanding sense. Brun's compositions are pastiches of classic material or medlies of rag and popular materials cemented with a consistent keyboard style.

So there was a large and diverse market for rags among musicians working in the style, and they in turn furnished ideas for ragtime melodies and rhythms. The gala ragtime contests current for many years must have been means for ragtime players and writers to exchange ideas and methods. Jelly Roll Morton is typical, in his idiosyncratic and individualistic way, of the working musician who listened carefully to his rivals, stole judiciously from them, and used any means of overtrumping them before the listening public. (Jelly Roll confessed, with

his usual shamefaced pride in his own cunning, to tricking
Tony Jackson out of a ragtime prize by applying rudimentary
psychological warfare techniques, essentially beating him
through gamesmanship.)

At any rate, the secondary ragtime composer could draw on
many sources for his work. The problems he faced were as
manifold, however. First was a continued pressure to produce
music that would sell, music that was novel and catchy yet
within the safe confines of current taste. Second was the severe
competition within the commercial music world—competition
with really first-rate composers like Joplin, Scott, or Lamb and
with the army of hack composers and would-be ragtimers who
flooded the market with an ocean of pastiche ragtime and vul-
garized ragtime songs. Third were the limitations of the piano
rag form, the tightness and self-imposed restrictions of the
genre, which kept the composer working with restricted materials or forced him to adapt forms like the ragtime song, which
simplified the classic rag form and allowed some looseness in
composition. Fourth, and most oppressive, was the utter whim-
sicality of both popular taste and the interpretations of public
demand by commercial publishers. The ragtime composer was
afflicted with demands that he conform to current trends, write
songs to fit topical interests, and otherwise tailor his work to the
imperative demands of money and fashion.

These were the same pressures that drove Joplin to his breakdown, turned Scott to eking out a living as a pit band musician,
turned Lamb to a steadier business than the precarious and
demeaning occupation of popular music. But the second-generation ragtime composers were less committed to ragtime as a
musical-aesthetic ideal. Most turned their hands to whatever
ephemeral demands came along, churned out ragtime songs and
stock works for vaudeville. Some, like Wenrich, Van Alstyne,
and Blake, succeeded as itinerant popular composers and kept
the original ragtime idea intact in their music. Others, like
Artie Matthews and Charles L. Johnson, simply stopped writing
rags, even if they kept them alive in memory. Others, like

J. Russel Robinson, Charles Thompson, and Luckey Roberts, went on to careers as ragtime/jazz solo pianists but ceased active composition, preferring to play what they had already written or to work in newer piano idioms. Whatever their response to public pressures and tastes, the second-generation ragtime writers only prolonged the short span of ragtime a few years. By the end of the second decade of the century, the genre was gone, submerged in the bypaths of the culture, though the style lingered on in the work of hundreds of ragtime-trained players.

The solid contribution of second-generation ragtime composers to the art of ragtime cannot be ignored. Collectively, if not individually, they developed and extended musical ideas and techniques of the classic writers. For instance, J. Bodewalt Lampe, although he worked for years as a prolific arranger of popular music and composer of marches, never again reached the ragtime standard of his early "Creole Belles." Carey Morgan produced, in "Trilby Rag," one interesting and inventive work, then followed a career of composing much more pedestrian popular songs. James Reese Europe, working as Irene and Vernon Castle's house arranger-bandleader, produced a solid work in ragtime with "Castle House Rag"; but he was employed to write diverse works to illustrate varying dance fashions, from the maxixe through the one-step, so he did not pursue ragtime composition. The history of ragtime is spotted with examples of composers who worked only incidentally with ragtime then turned to other genres of popular music. The extremely varied work of these men cannot be dismissed because it is not part of a self-consistent *oeuvre* or does not demonstrate a lifetime commitment.

Other secondary composers for various reasons wrote only a small number of genuine rags. Artie Matthews, known as an excellent ragtime player (Morton said he was St. Louis' best around 1910), published only his five "Pastime Rags" as a series of etudes for the pianist. He went on to a long career as a music teacher, and his ragtime works fit this pedagogical mold, as advanced exercises for the would-be ragtime performer. He apparently was not driven by the demon which inhabited Joplin, Scott, and Lamb—the drive to create works purely for themselves, to press the aesthetic frontiers of ragtime forward without practical motives. But his fine rags still constitute a compendium of ragtime techniques. Eubie Blake, whose long and busy lifetime in the music business testifies to his commitment and seriousness, wrote only a few rags, although he, like most ragtime entertainers, has a vast repertoire of unwritten original compositions. He then went on into commercial work with the musical stage and with jazz forms. Charles Thompson bothered to commit only his prize-winning "Lily Rag" to paper but carried the complete forms of others in his head and fingers, making phonograph records of a few original compositions but passing on no more. We must continually recall that ragtime was a folk tradition and form, that many more rags perished unscored than were written and printed. The most notorious loss is of Louis Chauvin's ragtime works, apparently as rich and complex a horde as Joplin's large published series but never committed to paper (except for "Heliotrope Bouquet," a direct collaboration with Joplin, and the scattered ideas of Chauvin that are said to live unacknowledged in the ragtime of Joplin, Turpin, and Scott).

Basically the second-generation men were writers and composers first and folk stylists second. Since they lived by selling compositions, much of their work has been preserved. In a sense, this is a basic aesthetic problem: how much is their work a simplification and modification of ragtime as played by the best virtuoso performers? As with most "ear-centered" folk musics, ragtime is difficult to annotate conventionally, and Joplin's whole revolutionary movement toward scoring is a trend away from the practices of folk players. As Joplin listened and reduced his observations to conventional notation, he compromised with his ears to simplify, clarify, and regularize the practices of folk ragtime styles. (However, since ragtime was oriented toward the standard tuning of the piano keyboard, this at least avoids the extremely knotty problems of annotating other black music forms — blues and jazz — where vocal-derived instrumental practices such as microtonal intonations make notation at best a vague approximation.) In essence, the entire structure of ragtime represents a compromise and regularization; its symmetry and order are imposed, after the fact. It is not an exact transcription of played ragtime of the 1890's but a deliberate expurgation and correction of some practices and a simplification of others, to bring the work within reach of an averagely gifted pianist. This practice of simplification of difficult folk styles is most vividly illustrated in the rag scores by Eubie Blake and Luckey Roberts, both virtuoso players with large, nimble hands, capable of playing incredibly demanding "trick" passages. The published scores of their rags are considerably simpler and less exhibitionistic than their performances of the same works. Publishers considered their works too "advanced" or complex for the music-buying public and accordingly demanded printed scores which are in effect outlines or synopses of the performance style. The legendary example is Luckey Roberts' "Ripples of the Nile," a very difficult piece written to be played at high speed and using very wide finger spans; rejected by the publisher as "unplayable," it was returned to Luckey, who later slowed it down and simplified a portion as the popular song, "Moonlight Cocktail."

Many second-generation composers came to ragtime composition at a great remove from a live folk tradition. Writing a rag was a straightforward problem in composition, not an attempt to communicate a style. Therefore, their compositional practices became conventionalized quickly, deteriorating into a process of pastiche arrangement, not original invention. In commercial imitations of folk ragtime, the clichés of the rag are repeated endlessly and mercilessly, without care for melodic clarity, coherence, or structural logic. Because the rag's form is open — a suite, potpourri, or medley — it is susceptible to bastardizing, jumbling of musical ideas in chaotic fashion. This is precisely what many hack composers proceeded toward — an

indiscriminate repetition of familiar rhythmic and melodic figures pasted together haphazardly, an anthology of echoes from
popular rags. More than most musical forms, the rag is vul-
nerable to mutilation by heedless grafting. This process of
collage-composition, more than any other single factor, corrupted the public ear for ragtime. Gresham's Law operates
with a vengeance in the popular arts, and bad art inevitably
drives out good in the open marketplace.

Not that all second-generation ragtime composers were motivated only by veniality or ignorance. However, because many
began with written compositions as models and proceeded to
write more compositions, the production of ragtime hastened
toward a consolidation of concepts and materials which it was
too immature to bear. An orthodoxy, a strict commercialization
set in, a form of premature rigor mortis. Only a few secondary
composers adhered closely to ragtime composition and produced works that are varied and inventive and which show a
progressive development of the composer's sensibility. Henry
Lodge's rags are distinctive and varied; they sound like no
one else's work, and each is different from its predecessor. His
"Temptation Rag" has continued to be popular because it employs a persistent habanera-like rhythmic pattern developed
through distinctive themes. But his more obscure "Sneaky
Shuffles," "Black Diamond Rag," and "Red Pepper" are
equally imaginative and melodic. His large and varied output of
rags ought to be better known. Charles L. Johnson, another
prolific and indefatigable composer, struck off a series of compositions that are far more than imitations of the black writers
from his native Southwest. Everyone knows his "Dill Pickles,"
but his "Powder Rag" and "Blue Goose Rag" (published under
the *nom de plume* Raymond Birch) are excellent works and were
once standard in the ragtime repertoire of 1910–1915. The same
process of cataloging could be applied to two dozen fine composers, all known, at best, by one occasionally played composition. A little investigation shows how fickle public taste and
memory prove. It is almost as if there existed an unwritten law

of popular culture alloting a popular composer just one hit, one second of glory. The same idea applies as much to the great genius of Joplin as to his followers. He is, after all, known to general posterity only as the obscure composer of "Maple Leaf Rag," which in turn stands as a symbol and portmanteau epitome for all of ragtime.

The importance of the second-generation writers comes in the aggregate, then, not in distinct musical personalities, because most never received enough recognition to be known popularly as individuals. Their work was simply part of a vast and varied flow of music loosely accepted as "ragtime," lumped together with songs from fifth-rate musical revues, popular marches, and two-steps, the detritus of the popular music industry. Only by dint of retrospective analysis is it clear that some composers understood ragtime from the inside out and felt an intuitive kinship with black musical expression, while others simply aped externals. But it is obvious that the ragtime pulse communicated itself clearly and whole to some white ears.

Among second-generation ragtimers, there was a meeting and fusion of the two earliest strands of ragtime—black folk traditions which had motivated Joplin and the Missouri ragtime men, and traditions of minstrelsy and vaudeville on which early commercial writers (e.g., Kerry Mills, Lampe, Van Alstyne) founded their work. In oversimplified terms, these are black and white traditions; but both are founded on ancestral musical forms no longer extant, and both ultimately derive from rudimentary black forms. The ragtime composers who came into prominence around 1910 made a synthesis of these early traditions, a thorough assimilation of both original folk materials as transmitted via classic ragtime and the innumerable corruptions of folk material passed into popular song via the minstrel show, vaudeville, and musical revues. Thus, we ought to find in second-generation work the structure and conventions of classic ragtime and the careless lyricism of the popular rag song—and that is an accurate description of the style.

By 1910 ragtime had ceased to be a black folk music and

become a universally accepted American popular music, despite the objections of moralists, conservateurs of the musical establishment, and elitist cultural observers. It had communicated a totally new approach to the popular song — a flexible, improvisational, pianistic style based on persistent broken rhythms — and shattered forever the old mode of strictly written-and-read music. After 1900 few popular musicians felt content simply to read off the notes printed in the score of a song; the improvisational practices of folk ragtime — "ragging" a tune — brought a whole new world of possibilities to the workaday musician. The practice of shifting accents and using syncopations was strongly ingrained in everyone in the ragtime tradition. The original folk style was thus communicated through the medium of printed scores as well as through the examples of hundreds of itinerant players.

One of the most important functions of the ragtime composers of 1910–1915 was their communication of ragtime traditions to later musical modes. If the early ragtime of 1895–1910 brought the first impact of a fully developed black musical style on white popular music, the late ragtimers solidified this tradition and perpetuated it. The ragtime style was carried into jazz modes of the 1920's through dozens of ragtime-oriented pianists. Jelly Roll Morton never lost his basic ragtime orientation, nor did J. Russel Robinson or James P. Johnson. Not only were the earliest jazz pieces adaptations of instrumental ragtime, but the pianist in most early jazz groups played a relatively "straight" ragtime part behind the band. Good examples can be heard on the Original Dixieland Jazz Band recordings, where Henry Ragas', J. Russel Robinson's, and Billy Jones's piano parts are clearly ragtime, or in the work of Walter Decou, a New Orleans pianist who played with the Sam Morgan Jazz Band in the 1920's and was recorded in 1942 with Bunk Johnson's band and whose parts in the ensemble are "pure" ragtime. So, even if active production of ragtime had nearly halted after 1920, the style itself was kept very much alive in jazz and popular music. Ragtime composer-performers of major stature,

like Eubie Blake or James P. Johnson, went on to write successful music for revues, thus preserving their ragtime-derived
ideas inside the various forms of popular music. The whole
nascent tradition of Harlem shout-piano styles stemmed from
ragtime-oriented players like Blake and Johnson and passed
conspicuously through the work of Fats Waller, Duke Ellington,
and many other pianist-composers of the next generation, right
down to the work of Thelonius Monk and many of the most
modern jazz pianists.

However, not all results of second-generation composition
were positive. Developing along with composers who listened
to and respected the work of classic ragtime writers was another group more directly derived from the tradition of the
razzle-dazzle ragtime contest and the exhibitionistic pianistic
improvisation. Composers like Zez Confrey and Roy Bargy
developed a pseudo-ragtime "novelty" mode designed to show
off virtuoso style, at the expense of ragtime's basic drive, form,
and consistency. Confrey's popular "Kitten on the Keys" is
typical of this bastard form. This branch of ragtime developed
into the empty pyrotechnics of the cocktail pianist, a style based
on cascades of arpeggios which mask deficiencies in rhythmic
motion, especially in the left hand. The drive of ragtime is subordinated to elaborately decorative figures, deliberately intricate
problems in keyboard articulation that are no longer melodic
units but raw exercises in ingenuity.

This branch of pseudo-ragtime transmitted itself through
popular music also, through cocktail pianists and piano showpieces, culminating in the debased ragtime styles of the barroom ricky-tick school of "ragtime." This style presses the
basic pianistic tendencies of ragtime to absurdity, abandoning
marchlike rhythms and evolving into a "pure" pianism divorced
from intelligible musical structure. When the works of Confrey
or Bargy are compared with the pianistic developments of Jelly
Roll Morton (e.g., "Perfect Rag," "Bert Williams," or "Fingerbuster"), there is a vast difference in conception and quality,
although Morton admitted an admiration for Roy Bargy's work.

Morton's piano pieces are conceived as compositions first, piano vehicles second, even though Morton was a virtuoso player capable of constructing difficult and elaborate works rooted in ragtime. The 1938 Library of Congress recordings of Morton give him an opportunity to play every conceivable ragtime and jazz style, and when he plays piano versions of his band compositions ("Jungle Blues" or "Hyena Stomp"), they immediately become pianistic under his fingers. It is this quality of musical flexibility that marks the best ragtime—it was conceived as music before it was designed as a means of exhibiting piano technic.

The end of the ragtime tradition, then, came in a debased pianistic absurdity which abandoned the dance rhythms and march structure of original ragtime for chaotic parades of arpeggios and trick fingerings. But this was not the end of ragtime's legacy to popular music and jazz. Its influence—in terms of musical structure and techniques, in terms of a demanding impulse toward form and symmetry—runs through all the popular music of the twenties. Another legacy of ragtime is the union of black and white musicians in a common musical tradition. The story of ragtime is one of men working across the strong color line of their time—Joseph Lamb working harmoniously with Joplin, drawing on Scott's inspirations and completely mastering the intricacies of classic ragtime. The same story is repeated among the secondary composers. Half or more were white composers at some remove from the basic folk sources of ragtime, yet they managed to assimilate the musical ideas and spirit of ragtime, to produce genuinely "black" music despite their distance from the black folk community. This demonstration of racial harmony is of great importance for American music and American society. The story of white musicians fascinated by black music and becoming immersed in it is repeated many times in the history of jazz. The story of talented and insightful men like John Stark, who eschewed purely commercial interests to help black musicians, recurs in the work of men like John Hammond, Alan Lomax, William Russell, and many other jazz historians and critics.

Ragtime was a potent force in uniting the nation in song. Even with the elements of blatant racism and commercialism which marred its career, ragtime provided a powerful outlet for black feelings and demonstrated the gifts of black musicians to a wider public than ever before. It was a triumphant overture for the great renaissance of black musical culture which has distinguished the twentieth century.

RAGTIME SKETCHES: SOME BRIEF LIVES
IN THE RAGTIME BUSINESS

Eubie Blake (1883–). Born in Baltimore, conservatory-trained in New York, Blake teamed with Noble Sissle in 1915 for a lifelong collaboration on musical productions. In 1917 he worked with James Reese Europe in the Clef Club Orchestra and went on with Sissle to create highly successful musicals like *Shuffle Along, The Chocolate Dandies,* and *Blackbirds of 1930.* Rags like "Fizzwater" and "Charleston Rag" demonstrate his personal version of volatile and difficult east-coast ragtime.

George Botsford (1874–1949). From Sioux Falls, South Dakota, Botsford worked as a commercial songwriter and small music publisher. Beginning early with a typical cakewalk, "The Katy Flyer" (1899), he went on to rags like his well-known "Black and White Rag" (1908), "Texas Steer Rag" (1909), "Chatterbox Rag" (1910). He also wrote "Grizzly Bear Rag" (1910), for which Irving Berlin contributed lyrics, initiating one of the many animal-fashion dance fads. His best-known rag song, "Sailing Down Chesapeake Bay" (1913), is still heard.

Charles N. Daniels (Neil Moret) (1878–1943). From Leavenworth, Kansas, Daniels worked as an important commercial songwriter-arranger and as a small music publisher. His "Hiawatha" (1901) brought him $10,000 and initiated the craze for "Indian intermezzos." Earlier, he had arranged Joplin's first published rag, "Original Rags" (1899), for publication. He tried to follow up the Indian song craze with "Silver Heels" (1909) and later became a standard popular tunesmith, with "Chloe,"

"Moonlight and Roses," and "She's Funny That Way" to his credit.

Abe Holzmann (1874–1939). Born in New York City, Holzmann was conservatory-trained and worked as an arranger-composer in the music trade. He contributed basic works to the cakewalk craze, with "Smokey Mokes" (1899), "Hunky Dory" (1901), and "Bunch O' Blackberries" (1900), all popularized internationally by Sousa's band. He continued to work as a composer, concentrating on march forms.

Charles H. Hunter (1878–1907). Hunter was born in Columbia, Tennessee, and ended his career in St. Louis. Self-taught and nearly blind, he worked as a piano tuner and composed rags in an early folk style. His best-known rags are "Tickled to Death" (1899), "A Tennessee Tantalizer" (1900), " 'Possum and 'Taters" (1901), and "Cotton Bolls" (1901).

Charles L. Johnson (*Raymond Birch*) (1876–1950). Born in Kansas City, Kansas, Johnson lived and worked there as a music publisher. Best known for "Dill Pickles Rag" (1906), he wrote one enduring Indian intermezzo, "Iola" (1906). Under the name Raymond Birch he contributed "Powder Rag" (1907), "Blue Goose Rag" (1916), and other highly skillful compositions in the classic tradition.

Joe Jordan (1882–1971). Born in Cincinnati and reared in St. Louis, in the hothouse atmosphere of early ragtime, Jordan moved to Chicago and professional music, working as a bandleader and arranger. He teamed with Ernest Hogan in songwriting, formed the Memphis Students singing/playing group, went on to team with Will Marion Cook and to a long career as an orchestra leader. His best-known rags include "Pekin Rag" (1904), "J.J.J. Rag" (1905), and "That Teasin' Rag" (1909).

J. Bodewalt Lampe (*Ribe Danmark*) (1869–1929). Born in Ribe, Denmark, Lampe arrived in the U.S. in 1873, was conservatory-trained, and worked as a composer-arranger-conductor in all phases of popular music. His enduring "Creole Belles" (1900) was an archetypal cakewalk, at the end of the craze. He wrote many stock arrangements of rags, rag songs, and music in the ragtime tradition for orchestra and band. Lampe ended his career as musical supervisor for the Trianon Ballroom in Chicago and musical director of Dell Lampe's dance orchestra.

Frederick Allen (Kerry) Mills (1869–1948). Born in Philadelphia, Mills worked for many years in New York as a publisher, following trends in the black music traditions. He wrote the most typical cakewalk, "At a Georgia Campmeeting" (1897), the standard and enduring Indian intermezzo, "Red Wing" (1906), and contributed dozens of other rag songs and related materials, including "Kerry Mills' Ragtime Dance" (1911). The most facile and skilled commercial ragtime composer, Mills's career reflects changing trends of 1895–1915 in detail.

J. Russel Robinson (1892–1963). Born in Indianapolis, a center of white ragtime activity (May Aufderheide, Paul Pratt), Robinson's career vividly links ragtime and jazz traditions. His ragtime compositions—"Sapho Rag" (1909), "Dynamite Rag" (1910), "The Minstrel Man" (1911), and "That Eccentric Rag" (1912)—lead directly to his jazz works—"Margie" (1920), "Aggravatin' Papa" (1922), "Beale Street Mama" (1923), "Lena from Palesteena" (1920), "Singin' the Blues" (1920), and "Rhythm King" (1928). The jazz pieces were featured by the Original Dixieland Jazz Band, Bix Beiderbecke's Gang, and other important jazz bands. Robinson replaced Henry Ragas in the Original Dixieland Jazz Band and toured with them to England, introducing ragtime and rag songs to British music hall audiences. The Original Dixieland Jazz Band recorded many of his early jazz numbers.

Tom Turpin (*ca.* 1873–1922). Born in Savannah, Georgia, Turpin moved early to St. Louis, following his father's trade as a saloon-keeper, opening his Rosebud in St. Louis and making it a ragtime center. As a pioneer folk player-composer, Turpin was catalytic in transcribing early folk ragtime styles, which appear in his rags: "Harlem Rag" (1897), "The Bowery Buck" (1899), "A Ragtime Nightmare" (1900), "St. Louis Rag" (1903), and "The Buffalo Rag" (1904). Turpin's early ragtime was a basic influence on all midwestern ragtime composers.

Egbert Van Alstyne (1882–1951). Born in Chicago and conservatory-trained, Van Alstyne worked as an itinerant ragtime musician with road shows and vaudeville, then set up as a commercial songwriter with Harry Williams and later with Gus Kahn. He contributed rag songs like "In the Shade of the Old Apple Tree" (1905) and shared credit with Tony Jackson on publication of "Pretty Baby" (1916).

Albert and Harry Von Tilzer (1878–1956; 1872–1946). From the Indianapolis ragtime clan, the Von Tilzers established a fantastically successful publishing empire in New York, producing dozens of enduring popular tunes. In the ragtime tradition they produced: "O By Jingo" (1905), "What You Gonna Do When the Rent Comes Round?" (1905), "Wait Till the Sun Shines, Nelly" (1905), "The Cubanola Glide" (1909), and many other standard rag songs.

Percy Wenrich (1880–1952). From Joplin, Missouri, Wenrich was directly linked with the folk-rag tradition. He established himself as a commercial songwriter and vaudeville performer with his singer wife, Dolly Connolly. Wenrich wrote rags — "Ashy Africa" (1903), "Peaches and Cream Rag" (1905), "The Smiler" (1907), "Dixie Darlings" (1907), and many others — plus popular songs in the ragtime tradition — "Put on Your Old Grey Bonnet" (1909), "Moonlight Bay" (1912), "When You Wore a Tulip and I Wore a Big Red Rose" (1914).

V

Ragtime Songs and Ragtime Bands

". . . many of the tunes played by the smaller marching bands were popular ragtime songs, not classic rags such as those composed by Joplin and out-of-town writers. Ragtime songs were all the rage. . . ."
— Roy Carew, 1966

". . . they did a lot of ad-libbing in ragtime style. . . ." — Jelly Roll Morton, 1938

> *I got a ragtime dog and a ragtime cat,*
> *A ragtime piano in my ragtime flat;*
> *Wear ragtime clothes, from hat to shoes,*
> *I read a paper called the "Ragtime News."*
> *Got ragtime habits and I talk that way,*
> *I sleep in ragtime and I rag all day;*
> *Got ragtime troubles with my ragtime wife,*
> *I'm certainly living a ragtime life.*
> *— Roberts and Jefferson, 1900*

Along with the work of the classic ragtime composers and their serious followers, there is a broad spectrum of popular rag songs and the folk ragtime style to be considered. In terms of wide influence, pseudo-ragtime and commercial rag songs are more important than masterworks by Joplin, Scott, and Lamb. What hack composers and publishers' arrangers did was to make ragtime available to everyone. If this was inevitably a process of cheapening and debasing the materials of folk ragtime, it was also a means of bringing the music directly into the mainstream of American life. They made ragtime a musical language, a common dialect anyone could understand.

There are two processes to consider: the ragtime song phenomenon and its directions, and the conversion of piano ragtime into ensemble music. Both these evolutions are complex, and both bear directly on the public effect of this first major black music form to become a popular music. We must try to understand how the Man on the Street of 1900 got his ragtime and what it meant to him—how he started "living a ragtime life." To do this, we must sift through many diverse kinds of musical materials from the turn of the century.

FROM "COON SONGS"
TO "INDIAN INTERMEZZOS"

If the modern business of popular music publishing—Tin Pan Alley—really had its genesis in the 1890's vogues of "coon songs," "plantation songs," and cakewalks, by 1900 it was a large, rapacious industry which lived and breathed competition. The struggle among rival tunesmiths was fierce and Darwinian, "red in tooth and claw" at least figuratively. The term "ragtime" became a catchword, and for a few years it was mandatory to label every new tune as ragtime. From the commercial presses rolled a torrent of hack work indiscriminately tagged as rags or ragtime songs, many of the products either worked-over versions of old sentimental parlor songs or grotesque imitations of genuine black folk music, or what a songwriter scrabbling for a living in New York City thought was folk music.

However, in the confusion of unchecked musical capitalism, a few genuinely gifted and perceptive composers worked; most of them were white, but trained in or acquainted with black musical traditions. The most gifted writers of the cakewalk craze were white musicians essentially trained in a "legitimate" tradition—perhaps explaining why the cakewalks are such highly structured and formalized music, a direct link with the strong march tradition of the nineteenth century. The three men who wrote cakewalks which have endured are Abe Holzmann, classically trained ("Smokey Mokes" [1899], "Hunky Dory" [1901], "Bunch O' Blackberries" [1900]); Kerry Mills, an astonishingly facile and prolific publisher-composer ("At a Georgia Campmeeting" [1897], "Whistlin' Rufus" [1899]);

and J. Bodewalt Lampe, a gifted immigrant composer, also classically trained and working chiefly as an itinerant arranger ("Creole Belles [1909]"). There were other cakewalks—Sadie Koninsky's "Eli Green's Cakewalk" (1896), William H. Tyers's "Aunt Mandy's Wedding March" (1899), and an early example, D. Emerson's "Kullud Koons' Kake Walk" (1892)—but it might justly be asserted that Holzmann, Mills, and Lampe captured the archetypal cakewalk in their handful of tunes.

An important aspect of the cakewalk craze, which led directly and logically to the rise of ragtime as a popular cult, was the connection of the cakewalk with brass band literature. The 1890's saw the maturation of a broad American movement in wind-band literature and styles. There were literally thousands of village, town, and city bands across the nation, all demanding music and musical examples. Patrick Gilmore died in 1892 after a lifetime of energetic and ingenious work with bands and their music; and his immediate heir was John Philip Sousa, who was destined to create and maintain the most successful band in history. The cakewalk craze occurred as Sousa was becoming nationally known for his touring band and for the new march music he was creating with it. Sousa, sensitive to popular tastes and new ideas, immediately incorporated cakewalk music into his band's repertoire as a bow to the folk music of the South, even though he had some difficulty in getting cakewalks arranged and played properly. His trombone soloist, Arthur Pryor, a Missourian with a feeling for the folk ragtime rhythms of cakewalk, took over the task of making these new syncopated arrangements. When Pryor went out on his own, he continued this tradition in his band's repertoire. Quite early, Sousa played arrangements of Holzmann's and Mills's cakewalks and commissioned other pieces in the style.[1] It was clear from the beginning that in some ways the cakewalk music was

[1] Sousa, in his own composition, was fascinated with the materials of ragtime. He dealt with Indian themes in two marches, "Powhatan's Daughter" and "New Mexico"; and in an ambitious suite, *The Dwellers of the Western World,* he incorporated Indian themes and a section on the black man which used cakewalk and early ragtime materials in a careful and inventive manner.

more suited to instrumental rendition than to the piano keyboard. The cakewalk, so closely akin to the traditional march, called for a rich, polyphonic treatment. Certainly the old band recordings from 1900–1910 by Sousa, Pryor, and others still show much life and power, despite cramped acoustic recording techniques.

Curiously, the cakewalk craze has survived most firmly in the brass band tradition, even more than in ragtime, which absorbed and reworked the cakewalk's flavor and rhythms totally. There is a strong movement in brass band literature toward a kind of cakewalk/minstrel/vaudeville/circus genre piece very much in a line of descent from the cakewalk. This appears in the series of "circus trombone" set pieces probably initiated by Pryor's work as a virtuoso trombone soloist with Sousa. There is a rather large literature of such pieces, all featuring robust trombone work, either in solo or in section, making heavy use of trombone "smears" or glissades in a folk or "nonlegitimate" manner. Works in this subgenre include a series by bandmaster Henry Fillmore (" 'Lassus Trombone," "Shoutin' Liza Trombone," "Sally Trombone," "Bones Trombone," " 'Hot' Trombone"); a work recorded on cylinder by Sodero's Military Band ("Slidus Trombonus"); and many others, leading logically on to jazz set pieces like Kid Ory's "Ory's Creole Trombone" or Wingy Manone's "Tailgate Ramble," which are really set in this circus-band tradition rather than in any direct jazz heritage. The connection of circuses with vaudeville and with the long-lived tradition, especially in the Deep South, of the traveling minstrel show is reflected clearly in the titles of Fillmore's works. The endurance of cakewalk music in this form is a fine example of the persistence of folk ragtime rhythms and folk styles in out-of-the-way corners of Americana.

The intermixture of jazz and brass band traditions is widely documented, but there is a curious cross-connection with the cakewalk here also. One of the finest and longest-lived New Orleans street bands, the Eureka Brass Band, recorded in 1958 a circus-band specialty, "Trombonium," by Buell N. Withrow

(1914). The Eureka Band read the piece from a stock arrangement, obviously infusing it with a great deal of their own improvisational fervor. This arrangement was made by a Jerome H. Remick house arranger, one Ribe Danmark—a pseudonym for J. Bodewalt Lampe, the "Creole Belles" cakewalk man of 1900. The trio of "Trombonium" bears a suspiciously marked resemblance to the verse of Lampe's own "Creole Belles." (Another Lampe composition, "Georgia Sunset Cake-Walk," recorded in 1908 by Arthur Pryor's band, also sounds much like "Creole Belles.") Thus there is a long and complex series of connections between the original cakewalks and long-standing brass band/circus band/vaudeville pit band/jazz group traditions. The cakewalk has been sustained as a basic part of this diffuse instrumental tradition.

The cakewalk craze provided a link between folk ragtime styles and a more polished and structured music, largely through the musicians who wrote and arranged the music. This is a significant point, for the cakewalk craze was subsumed by the much larger boom in ragtime in the last years of the 1890's, and the turn to a piano form has obscured the instrumental nature of the cakewalk. It forms a major connection with later ragtime instrumental fashions, when arrangers began making ensemble transcriptions of piano rags. We need to recall that the cakewalk craze attracted a strong following of listeners oriented toward dance music and toward ensemble versions of dance music at that. This major impulse exists side by side with the pianistic motives of classic ragtime. The strong march rhythms of the cakewalk were absorbed into a piano style and used in subtle ways by classic ragtime composers, but they still show traces of their origin and place in band literature.

The meteoric rise of ragtime as a vogue, occurring simultaneously with the peak of the cakewalk craze, quickly obscured the earlier fads of the nineties, including the "coon songs" and other vestigal minstrel ideas; but it did this through the same process of synthesis and absorption. Ragtime satisfied both the people looking for a vigorous, steady dance music and the

audience for folk-flavored songs redolent of Old South mythology and downhome allusions. Ragtime also solidified the
economic positions of many major publishers. In effect, it created Tin Pan Alley as a going business proposition. Before the
1890's and the diffusion of black-derived musics sprouting
from minstrelsy's corpse, there was no large-scale commercial
operation. After 1900, when the ragtime vogue peaked, there
was a massive music industry centered in New York City but
competing with healthy operations in Detroit, Indianapolis,
Cincinnati, St. Louis, and other midwestern cities. To be fair,
recovery from the depressions of the 1890's also spurred on
the enlargement of the whole entertainment industry, but ragtime was nevertheless a basic attraction which helped many
publishers and writers get a leg up into the business.

Significantly, most histories of popular music have slighted
the direct influence of ragtime and original black composition
in the rise of the commercial business. The mythology of Tin
Pan Alley has been developed through countless films and
novels, stories of rags-to-riches show-biz success, fictionalized
biographies of Irving Berlin, Rogers and Hart, George M.
Cohan—an interesting formula dependent on a standardized
version of the American Dream: America the Land of Opportunity. The archetypal story depicts a struggling man of genius
walking into the dingy office of a cigar-chewing, cynical old
song-plugger and singing his heart out, moving swiftly thence
to the footlights, with a Good Woman backing him against
adversity, until suddenly all America is singing and dancing
to the young genius' inspiration. This popular folktale, a variant
of the literary folktale of the Young Man from the Provinces,
has helped gild and gloss over the crassness and veniality of
the commercial music industry and has masked the unbridled
capitalism inherent in the business. This myth carefully sup-
presses details of thefts from talented composers, black and
white, as a matter of course. The tales told by Jelly Roll Morton,
Perry Bradford, and other creators of black music are quite
different from the authorized version of Tin Pan Alley poetic
justice.

For instance, ragtime's role in creating a mass market for sheet music is minimized in one recent standard history of popular music. Further, the author garbles the simplest facts of ragtime's history to the point of unintelligibility, demonstrating again that the history of black music has consistently been distorted, misread, and mislaid through the myopic vision of white commentators. David Ewen attempts to describe the genesis of ragtime and makes what must be a record number of howlers in one brief expository paragraph:

> The first to write down a rag was Scott Joplin, a Negro pianist from Missouri. [The first composition formally titled as a rag was "Mississippi Rag," entered for copyright by William H. Krell, who used it as an instrumental piece with his band as well as in a piano arrangement.] When he was working as a ragtime pianist at the Maple Leaf Club, he attracted a local publisher, John Stil[l]well Stark, who offered to publish some of his rags. *Oriental Rag* [*sic*] in 1899 was not only Joplin's first published piece of music but also the first piano rag ever printed. [The correct title is, of course, "Original Rags"; it was not Joplin's first publication. See above for the first-ever business. The first Negro rag printed was Tom Turpin's "Harlem Rag," in 1897.] Later the same year Stark issued Joplin's *Maple Leaf Rag* — to this day a classic in piano ragtime. Among Joplin's later pieces were *Sunflower Rag* [*sic* — "Sunflower Slow Drag"]. . . .[2]

Nearly every fact here is wrong; and if this is typical of writing on the backgrounds of popular music, it is no wonder that black music has been devalued in the minds of the white middle-class reader/listener. There is no excuse for such glaring errors when Blesh and Janis' *They All Played Ragtime* has laid out the basic facts for anyone to find. It is only a blindness to black music's history and significance which creates such error, plus a concomitant feeling that popular music doesn't matter too much, and who really cares if it is treated shoddily?

Whether the history of black music is garbled by deliberate distortion or by carelessness, the effect has been to minimize or dismiss the facts of black music's seminal role in the whole

[2] David Ewen, *The Life and Death of Tin Pan Alley* (New York: Funk and Wagnalls Co., Inc., 1964), 170.

range of twentieth-century music. This is symptomatic of the dominant white culture's urge to shape its social myths in its own image. The hackneyed story of rags-to-riches success by a poor-but-honest White Anglo-Saxon Protestant is preferable to the truth of black composers working against impossible odds to reshape the course of white culture. At any rate, the ragtime revolution was a significant force in the development of a multimillion-dollar popular music industry. Then, the publishing houses moved to control and exploit the demand for ragtime. This was done first by the production of ersatz ragtime and rag songs starkly reminiscent of the recent "coon song" craze.

A principal rule of commercial music exploitation is: Ride with the tide, follow a trend and milk it for all it's worth. A corollary or logical extension is: Be ready to change the trend, but change it as little as possible—find the next step in the popular imagination to which you can relate. The result of this looking-glass logic led directly to the vogue, beginning about 1902, for the "Indian intermezzo," relevant as an integral part of the ragtime movement, with the best Indian songs written by experienced ragtime composers. Further, it is evidence of the direction that popular music took—from derisive "coon songs" to sentimental and nostalgic hokum about America's other persecuted and despised minority, the Indian. After the recent final defeat of hostile tribes, the American Indian was a defused threat, an object now of pity rather than of fear and hatred. The evolutions of the popular imagination in regard to the Indian are almost as complex as toward the black man, but without the potent residual guilt of the slavery issue.

On December 29, 1890, at Wounded Knee, South Dakota, elements of the U.S. Army massacred the last significant hostile Indian force, in one horrific genocidal gesture settling the problem of "Indian Violence" on the closing frontiers. From this time, there was no more real threat from American Indians as an organized and free group in our society. The ambivalent attitudes of white society could coalesce quickly. There had always been a strong strain of "Noble Savage" philosophy in the popular imagination, side by side with the usual malicious doctrines of inferiority, bestialism. "Hard" and "soft" versions of primitivism were always in conflict over the presence of the Indian. Popular songs celebrated the "Noble Red Man" through the eighteenth and nineteenth centuries, after the most active threats of the French and Indian War and the virtual expulsion of eastern tribes from New York state and the seaboard. And literature had treated the Indian generously as a piece of intriguing exotica, from Philip Freneau's and J. F. Cooper's portraits onward. By the turn of the century, the Indian question was settled for good and all in the public mind — the Indian could be treated comfortably as a harmless object of compassion, with an overt romanticism and nostalgia. We, as a culture, very thoroughly followed the pioneer doctrine that "the only good redskin is a dead redskin," and then sat back to sentimentalize our late, dead adversaries.

The final passing of the threat of Indian violence and the gradual fading of the surviving Indian population into relative obscurity on the remote reservation areas occurred during a period of controversy in art, and specifically in music, over the existence and feasibility of an American national music. While the concern with this issue dates from the middle decades of the nineteenth century, a certain discouragement over the apparent failure of American culture to produce an identifiable national music had set in by the turn of the century. Despite some vigorous attempts to rationalize this failure — notably by Reginald Dekoven, writing in 1909 — self-conscious efforts to create an American music continued.

The crux of the difficulty in creating a national music was the notion that national music should incorporate folk or indigenous music of the people. However, the identification of indigenous American folk music proved a difficult problem in itself. In 1906 H. E. Krehbiel suggested that would-be composers of American national music reconcile themselves to the current paucity of indigenous folk materials in the United States and use Indian and Negro folk themes, at least until the ultimate American folk music surfaced. In suggesting the use of Negro and Indian materials, Krehbiel, by his own admission, was following the lead of Bohemian composer Anton Dvořák, who had lived in the United States between 1892 and 1895 (see the discussion of Dvořák's theories in the ragtime controversies outlined in Chapter II above).

With the turn of the century, a generation of American composers desperate to create an American music witnessed the passage of the Indian and his lore out of threatening reality into remote ideality. Under these circumstances Dvořák's suggestions, which had originally fallen on deaf ears, seemed more palatable.

In 1882, Theodore Baker published a set of transcriptions of Indian melodies.[3] Baker's work provided an initial corpus of folk materials upon which would-be American national composers could draw. Even Edward MacDowell (who vehemently disdained Dvořák's suggestions as a "nationalism . . . cut in Bohemia"[4]) used themes from Baker's transcriptions in his *Indian Suite,* first performed in 1896. MacDowell, however, was only one of many American art-music composers to use Indian materials. A whole genre of cantatas on Indian subjects developed after Arthur Foote's cantata, *The Farewell of Hiawatha* (1886), a setting of Longfellow's "Song of Hiawatha." Although Foote did not use actual Indian themes in his cantata, two other cantatas — Frederick Burton's *Hiawatha* and Henry Kimball Hadley's *Lelawala, a Legend of Niagara,* both of which appeared in 1898 — dipped into the ethnomusicologists' newly found reservoir of Indian musical materials and thus set the pattern of using Indian materials in cantatas on Indian subjects.

Perhaps the most surprising setting for Indian musical materials was the opera house. Although the fad for Indian operas was relatively short-lived, it was vigorous while it lasted. Con-

[3]Theodore Baker, *Über die Musik der Nordamerikanischen Wilden* (Leipzig: Breit-kopf and Härtel, 1882).

[4]Gilbert Chase, *America's Music from the Pilgrims to the Present* (New York: McGraw-Hill, 1955), 355.

tributors to this fad include Charles Sanford Skilton, with his *Kalopien* and *The Sun Bride;* Arthur Nevins, with his *Poia;* and Charles Wakefield Cadman, with his *Sunset Trail* and *Shanewis*. Both of Cadman's operas are concerned with the relation of Indian culture to white western civilization. *Shanewis,* first performed by the Metropolitan Opera Company in New York in 1918, has special interest in its rather poignant picture of the alienated educated Indian, at home neither in his traditional world nor in the white man's. Cadman used actual Indian musical materials in his music for *Shanewis,* including an Omaha love song. Cadman's identification of his Indian opera with American opera is demonstrated in his suggestion that the guests at the ball associated with *Shanewis'* opening should come in costumes identifying them as persons central to the creation of America — Queen Isabella, Ralph Waldo Emerson, Leif Erikson, the Salem witches, George Washington, Abraham Lincoln, and others.

Other musicians and scholars developed an interest in Indian musical lore. Arthur Farwell responded to Dvořák's challenge by founding the Wa-Wan Press, through which he hoped to provide a platform for music made of American folk materials.

While the extent of activity surrounding the creation of an American art music using Indian materials could easily qualify as a movement in itself (these examples only scratch the surface), the interest in Indian materials in the early twentieth century reached far beyond the boundaries of art music into American popular culture, specifically into American parlor and ragtime music.

In parlor music, the work of Charles Wakefield Cadman has had the widest impact. His parlor song, "The Land of the Sky Blue Water," based on an Omaha tribal melody collected by Alice C. Fletcher, has long survived the passing of the Indianist movement and implanted itself inextricably in the heart of American popular culture.[5] In his parlor songs, Cadman skillfully adjusted Indian materials to the stylistic and technical

[5] Cadman's sentimental songs have recently been edited and published. See: Mischa Portnoff, ed., *The American Indian in Song: Piano Solos with Words* (New York: Edwin H. Morris and Co., Inc., 1968).

vocabulary of the American parlor amateur. He transformed Indian themes into a vocal solo and piano accompaniment form vaguely reminiscent of the standard nineteenth-century drawing room ballad. "Jeanie with the Light Brown Hair" and "The Land of Sky Blue Water" belong essentially to the same world.

Despite a veritable craze for Indianist materials in all of American musical culture at the turn of the century, it was a passing fancy. Today, interest in Indian culture focuses mainly on study of Indian culture for its own sake. However, vestiges of the impetus to comingle the Indian and western musical traditions still exist. Efforts such as Fred Waring's commercial arrangement of "Red Wing" for high school chorus and piano accompaniment fall into this category, and while such materials have novelty appeal, the identification of Indian musical materials as the key to creation of an indigenous American music seems doomed.

Ragtime, however, was not immune to the Indianist craze. The Indian intermezzos in vogue from 1903 to 1910 created a wildly romantic and sentimental version of the Indian. They are melodramatic tales of tragic, thwarted Indian romances — lovers separated by fate or nature, a dusky-but-beautiful Indian maiden cruelly slain or snatched from her noble, handsome Indian brave. The public was ravished by such pathetic situations and doubtless shed an honest tear or two for such heroines as Red Wing, Iola, Anoma. The Indian's own vision of his fate in the 1890's is one of profound sorrow and genuine tragedy, a sense of defeat and desolation as he was forced from his land, his tribe, his connections with a living nature. A survivor of the Wounded Knee massacre gave his story a powerful dignity and simplicity:

> I did not know then how much was ended. When I look back now from this high hill of my old age, I can still see the butchered women and children lying heaped and scattered all along the crooked gulch as plain as when I saw them with eyes still young. And I can see that something else died there in the bloody mud, and was buried in the blizzard. A people's dream died there. It was a beautiful dream. . . . you see me now a pitiful old man who has done nothing,

for the nation's hoop is broken and scattered. There is no center any longer, and the sacred tree is dead.[6]

But for the songwriter's hack of 1903, the Indian was neither a threat nor an object for understanding. The Indian that he saw was a type-figure, straight out of sentimental melodrama—a cardboard variant on the Juliet figure, the simple, virtuous maiden wronged by hard destiny.

The lyrics for the typical Indian intermezzo present a rigidly conventionalized portrait of the mythic Red Man and of nature, as much a period piece as such nineteenth-century genre paintings as "The Dying Indian":

> Oh the moon is all agleam on the stream
> Where I dream here of you my pretty Indian maid.
> While the rustling leaves are singing high above
>   us overhead
> In the glory of the bright summer night
> In the light and the shadows of the forest glade
> I am waiting here to kiss your lips so red.
>
> There's a flood of melodies on the breeze
> From the trees and of you they breathe so tenderly
> While the woodlands all around are resounding your name,
> Oh my all in life is only you
> Fond and true and your own forevermore I'll be.
> Hear then the song I sing with lips aflame.
>
> (*Refrain*)
>
> I am your own your Hiawatha brave, my heart is yours
>   you know,
> Dear one I love you so,
> Oh Minnehaha gentle Indian maid decide, decide
>   and say you'll be
> My Indian bride.
>
> ("Hiawatha," lyrics by James O'Dea)

The rushed phrases and internal rhymes seemed to be trademarks of the Indian songs, just as the characteristic rumbling rhythm and minor chords tried to suggest Indian drums and

---

[6] John G. Neihardt, *Black Elk Speaks* (Lincoln, Neb.: University of Nebraska Press, 1961), 276.

pentatonic harmonies. "Red Wing" encapsulated all the clichés, musical and literary:

> There once lived an Indian maid,
> A shy little prairie maid,
> Who sang a lay, a love song gay,
> As on the plain she'd while away the day;
> She loved a warrior bold, this shy little maid of old,
> But brave and gay, he rode away one day to battle
>   far away.
>
> (*Chorus*)
>
> Now, the moon shines tonight on pretty Red Wing,
>   the breeze is sighing, the nightbird's crying,
> For afar 'neath his star her brave is sleeping,
> While Red Wing's weeping her heart away.
>   ("Red Wing," lyrics by Thurland Chattaway)

It would be hard to match the simplemindedness and repetitiousness of these once-popular parlor classics.

The fatuousness of this stereotype notwithstanding, the Indian intermezzos were a great vogue; and they gave ragtime a strong forward impetus, for this additional injection of exoticism helped make ragtime that much more popular, gave it a spice of sentimentality and drama that the peppy ragtime songs lacked. It was no longer the vogue to perpetuate slander against the black man but to develop a mythology to accommodate the nearly extinct Indian. The Indian intermezzo rage began in 1902, in the usual accidental manner that marks the genesis of popular crazes:

> It was John Philip Sousa who helped spread the Cakewalk all over America and Europe, and it was Sousa who inadvertently did the same thing for the Indian song when he helped popularize an instrumental number by Charles N. Daniels named "In Hiawatha" after a small town in Kansas. Daniels, who wrote this composition under the pseudonym Neil Moret, hired lyricist James O'Dea to convert it into a successful song. It was O'Dea who saw the possibility of an Indian love story, and the result so caught the public fancy that Daniels was able to sell his work to Whitney Warner in Detroit for $10,000 late in 1902.[7]

[7] Roger Hankins, "Those Indian Songs," *The Ragtimer* (May/June, 1970), 5. This excellent article supplies both commentary and musical examples with analyses.

The combination of raggy, marchlike rhythms coupled with a sentimental and exotic love tale seemed unbeatable. Soon there was a mass of closely derivative pieces retailing pathetic Indian tales to the familiar broken rhythms of ragtime.

There seems a rather obvious debt in the Indian songs to the nineteenth-century fashions for Indian poems, the standard for which was, of course, Longfellow's "Song of Hiawatha." A longstanding schoolboy classic, Longfellow's poem was written in bumpy and hypnotic trochaic rhythm, with simple repetitious rhymes, in imitation of Indian chants and ceremonial music — or what Longfellow's excellent ear for rhythms and shape took to be authentic Indian speech/musical patterns. Certainly, thousands of middle-class Americans would have accepted the monotonous chanting quality of the "Song of Hiawatha" as exactly what those mysterious and exotic Indians must have sounded like at their heathen rituals. James O'Dea picked up the device of multiple rhyme and short, bumpy rhythms which fit perfectly the locomotive rhythms of Daniels' music (Daniels claimed he conceived the tune while riding a train through Hiawatha, Kansas). Daniels and O'Dea had in one stroke cast a pattern for hundreds of Indian intermezzos that followed "Hiawatha."

The song was popular enough and simple enough to elicit parodies of the jerky rhythms and rhymes, such as "Does your mother like to hike, down the pike, on a bike, with her baby on the handlebars?" (which catches the rhythm of the chorus exactly). It was also popular enough to pass into the repertoires of bands, singers, and pianists everywhere and to endure hardily. New Orleans jazz bands still played the tune, sometimes under the title "Lizard on a Rail," a half-century later. The imitations of "Hiawatha" were cast closely in its mold, and a few of them achieved some independent success. The best commercial writers tackled the vogue with their usual craftsmanship. Charles L. Johnson wrote "Iola" (1906); Percy Wenrich wrote "Silver Bell" (1910) and "Golden Deer" (1911); and Daniels and O'Dea tried for the laurel again with "Silverheels" (1905). But of all the Indian songs with color-coded names, it was "Red

Wing" (1907) by the indefatigable Kerry Mills which was the formula's definitive work. This tune is the single most enduring and widely known work of the vogue, a song which has passed into public consciousness as one of those apparently anonymous but universally known works.

Once again, after having written the perfectly characteristic cakewalk, "At a Georgia Campmeeting," Kerry Mills demonstrated his musical shrewdness with "Red Wing." He captured in summary the conventions of the Indian intermezzo and used the clichés of musical structure and lyrics so perfectly as to define the idea for good and all. The song creates a bittersweet mood, walks a tightrope between seriousness and self-parody: "Perhaps the secret of Red Wing's success is that it didn't take itself seriously. It dared to tell a sad story of Indian love, while the music alternated between a jolly little verse and a lyrical 'Indian theme.' "[8] Mills had almost note-for-note lifted for the verse of "Red Wing" the melody of one of Robert Schumann's minuscule piano compositions, "The Happy Farmer," a keyboard exercise from the *Album for the Young* (Op. 68) known to nearly every beginning piano student. "Red Wing's" typical chorus is similar to that of Charles L. Johnson's "Iola." Kerry Mills showed a remarkable ability to synthesize the materials of a musical trend and assemble them in a memorable fashion, even if his attempted sequel, "Sun Bird" (1908), never equaled the success of his original work in "Red Wing."

The vogue for Indian intermezzos, like all such fads, ran its course in a half-dozen years. It had several lasting effects, however. First, it introduced a new strain of material to the stream of ragtime songs, broadening them and probably keeping them from drying up as a fad themselves. Second, it contributed a small but solid subgenre to popular music. While the Indian intermezzos of 1902–1910 were never revived on a large scale, such later popular versions of Indian material as "Indian Love Call," "By the Waters of Minnetonka," and even swing-era standards like "Cherokee" owed something to the first period

[8] *Ibid.,* 6.

of popular Indian themes. Third, the Indian intermezzos contributed a flavor and a set of songs to classic jazz, that massive and intriguing repository of turn-of-the-century taste. Jazz musicians who were discovered in the 1940's revival relied on popular music of their youths as a basis for their repertoires, and Indian songs were one staple. Tunes like Mills's "Red Wing," Thomas S. Allen's parodic "Big Chief Battle Axe" (1907), and Daniels' "Hiawatha" were still played by bands fronted by Bunk Johnson, George Lewis, and Avery "Kid" Howard. Kid Howard showed a further folk connection of the ragtime Indian songs with a spectacular piece in his repertoire, an instrumental with strong ragtime feeling (said to have come from a medicine-show band) called "Indian Sagua."[9] As recently as 1971, Bill Williams, an old and neglected folk-blues guitarist from Greenup, Kentucky, still used the chorus of Percy Wenrich's "Silver Bell" as a "signature" tune for his routines. The Indian music found its way, with its ragtime beat, directly into a basic part of our national popular imagination.

Along with the Indian intermezzo vogue during the first years of the ragtime era, there were many other trends in popular music which assimilated the broken rhythms and exuberant feelings of ragtime. Every conceivable formula for capitalizing on ragtime was attempted—synthesis with oriental motifs, Spanish rhythms, patriotic themes, every standard "novelty" device. The peculiar hybrids and mutations are not worth detailing, but one fact remains clear: ragtime itself was strong enough to absorb and transmute all the influences around it, all attempts to reorganize or corrupt it.[10] From 1900 to 1910, Scott Joplin and James Scott wrote the bulk of their classic

[9]One old trouper mentions this particular medicine-show tradition: "They had played together in a medicine show, working for a 'Doctor' who was peddling a product called 'Kickapoo Indian Sagwa' which was supposed to cure anything from corns to rheumatism and could be used internally or externally." Tom Fletcher, *100 Years of the Negro in Show Business* (New York: Burdge and Co., Ltd., 1954), 209.

[10]One curious hybridization which became a momentary fad around 1915 was a series of so-called "half and half" dances—ragtime tunes written in ⁵⁄₄ time which were supposed to be half-waltz (³⁄₄) and half foxtrot (²⁄₄). The dance craze and its music were (mercifully) short-lived.

rags; Joseph Lamb followed quickly, with most of his writing done by 1915. Their work developed by an inner logic, by rules of composition they discovered on their own, amidst all the chameleon transformations of Tin Pan Alley. And secondary ragtime composers also generally avoided the clichés and temptations of commercial vogues as they developed the basic ideas of classic ragtime into a new dance music in the years after 1910. In the kaleidoscopic change of the commercial industry, the few stubborn souls infected with the real ragtime virus kept on with their work despite shifts in taste and money-making trends.

A strong vaudeville tradition of black music, dating from the "coon songs" and cakewalk routines, continued with both rag songs and instrumental ragtime. In the Deep South a tradition of black minstrel shows flourished, including various touring companies using such names as "Georgia Minstrels" and "Rabbit Foot Minstrels." These groups perpetuated a ragtime tradition for several generations. Also, a strong tradition of musical shows and revues depended on the fecundity and variety of commercial songwriters. By 1905 every show or revue included at least one ragtime number — a "coon song," a ragtime dance, a rag song tailored for the show's theme. While these shows were not precisely operettas (somewhat closer to the British music hall revue or even the old pantomime), they did give a context for ragtime songs that was more "genteel" or conventional than the barroom-bordello image early attached to the music. Long on novelty and spectacle and short on imagination and logic, these precursors of the full-scale Broadway musical helped bring ragtime singing and playing into the mainstream of popular music. It was considered *de rigeur* for a half-dozen years for each new revue to incorporate ragtime music and ragtime allusions. Quickly enough, ragtime was accepted as a basic part of this vaudeville musical tradition, losing both its initial "sinful" overtones and its association with black folk musicians. It was complacently accepted by middle America as a popular novelty — a little boisterous, perhaps, but not downright distasteful. Nearly every "respectable" musical medium had by 1905 accepted ragtime as part of the gamut of popular music, from folk-minstrel performers to Sousa's band to run-of-the-mill performers of Tin Pan Alley and vaudeville. It was clear to every observer that America had taken readily to her "ragtime life."

FROM "THE RED-BACKED BOOK OF RAGS" TO CLASSIC JAZZ

If the ragtime song flourished by virtue of commercial opportunism, ragtime was simultaneously assimilated into broad popular acceptance from another direction—as part of several divergent streams of instrumental music, separate from song-pluggers' routes in the publishing world. Very early in its history, ragtime was adapted as an instrumental music, either by a "legitimate" process of written orchestral scores or by improvisational borrowing by instrumentalists. There are basically about five classes of instrumental adaptations to consider: (1) orchestral scores transcribed from piano rags, designed to adapt the piano score accurately and completely to an ensemble; (2) instrumental arrangements/accompaniments for ragtime songs, usually written for vaudeville groups, etc.; (3) brass band ragtime, either transcriptions or original compositions; (4) borrowings of ragtime style for instrumental combinations in other genres—e.g., string bands and country dance bands; and (5) jazz originals deriving from ragtime style and structure.

Ragtime was naturally adapted by instrumental ensembles of all sorts, as its appeal spread.[11] There was more than enough interest in ragtime to keep all the itinerant piano players in America busy day and night. But when ragtime was transcribed for instrumental ensembles, the music was substantially changed. Ragtime was, as conceived by pioneer folk-rag composers and classic ragtime writers, a highly pianistic music tailored

[11] For a thorough description and discussion of a representative "ragtime band," see Tom Shea, "Finney's Orchestra," *The Ragtimer,* IV (May/June, 1965), 34–38.

for the percussive resources of the piano keyboard and its fixed
sonorities. Since some ragtime styles, like brass-band cakewalks, developed quite early, they stimulated composers who
wrote exclusively for the keyboard. But the basic flow of influence was one way, the problem being to devise instrumental
transcriptions to duplicate ragtime's form without losing its
basic feelings and textures.

The first class of instrumental transcriptions to consider is
the collection loosely called "The Red-Backed Book of Rags."[12]
This collection of "Standard High-Class Rags" was published
around 1912 by Stark Music Company of St. Louis; it was an
anthology of fifteen transcriptions for small ensemble, basically
of classic rags. The fifteen classic rags included in "The Red-
Backed Book of Rags" were:

1.	Maple Leaf Rag	Scott Joplin
2.	The Cascades	Scott Joplin
3.	The Easy Winners	Scott Joplin
4.	The Ragtime Dance	Scott Joplin
5.	The Chrysanthemum	Scott Joplin
6.	African Pas	M. Kirwin
7.	Ophelia Rag	James Scott
8.	Hilarity Rag	James Scott
9.	The Minstrel Man	J. R. Robinson
10.	Frog Legs Rag	James Scott
11.	Sensation	Joseph Lamb
12.	Kinklets	Arthur Marshall
13.	Grace and Beauty	James Scott
14.	Sunflower Slow Drag	Joplin-Hayden
15.	The Entertainer	Scott Joplin

The transcriptions were designed for a small orchestra of
the sort used in theater pits or cabarets, scored loosely enough
that various combinations of instruments could play the rags
without serious distortion. The arrangements follow the original
structure of the piano rags closely, only changing keys to facili-

[12] A complete analysis and discussion of the Stark folios is in Samuel B. Charters,
"Red Backed Book of Rags," *Jazz Report*, II (July, 1962), 7–8.

tate instrumental sound or changing figures slightly to allow for brass, woodwind, or string techniques. John Stark, a thorough musician and a "ragtime literalist," wanted to keep the music pure, so these adaptations are careful transferrals of the piano style to a standard ensemble of the period.[13]

The transcriptions have considerable charm, albeit a slightly archaic flavor, when played "straight" by competent musicians. They were designed, undoubtedly, for musicians largely unacquainted with folk instrumental ragtime styles (*e.g.,* "alley fiddle" techniques, vocal instrumental tone, and other "ear" practices). Modern recordings using the "Red-Backed Book of Rags" are successful in transmitting the sentimental and romantic sound of the period.[14] There were undoubtedly other similar sets of orchestrations used by pit orchestras and dance groups throughout the country.

One staple of music publishing has always been the creation of stock arrangements of hits, sold to instrumental groups too small, insolvent, or unsophisticated to have a resident arranger. Ragtime stock arrangements were constructed according to the standard procedures of the time; consequently, they sound much like a small string/wind danceband of the turn of the century. In other words, ragtime arrangements follow musical conventions and flavor of non-ragtime music, imposing this set of practices on top of ragtime compositions, creating an intriguing collage effect:

> An examination of the orchestrations began to reveal a technique and approach to orchestral music almost forgotten. The prime lead was always played by the first violinist. In many cases he was the leader of the orchestra. Second violinist was seldom called on for much other than double stop figures (two notes on the same beat) on the second and fourth beats. This tended to fill the basic mission

---

[13] It is instructive to compare the practices of ragtime transcription with the chamber-orchestra writing of Charles Ives, of the same period. Ives wrote for miscellaneous and interchangeable groups of instruments, obviously from his own experience with pit bands and assorted ragtime ensembles which he enjoyed.

[14] Two modern recordings from the "Red-Backed Book of Rags" show the style and flavor of the transcriptions: *Peter Bocage with the Love-Jiles Ragtime Orchestra* (Riverside RLP-379) and *The New Orleans Ragtime Orchestra* (Pearl PLP-7/8).

of the guitar or banjo which had not yet appeared in the orchestra. Viola and cello were only slightly more important, but their position was not necessarily critical to the orchestral effect. Bass viol played first and third bass line with bow for the most part. This string quartet could be said to form the backbone of the orchestra. The woodwinds such as piccolo, flute and clarinet, played harmonic second parts obbligato or doubled as needed. First cornet generally played lead except in passages beyond the range and facility of the instrument. Second cornet, if included, would play second harmony to first cornet. Trombone played the bass line with lead and modulation figures and some simple counterpoint. Drums played strict $\frac{2}{4}$ time much in the manner of a march drummer.[15]

This describes "Alexander's Ragtime Band" as it was constituted around 1910—essentially a dance orchestra of the era playing a straight-forward and literal transcription of piano music. To modern ears, straining for jazz intonations and improvisational creativity, ragtime stock arrangements will sound quaint, tame, and uninspired.

A tension is created in transcribing music from one basic form to another—in this case, from a percussive keyboard style to a "slick" dance-orchestra style. Some spectacular and effervescent effects of ragtime depend on keyboard virtuosity and on the subtle continuity of rhythm created by the two hands of one musician, a eurhythmic sensation only possible in solo playing. In stock arrangements, such effects are muffled or lost. The arrangements, even though clever and facile, often sound oddly awkward or empty. However, even these literal transcriptions contribute an important perspective on ragtime in that they accentuate the polyphonic elements of the form. The multiple instrumental voices illuminate clearly—in musical silhouette—the multiple lines of the writing, which may be obscured by a pianist. The stock scores are like three-dimensional working models of piano rags, and as such can be useful in study.

[15] Frank Powers, "Ragtime Stock Orchestrations," *The Ragtimer,* V (November, 1966), 46–48. This article includes examples and analyses of typical stock scores of the era.

A second class of instrumental ragtime, distinct from transcriptions of piano rags, is the group of arrangements of ragtime songs. An essential difference is that these arrangements
were closer in shape and flavor to standard vaudeville orchestral
work common since the 1890's. Further, there is a basic difference between the form of the piano rag and the form of the
conventional popular song. Transcriptions of classic rags re-
tained the stylized quadrille-like structure of the rags, with all
repeats and the "folded" multithematic development. Many
popular tunes of the era, however, used no more than a simple
verse-chorus structure. Some composers of rags and rag songs
used a compromise structure, with an introduction, verse,
chorus, and instrumental trio incorporated. The trio is usually
omitted in modern arrangements and the verse might be dropped
also, but for instrumental combinations a full and varied arrangement was available.

Stock arrangements of rag songs follow the general pattern
for classic rags, in terms of instrumental style and techniques.
Most are stiff by modern standards, again aimed at "reading"
bands, not players familiar with folk ragtime styles. Expanded
versions of ragtime songs show awareness of the demands of
instrumental music, however. Instrumental arrangements were
clearly envisioned by the composers, who did not write specifically for the piano keyboard or the keyboard technician,
as did classic ragtime composers. For instance, one feature
of many ragtime songs is the *interpolation* — a musical allusion
or quotation from a familiar folk ditty, hymn, or march. Some
ragtime songs contain trios or interludes which are virtually
pastiches of allusions. This had always been a sure-fire gimmick
of popular music: "When all else fails, play 'Dixie' or 'Hail,
Columbia.'"

The tradition of the medley-pastiche musical offering is a
strong one in the nineteenth century, and the most popular
music of the era often used this form of collage construction.
Sousa's programs often included pastiches of light classics or
popular-folk melodies. His marches, also, often reflect this

structure. "Riders for the Flag" and "Semper Fidelis," for instance, are built up from standard bugle calls interpolated into original march melody strains; "Ancient and Honorable Artillery Company" interpolates "Auld Lang Syne" into the trio; "New Mexico" is a complete pastiche of Indian, Mexican, and bugle corps motifs interwoven into a regular march structure. Other composers of light classics, such as Victor Herbert, also followed this practice of musical quotation or allusion as a basic means of construction.

Examples of pastiche in the ragtime mode are Jay Roberts' "Entertainers Rag," which features "Dixie" in the right hand against "Yankee Doodle" in the left (a gimmick often used by nineteenth-century concert virtuosi to wow the rubes in the provinces). Others, memorable for instrumental arrangements, include Anthony Zita's "Slavery Days" (1906) and Ted Snyder and Irving Berlin's "I Want to Be in Dixie" (1912). Even Berlin's universally known "Alexander's Ragtime Band" includes a trio (usually omitted) built around Stephen Foster's "Swanee River," reminiscent of the evergreen Civil War celebration in marchtime, "Marching Through Georgia." The pastiche method was often used with Old South nostalgia materials, probably because brief allusions to familiar black folk themes fit ragtime's broken rhythms.[16] The allusion/pastiche method of organizing and synthesizing folk materials is an old and honored tradition in American music. Charles Ives depended on the technique for his most ingenious effects, as did so early a composer as James Hewitt (1770–1827) who is remembered for spectacularly allusive patriotic suites like "The Battle of Trenton." In any event, many ragtime songs were conceived as instrumental versions, transcending both keyboard and vocal interests.

A third category related to standard arrangements of popular ragtime songs is brass band arrangements and original com-

---

[16] An excellent recreation of the ragtime band sound is a modern recording from assorted stock ragtime scores, *The Dawn of the Century Ragtime Orchestra* (Arcane Records).

positions. As noted earlier, band versions of cakewalks and early ragtime songs helped broadcast and popularize the whole ragtime movement. Further, composers like Abe Holzmann and Arthur Pryor, who had a thorough understanding of both the wind idiom and the new rhythms of ragtime, created a new genre of band music. There is no need to reiterate the debts of classic jazz to street bands and the New Orleans tradition of marching jazz. From the initial interest in black ragtime/dance music the marching band repertoire expanded to include new forms of syncopated marches.

Brass bands and concert bands helped spread ragtime rhythms both directly and indirectly. Scott Joplin was a member of the Queen City Concert Band in Sedalia, and many of the earliest cylinder recordings of ragtime are by miscellaneous wind ensembles in the brass band tradition. The fusing of such powerfully emotional and rhythmic musics as marches and ragtime created a strong repository for new black expressions.

The fourth group of ragtime accretions — borrowings in miscellaneous folk genres — is hardest to describe concisely. There has existed since well before published ragtime scores a strong country-music tradition of ragtime string-playing. This surfaces repeatedly in country music recordings of alley-fiddling and virtuoso guitar work. This tradition is independent of specialized adaptations like Fred Van Eps's ragtime exhibitions or the work of string groups playing from standard ragtime transcriptions. It can be heard on country/folk recordings from Gid Tanner's Skillet Lickers through the Sons of the Pioneers and on into modern bluegrass music. It surfaces in skiffle-hokum music like that of the Memphis Jug Band, the jazz-skiffle of the Dixieland Jug Blowers, and in sophisticated guitar jazz like that of Lonnie Johnson and Eddie Lang. It is still customary to call virtuoso country tunes "rags" (see Chet Atkins' "Steel Guitar Rag" or Woody Guthrie's mandolin piece, "Woody's Rag"), even though the tunes may not reflect ragtime structure. Here the term refers clearly to the folk style, techniques, and rhythms.

Country music ragtime influences reveal many cross-cultural musical borrowings. Black and white country music traditions meet in small string combinations playing versions of blues and rags, a repertoire of musical styles and devices common to both white and black country musicians.[17] There is recorded evidence of classic ragtime material used by country string-band musicians, in recordings made for Okeh (Memphis, 1928): two records, "Somethin' Doin'" and "Easy Winner," are derived from Joplin's "Something Doing" and "The Entertainer" and Lampe's "Creole Belles," plus original folk-rag material, played by a guitar-mandolin-violin combination. These recordings show how folk musicians in a ragtime tradition used materials of classic ragtime in a folk fashion.[18] Other examples of ragtime-derived work include the Dixieland Jug Blowers' "Banjoreno" and "Southern Shout"; the Kentucky Jug Band's "Walking Cane Stomp"; and Gus Cannon's Jug Stompers' "Mule, Get Up in the Alley" (all recorded in the late 1920's).[19]

While classic ragtime, in its complex structured form, did not appear in the repertoires of rough-and-ready country bands, the original "primitive" ragtime style was a basic point of departure for the groups, who were able to produce on demand almost any kind of dance music—from waltzes and polkas through a whole gamut of white and black folk dance forms. One of the standard sources of country music, well through the 1930's, was various corrupt versions of old rag song hits. Besides the various parodies of "Hiawatha" mentioned earlier, another tune that lived through parody versions was Lampe's ubiquitous "Creole Belles." One enduring parody set words to the chorus: "My mama told me/If I was goodie/That she would buy me a rubber dolly."[20] This was recorded in the twenties by a typical southern

[17] For a thorough and completely documented discussion of black-white cross-cultural interchange through country folk music traditions, see Tony Russell, *Blacks, Whites and Blues* (New York: Stein and Day, 1970).

[18] Richard Spottswood and David A. Jason, "Discoveries Concerning Recorded Ragtime," *Jazz Journal*, XXI (February, 1968), 7.

[19] A thorough discussion of the skiffle tradition appears in Paul Oliver, *The Story of the Blues* (London: Design Yearbook, Ltd., 1969), 47–57.

[20] Lyrics relayed in correspondence with J. Bodewalt Lampe's daughter, Mrs. Dorothy Lampe Krackehl, November 4, 1971.

white string band, the Georgia Yellow Hammers, under the title "Rubber Dolly Rag." (As if to demonstrate the hardihood of folk ragtime, the same theme turned up in the 1950's as a rock and roll tune called "Slap Clap.") The white string-band tradition was a close parallel to black jug band/hokum band traditions, as deeply imbued with ragtime origins as the black music. Other ragtime-derived tunes include "Carbolic Rag" by the Scottsdale String Band and "Dallas Rag" by the Dallas String Band, also from the twenties. While the rags are often simplified, usually including only one or two original strains and often coupled with other traditional blues or dance material, they are still recognizable, and the persistent ragtime style in which they are couched is an obvious descendent of piano rag-time's basic idioms.

Mention of country string bands and hokum bands should recall that before the advent of country-music radio programs and specialized interests, vaudeville (plus touring minstrel/medicine-show troupes) was the common background for all these groups. Strong traditions of minstrel humor and music inform many of these folk ragtime works. Continuity of a rag-time tradition within show business was fed by the apparently endless nostalgia for the old patterns of the minstrel show, the circus, the carnival, and other roadshow traditions in American music. Itinerant musicians, working essentially in a ragtime tradition, continued to job across the country for many years after the classic ragtime era and even after the advent of electronic mass media. It is still possible to hear a kind of "eclectic ragtime" piano style (compounded of ragtime phrasing, blues-piano bass lines, and country-western harmonies) in the work of pianists with black and white gospel groups and commercial country-western combos.

The last source of ragtime style in later music is the most difficult and controversial to describe—the continuity of ragtime in the jazz tradition. Arguments rage about whether jazz derives mostly from the blues tradition or the ragtime tradition, whether ragtime is "an early form of jazz," about the "purity" of rag-time, about jazz "killing" ragtime. Most arguments spring from desires to make absolute distinctions and definitions, to find sharp demarcations in chronology; most have little to do with the reality of black music.

Clearly, ragtime was a strong influence on jazz. Early musicians used the term "ragtime" as a catchall to describe their music, much of it derived directly from ragtime standards – both rag songs and classic rags. Musicians of Bunk Johnson's generation considered their ensembles "ragtime bands," and the music they played was derived in both style and technique from folk rag sources. It departed quite early from the pianistic traditions of the Missouri ragtimers and became a folk instrumental ragtime style. "Ragging" was the process of syncopating a melody, of adapting it to various standard ragtime rhythms. Most important, early jazz musicians took from ragtime a sense of structure. Their own compositions are often shaped like classic rags, with multiple themes, repeats, a complex organization different from either folk blues or commercial popular songs. This is apparent in works by two of the earliest recording bands – the Original Dixieland Jazz Band (1917–1920) and King Oliver's Creole Jazz Band (1923). Many of their compositions are even labeled as rags.

The whole approach of the Original Dixieland Jazz Band was closely linked with ragtime. Their tunes were originals (meaning, basically, melodies and motifs absorbed in working the New Orleans jazz circuits) constructed of three or more themes formally organized and repeated in a fixed pattern. Their rhythms were marchlike, reminiscent of cakewalk and ragtime two-step patterns of the preceding decade. Further, their records show that they adhered strictly to "head" arrangements of the tunes, with only rare variations or improvisations – a pattern almost as fixed as a written classic rag. (Compare Victor and English Columbia versions of tunes like "Tiger Rag" or "Sensation Rag" to see how closely the Original Dixieland Jazz Band followed a standard "head" arrangement.)

The Original Dixieland Jazz Band departed from ragtime traditions in the free polyphony they used, much different from the sedate harmonizations of ragtime transcriptions, and in their use of blues materials. They borrowed the organization of ragtime and injected it with blues harmonics and timbres and improvised polyphony (largely from the brass band tradition), but their strong ragtime feeling cannot be dismissed as archaic or accidental. Not only is Henry Ragas' (or Billy Jones's and J. Russel Robinson's) piano playing in the ragtime idiom — the phrasing of LaRocca, Shields, and Edwards corresponds to piano patterns of ragtime, and Spargo's vigorous drumming underscores the march/ragtime rhythms of the ensemble. The musicians and their first northern audiences recognized the Original Dixieland Jazz Band's music as an extension of the foxtrot ragtime of the Castles and James Reese Europe — a more abandoned version, perhaps, but the same "advanced" ragtime style in fashion in New York City since 1915.

In the case of the Oliver band, the first great creative black jazz group on records, ragtime influences are also obvious, if more coherently synthesized with blues and improvisational elements. Oliver's compositions are organized in the ragtime mode, with multiple themes, scored for a band more capable of genuine improvisation. The tunes — "Snake Rag," "Weather-bird Rag," "Canal Street Blues," "High Society," "Mabel's Dream," "Southern Stomps," — are multithematic and poly-phonic, but they too are "head" arrangements, fairly fixed in pattern (compare Okeh and Gennett versions of tunes like "Snake Rag" or "Mabel's Dream" to see how fixed these ar-rangements were). Joe Oliver's band was basically a dance orchestra, and its music was built on standard dance arrange-ments; also, while the music on record is probably more tightly controlled and organized than their on-the-job work, the multi-thematic structures of ragtime are still clear. Further, the Creole Jazz Band's instrumental techniques recall ragtime: Honore Dutrey's trombone parts are essentially "straight" cello parts from stock arrangements or simple doubling of the bass line, and other instruments often play parts similar to transcription harmonies. Almost as many of Joe Oliver's early recordings are called rags as the standards of the Original Dixie-land Jazz Band. Both bands considered themselves to be work-ing in the vein of ragtime as it was understood around 1920, *i.e.*, as foxtrot music organized around a medium-fast tempo, with contrasting themes played "straight" by jazz musicians.

Other early jazz/dance bands also attest to continuity in the ragtime tradition: Piron's New Orleans Orchestra and the Original Tuxedo Jazz Orchestra recorded dance tunes in the ragtime mold, following the example of Oliver's band. The Tux-edo Orchestra's "Black Rag" (1925) is a reorganization of Wilbur Sweatman's "Down Home Rag" (1911), with room for improvisational solos. Piron's "Red Man Blues" (1925) and "Bouncing Around" (1923) are ragtime-derived dance music in the New Orleans tradition. Through the 1920's the dance band tradition in New Orleans developed these principles of folk ragtime style and composition. The great Sam Morgan Jazz Band (recorded in 1927) used a repertoire of homemade originals derived by transforming themes from popular songs, folk tunes, ragtime, and marches and assembling them in simple multithematic structures. Their "Bogalusa Strut" is a good example of this method of synthesis, a way of creating pastiche ragtime effective as instrumental dance music. Again, the Morgan band left room for improvisational solos and passages of brilliant ensemble jazz, but the tight arrangements are in-dicative of an enduring New Orleans concept of instrumental ragtime.

Without stretching the definition of ragtime to encompass all jazz, it is obvious that ragtime style and structure were crucial in early jazz composition. The crowning example is the work of the first great jazz pianist-composer, Jelly Roll Morton, a ragtime-trained musician who spent his long career transforming early ideas of ragtime into his unique version of black music. His piano work of the 1920's and the brilliant series of Red Hot Peppers recordings show how far Morton carried the ex-ample of ragtime. Again, style and structure both begin with ragtime—this time with classic rags, since Morton, a highly literate musician, knew ragtime from the inside out. If his great idol was Tony Jackson ("the world's greatest single-handed entertainer"), Jelly Roll also knew the printed works of ragtime composers and ragtime styles of competitors up and down the Mississippi. The playing-singing style of Tony Jackson set a pattern for Morton, a great jazz composer who also wanted to succeed as a famous entertainer, in Jackson's footsteps.

Morton's piano recordings of the early 1920's show him at the peak of his powers as a creative composer for the piano. "Perfect Rag" (1924) sums up Jelly Roll's past, his training as a ragtime writer and interpreter. Already, when he made these recordings, Morton had moved from the pianistic conceptions of his earliest days toward an orchestral music, ragtime *conceived* as instrumental music, not merely transcribed from keyboard to ensemble. In a few years he was able to realize compositions like "Grandpa's Spells," "Kansas City Stomps," and "Shreveport Stomp" as instrumental recordings, but the Gennett recordings of 1923–1924 serve as a prelude to his band work with the Red Hot Peppers. Comparing piano and band versions of a few of Jelly Roll's ragtime-derived tunes quickly shows how much he owed to ragtime structure and rhythms and also how much he liberated himself from ragtime conventions as he began thinking in terms of complex polyphonic instrumental music. Coupled with his discussions and demonstrations of early ragtime piano styles on the Library of Congress records, Jelly Roll's 1920's records constitute a short course in the history of ragtime-into-jazz. Yet the ragtime heritage, even while Morton transcended and revamped it, was the single most important part of his musical education. It gave him basic concepts of musical organization and style on which he built all his later work.

These two interconnected trends—ragtime as a vehicle for popular songs and instrumental transcriptions of ragtime—brought ragtime directly to the front of American popular music in the twenty years after Joplin wrote "Maple Leaf Rag." If classic ragtime had remained an isolated phenomenon, a handful of men dedicated to creating a genuine black piano art-music, it is doubtful that anyone would have noticed it. All the rag-time composers, great and merely competent, were basically popular entertainers, and the diffusion of their music through existing musical media brought at least the idea of ragtime to a huge audience. That the music was eventually bastardized, debased, distorted is unquestionable, but its popularization also gave serious ragtime a chance to be heard and to endure. The paradox involved is at the heart of America's popular culture and seems inescapable. The idealism of Scott Joplin, as he ground away his life at work on *Treemonisha,* a genuine folk-opera, is that of Thoreau at work on his journals or Charles Ives at his symphonies. The hope that springs eternal is that once the mass public takes the easiest steps to Parnassus it will work to scale the giant steps. Joplin broke himself on the hard reality of the indifferent public, which had turned from the clear classicism of "Maple Leaf Rag" or "The Easy Win-ners" to the (relative) simplicities of the ragtime song or the novelties of vaudeville prestidigitators who rendered ragtime on the xylophone. Joplin never heard the voice of the people which says, "Give us this day our daily novelty — so long as it is not *too* new!" After *Treemonisha,* after "Magnetic Rag," Joplin was deaf to the thousand renderings of "Maple Leaf Rag" that every band and every itinerant musician played, and deaf to all the voices that sang new words to his old rhythms.

∽◁ VI ▷∾

"Try This on Your Piano"
Ragtime Style and Performance

They brought me all Scott Joplin's tunes—he was the great St. Louis ragtime composer—and I knew them all by heart and played them all off. They brought me James Scott's tunes and Louis Chauvin's and I knew them all.—Jelly Roll Morton, 1938

IN A NUTSHELL

*Tell me ye winged winds that 'round my
    pathway roar.
—We know one house of classic rags—pray
    are there any more?
The answer filtered through the leaves and
    whispered 'long the shore:*

"There's only one classic Rag House."

We mean just what we say when we call these instrumental rags classic.

They are the perfection of type. "The glass of fashion and the mold of form." They have the genius of melody and the scholarship of harmonization. They are used in the drawing rooms and the parlors of culture. Of course the name "Rag" is a scurrilous misnomer, and filthy songs have done much to drag the name in the dirt, but no name could hold down our classy instrumental numbers. That person who flouts them at this date is exposing a verdancy and ignorance that is pitiful.

*Breathes there a man with soul so dead
Who never to himself hath said:
    "I'll get the hul bloomin' bunch. By Heck."*
                    —John Stark advertisement, ca. 1910

The most controversial and difficult topic connected with ragtime is the most basic one: How is ragtime to be played? There are central questions to be raised, if not resolved, in a discussion of ragtime performance: (1) *Ragtime tempo:* slow or fast, fixed or variable? (2) *Improvisation vs. strict reading:* should ragtime

143

be embellished, developed, or decorated, or should it be read note-for-note from the printed score? (3) *Ragtime and the jazz pulse:* should ragtime rhythms be interpreted ("translated") as jazz ("To Swing or Not to Swing")? (4) *How to become a ragtime pianist*—how to practice ragtime? These are questions of the aesthetics of performance and cannot be settled conclusively; they can only be demonstrated in playing. However, it is possible to look at ragtime traditions and conventions for some guides to performance.

Only a few sources of information can be considered authoritative or reliable: statements on style by ragtime composer-performers—instructions on scores, expository works like Joplin's *The School of Ragtime,* interviews like those with Eubie Blake, Joseph Lamb, or Brun Campbell, recorded performances, either on disc or piano roll; and the printed scores themselves. All these sources should be consulted by a pianist seriously interested in ragtime, to find a balanced view of ragtime style. The basic ideas expressed below can be stated unequivocally.

RAGTIME TEMPO

Classic ragtime composers repeatedly asked that their works be played at moderate tempos. The scores of Joplin's, Scott's, and Lamb's rags are customarily marked "Not Fast" or "Do Not Play Fast." This prohibition seems to have been necessary quite early; apparently exhibitionistic players accelerated the tempos to emphasize keyboard pyrotechnics—still a temptation in performance. John Stark wrote a special note of instructions to James Scott's "Grace and Beauty" (1910) to emphasize this point: "Play every note of Grace and Beauty in slow march time. . . ." He went on to define this as a metronome setting of $\rfloor = 100$. This seems to indicate a clear concept of classic ragtime from the beginning, and "slow march time" may be the clearest description of what some early scores playfully indicate as "Tempo di Rag."

The tradition of ragtime style calls for a fixed tempo and a steady rhythmic pulse. Ragtime scores rarely indicate shifts of tempo or allow for a free *rubato* style. The tradition of playing indicates that ragtime, like jazz, was based on a steady dance tempo, which creates a subtle sensation of forward momentum through the elasticity of inner rhythms, not through gross shifts in tempo. Arbitrary changes in tempo or application of frequent *rubati* tend to destroy the contrasts in rhythm which are built into the score, shifting the emphasis from the music to the interpreter—a hangover from nineteenth-century ideas of the virtuoso pianist. One folk ragtime tradition, often observable in country blues/dance playing (for example, Leadbelly's playing of dance tunes in archaic ragtime style) is to accelerate the tempo steadily through a performance, to build a tension or suspense. Brun Campbell practiced this pattern habitually in his recordings, but they were made when he was quite old and out of practice; and his shifts of tempo may be as much uncertainty as a conscious device. Jelly Roll Morton deplored the habit of acceleration and demonstrated it as an illiterate error in his Library of Congress recordings. Evidence seems to point to a strictly maintained tempo as a ragtime standard.

IMPROVISATION VERSUS STRICT READING

On the complex question of improvisation, interpolation, or embellishment, there are many ambiguities within the tradition. Classic composers often stressed note-for-note reading as their expectation. Joseph Lamb explained on several occasions that he could not imagine changing his rags in any detail in performance once they were written. Scott Joplin was severely strict in *The School of Ragtime:* "We wish to say here, that the 'Joplin Ragtime' is destroyed by careless or imperfect rendering, and very often good players lose the effect entirely, by playing too fast. They are harmonized with supposition that each note will be played as it is written, as it takes this and also the proper time divisions to complete the sense intended."[1] However, as numerous piano rolls reveal and as Brun Campbell always insisted, there were equally strong conventions for additions of sounds, of "ear playing," in ragtime.[2] Often melodic variations were introduced on the repeat of a strain—e.g., the melody would be played an octave higher to heighten treble brilliance, or slight variations in the bass line might be introduced. (A "Connorized" piano roll of "Magnetic Rag" [1914], reputedly cut by Joplin himself, uses brief passages of "walking bass" not in the score.) Further, piano rolls, mechanically made, could be altered by "overcutting" or adding more notes after the fact, and they often incorporate trills and arpeggios beyond the capacity of a live performer. Obviously there was quite early a tradition of "decorated" playing, analogous to traditions of improvisational embellishment in eighteenth-century keyboard works. However, no manuals of decoration or bass realization exist for ragtime, as they did in the eighteenth century, to give us an exact idea of the improvisational styles represented at the turn of the century. Even the various ragtime instruction books touch on this problem only slightly.

Brun Campbell always defended the inventive "ear" tradition as perfectly consonant with classic ragtime composition. However, careful addition of figures is different from the wholesale transfiguration of ragtime by jazz-oriented pianists, which is often passed off as ragtime playing. When rags are treated as vehicles for improvisation and variation, they become simply another source of jazz material, like popular songs and jazz standards given the full treatment. This is not ragtime performance and should not be so represented. (See Appendix II

[1] Scott Joplin, "The School of Ragtime," in Vera Brodsky Lawrence (ed.), *The Collected Works of Scott Joplin* (New York: The New York Public Library, 1971), I, 286.

[2] Brun was very positive in his reminiscences of the early ragtime stylists: "None of the original pianists played ragtime the way it was written. They played their own style. Some played march time, fast time, slow time and some played ragtime blues style. But none of them lost the melody and if you knew the player and heard him a block away you could name him by his ragtime style." Campbell, "The Ragtime Kid (An Autobiography)," 12.

for a discussion and analysis of ragtime-derived jazz piano performances.) Jelly Roll Morton was very clear in his description of his "transformation" of ragtime into jazz and demonstrated both a "legitimate" ragtime style and his own evolution of jazz style in two superb renditions of "Maple Leaf Rag," on the Library of Congress recordings.

RAGTIME AND THE JAZZ PULSE

Ragtime remains distinct from jazz both as an instrumental style and as a genre. As a style, it is dependent on repetition of rhythmic conventions, whether read strictly from a score or repeated in a "head" arrangement. The style stresses a pattern of repeated rhythms, not the constant inventions and variations of jazz. Thus, ragtime stylists often strike jazz listeners as being stiff, monotonous, or "archaic" in approach. As a genre ragtime also relies on formalistic principles — the establishment of a series of contrasted melodic/rhythmic structures in a carefully designed order. The aesthetics of the genre depend on this sense of structure, not on inventiveness or virtuosity. "Jazz is defined not by *what* is played but by *how* it is played. Jazz music is that which is played by jazz musicians. It only exists by virtue of the musician or group of musicians creating it."[3] In contrast, ragtime — as style and genre — has existed as a tradition, a set of conventions, a body of written scores, separate from the individual players associated with it. In this sense ragtime is more akin to other folk musics of the nineteenth century than to jazz.

Can these general principles be assembled into a reasonably simple statement on piano style? Again, it is not easy to prescribe technic for piano ragtime, but a few ideas may help a player beginning to read a ragtime score.

Rhythm. Ragtime must be at once fluid rhythmically and clear and percussive in accent. The large rhythmic patterns which

[3] David A. Jason, "Ragtime: A Re-evaluation," *Jazz Journal,* XXI (April, 1968), 22.

compose the structure as well as the consistency of the syncopations or broken rhythms within single measures should be intelligible to the listener. Since rhythm is the most basic distinctive characteristic of ragtime, it must be executed and maintained precisely. Phrases must be articulated cleanly and clearly, so that the rhythm is fluid, intact. (Where specific phrasing marks are included in the score, they should be observed exactly.) This calls for evenness of playing, consistent attention to both large rhythmic structures and to internal rhythms — the contrast and combination of bass and treble lines. Most scores show clearly how phrases should be accented, and playing and listening to ragtime will help make the idiomatic or conventional rhythmic phrasing clear. The tension built up by varied rhythms within a consistent tempo is a very exciting but subtle technique. The player must work to achieve a flow of phrasing characteristic of all good keyboard work. Keyboard artists like Wanda Landowska and Vladimir Horowitz in their classical recordings maintain the brilliant rhythmic flow, a logic or syntax of phrasing, that a good ragtime pianist seeks. Piano rolls may also help clarify rhythms; even if they are stiff and mechanical, at least they sharply outline the rhythmic structures.

Rhythmic pulse. Also at the heart of ragtime is the continuity of the rhythmic structure, steadiness of tempo. Without raising the chimerical question of jazz phrasing, it is possible to say that the ragtime pianist ought to play with the rhythmic consistency and steadiness of the jazz ensemble pianist. A fixed, steady tempo underscores the rhythmic integrity of classic ragtime; in a sense, the steadiness of a basic march tempo opens out the rhythmic structure so that the internal rhythms are revealed.

"Tempo di rag." Restrained tempos, as recommended by the classic ragtime composers, will accentuate the rhythmic structures and the melodic lines. John Stark's prescription of "slow march time" gets us closer to the concept of ragtime around 1900, before jazz and its variants gave us new ideas of dance rhythms. The classic rags have a stately, crystalline beauty

which moderate tempos underscore—if rhythmic vitality is maintained.[4]

Melodic conceptions. Middlewestern ragtime—the work of Joplin, Scott, Lamb, and their followers—exhibits a lyrical beauty, a graceful style. The melodies of the different strains of a rag are apt to be contrasted sharply, but they are similar in that they follow lyrical, vocal lines. They can be hummed or sung easily, and they often sound like simple folk songs when isolated from the rag structure. In fact, the melodies often are folk tunes or folk rag themes found in many other contexts (*e.g.*, the "Buddy Bolden's Blues" theme which was apparently a levee work song and appears in Barney and Seymore's "St. Louis Tickle" and in a half-dozen other ragtime contexts). Clearly, the pianist ought to strive for a *cantabile* melodic line, even against hard rhythms or sharp accents.

Pianistic conceptions. Eastern ragtime tends to accent the percussiveness of the keyboard and the virtuoso skills of the player, making demands on technic which contribute to rhythmic vitality more than to lyricism or extended melody lines. Rags like those of Luckey Roberts, Eubie Blake, and their followers often strive for brilliance and virtuosity rather than melodic invention. They seem to demand brighter tempos and harsher rhythmic accents than Missouri ragtime.

The ragtime student ought to immerse himself in scores, in the few recordings of traditional ragtime pianists (Joseph Lamb, Jelly Roll Morton, Brun Campbell, Eubie Blake, Charles Thompson, Joe Jordan), in piano rolls or recordings of rolls, in the few recordings of authentic ragtime ensembles or jazz

[4]Those few classic rags which show metronome markings in original editions add confusion to the debate over ragtime tempo. They carry various markings, ranging from $\downarrow = 100$ to $\downarrow = 120$, all fairly brisk tempos in $\frac{2}{4}$ time. This is hard to construe as Stark's "slow march time." A basic (and insoluble) problem is the *author* of these metronome settings—were they indicated by the composer, by an arranger, or by the publisher himself? Since they are both rare and inconsistent, they are little help to the ragtime interpreter. Only Joplin's last rags use European tempo notations, although many carry injunctions (possibly John Stark's) warning the player "Do Not Play Fast." Artie Matthews' five "Pastime Rags" all are marked *moderato,* and numbers 1, 2, and 4 also carry the warning "Don't Fake"—*i.e.,* play as written, without improvised interpolations.

groups in the ragtime tradition. In sum, he ought to *hear* ragtime as much as possible, as well as read it from scores. Ragtime certainly deserves the same study and care that the serious pianist gives Bach, Chopin, or Bartok; further, since ragtime is a style as well as a genre encompassed in scores, the pianist must have a concept of the sound of folk ragtime firmly in mind.

It may be argued that piano rolls are misleading sources of information on ragtime style, because they are stiff and mechanical in sound. Yet the best rolls (and there are considerable variations in quality of execution of rolls) impart a strong feeling of ragtime's drive and vitality, the brilliant effects of complex polyrhythms and persuasive melodic invention. Further, rolls do date from the period of ragtime's wide popularity, and they are permanent records of the response to ragtime. Thousands of Americans heard classic ragtime only on rolls. The intelligent and sensitive performer can learn from these relics of ragtime's glory.

Some rags which give excellent demonstrations of the range and variety of ragtime rhythms and lyrical invention are: Joplin's *The Ragtime Dance* (1906), an anthology of rhythmic devices and figures as illustrative as any of Bach's exercises from *The Well-Tempered Clavier* or the *Anna Magdalena Notebook;* Joplin's "Euphonic Sounds" (1909), a crystalline structure of perfectly lucid melodies; his "Something Doing" (1903) or "Stoptime Rag" (1910), which demonstrate the contrast of lively rhythms and strategically placed silences. "Stoptime Rag" is especially intriguing for its use of silences, which constitute the three specific "stop" and "break" designs in the composition. (Stoptime was a dance pattern used in vaudeville and minstrel routines to accompany tap or soft-shoe routines, and Joplin has marked his score for the pianist, indicating that he should stamp his foot in the silences which lace the rag.) The breaks are superimposed on a marchlike linear rag composition: AA BB A C C_1 C C_1 DD EE DD FF GG. The most prominent occurrence is in the third measure of the A strain. It stops and breaks very effectively the continuity of the four-measure phrase:

STOPTIME RAG
A strain

The second stop-break pattern is used in the D strain. Eighth-note rests surround the syncopated two-measure unit. It forms a very lively contrast with the arabesque-like C strain:

STOPTIME RAG
D strain

The F strain shows a synthesis of the two previous stop-break patterns used in strains A and D. It occurs in the third measure of the four-bar phrase after very pronounced syncopation occurs in the first two measures. These strategically placed uses of silences of different kinds give this composition its unique design and continuum of time and space:

STOPTIME RAG
F strain

Joplin's "Stoptime Rag" suggests many insights into the possibilities for rhythmic devices and for the contrast of sound and silence within ragtime.

Artie Matthews' "Pastime Rags Nos. 1-5" (1913-1920) are a whole folio of variations in ragtime bass lines and complex rhythmic patterns. Good exercises in the variety of ragtime problems can be found in Joplin's late studies like "Scott Joplin's New Rag" (1912) and "Magnetic Rag" (1914), which show a subtle development of his earliest conventions, and even in anomalies like Joplin's ragtime waltz, "Bethena" (1905), which reveals the possibilities of ragtime phrasing imposed on a triple meter. All these works, and many more in the canon of classic ragtime, can give the pianist a taste of the beauty and scope of this most vigorous piano music.

How to Become a Ragtime Pianist

Other questions concerned with ragtime performance are more basic still: how do you become a ragtime pianist? how do you go about practicing ragtime music? To answer these questions, we must assume that you are acquainted with basic procedures in studying piano music, i.e., that you have learned the importance of fingering; correct articulation (rests, staccato, legato, etc.); dynamic markings; voicings (balance between left and right hands); use of pedal(s); consideration of style. It must also be assumed that you are acquainted with basic piano techniques, such as scale exercises (staccato, legato) in octaves, thirds, sixths, tenths; arpeggios (based on major, minor, seventh and other chords). If you are such a practicing pianist, specific exercises must be realized. Through them you will obtain accuracy in playing groupings, motives, patterns of notes in the left and right hands. You will learn how to play the boom-chick bass sequences of the left hand — i.e., how to hit the octaves of the boom-chick bass by themselves and how to combine them with the corresponding chord progressions. You will learn how to preset the right hand to an extended finger position which will allow you to play many of the phrases or periods of the corresponding rag strains correctly; how to use a hammer finger technique (closer to a legato than to a staccato) for the frequent sixteenth-note passages of the right and left hands; and how to combine these left and right hand exercises to obtain the correct balance of rhythm and volume in both hands.

The first type of group-accuracy exercises are the boom-chick exercises for the left hand. They use the descending left forearm only. The following examples are octave exercises only:

Octaves using the notes of the scale, ascending and descending.

Octaves using the tones of the major or minor triads, ascending and descending.

Octaves using the tones of the scale in other octave levels.

The following examples are octave exercises in combination with chord progressions:

Octave followed by one chord (triadic).

Octave followed by one chord and an octave.

Octave followed by one chord, an octave and another chord.

Octave followed by two chords.

etc.

Octave followed by two chords and an octave.

etc.

All exercises should be played in all keys. All should be practiced over and over again. Begin with a very slow speed and build the exercises up to the tempo of an allegretto.

The second type of group-accuracy exercises occurs in the right hand. They can be illustrated well with the right-hand part of Joplin's "Maple Leaf Rag." Before playing the first six measures of its A strain, the player extends his right hand in such a way that the fingers are ready to drop on the tones to be played. To extend the right hand after having played the very first note of the right-hand part would be too late. The following illustration shows the positions of the first eight notes (played by five fingers) in these first measures. Hand position on first measures, A strain of "Maple Leaf Rag":

For the first four measures of the trio part from the same rag, the player should note that he would have two hand positions, one on the first two measures, the other in the third and fourth measures; thus, he would have to plan his two positions, and never contract the hand while moving from one position to the other. Hand positions, trio of "Maple Leaf Rag":

Position one

Position two

The same procedures would be used by the player in the D strain of the same rag. He should note that he would have five hand positions. It would again take some planning to see that the hand would never contract while moving from one position to the next.

Position one: ms. 1 (9)

Position two: ms. 2 (10 and 10¹|₂)

Position three: ms. 3–8

Position four: ms. 11 and 12

Position five: ms. 13–16

In addition, the A strains of Joplin's "The Chrysanthemum" or "The Cascades" provide excellent examples of the hammer finger legato technic.

A final word: Ragtime is an art, a complex and sophisticated music derived from black folk sources. It requires skill, taste, and imagination in execution. Use of dynamic contrasts, of limited *rubato,* of a sensitive ear for the melodic and rhythmic thrust of a rag all contribute to the effect of ragtime performance. Acquaintance with the whole range of ragtime — from the early rag songs and cakewalks through the documentation of Jelly Roll Morton, Brun Campbell, and Joseph Lamb — will help the performer with any individual rag. The art of ragtime is more than an exercise in piano technic. It is finally a labor of love for the variety, depth, and richness of America's heritage of black music.

RAGTIME REDUX?

The past twenty years have seen a rediscovery of ragtime across the nation. Some three generations after its birth, the music has been accepted and recognized by people interested in American music as a valid and "respectable" form. This is perhaps the last large irony connected with Scott Joplin's sad life. He did receive the recognition he sought so desperately, but only as the posthumous dignity we seem always ready to grant our artists when they are safely buried and out of our way.

The revival of ragtime in the 1940's and 1950's cannot be traced to any single event or person, but there were clear milestones on the comeback road. In the early 1940's, Wally Rose, the pianist with Lu Watters' Yerba Buena Jazz Band in San Francisco, introduced a broad repertoire of rags to the audience for traditional jazz. Rose and the Yerba Buenans did much conscientious research and rehearsal, presenting piano and band ragtime in many forms, as a concurrent stream with the early jazz they also reintroduced. Watters even composed some ragtime-cakewalk music for his group. Paul Lingle and Burt Bales, pianists also associated with Watters, worked in the traditions of ragtime, too. At the same time, many rediscovered New Orleans musicians of the jazz revival (*e.g.,* Bunk Johnson and Mutt Carey) still recalled and played ragtime, since their basic repertoires stemmed from music of the first two decades of the century. These musicians featured both classic ragtime and the common ragtime songs of the era, all played in the same style of the years around the time of World War I.

In the late 1940's other events helped bring ragtime to a wide national audience. Pee Wee Hunt, an accomplished New York trombonist once associated with the jazz school of Eddie Condon, made a number of popular recordings in a skillfully nostalgic "doo-whacka-doo" vein of ricky-tick band ragtime, including Euday Bowman's enduring "Twelfth Street Rag," which became an instant pop classic and lingered on jukeboxes and radio programs for years. This recording rekindled memories of ragtime in a broad popular audience just when Rudi Blesh and Harriet Janis finished and published *They All Played Ragtime,* the first (and only) thorough study of ragtime and its social and aesthetic meanings. The combination of jazz revival work, Pee Wee Hunt's Top-40 breakthrough, and the massive amount of detailed information in the Blesh-Janis study made ragtime suddenly both interesting and accessible to many people.

Many musicians added impetus to this small wave of interest in ragtime: Tony Parenti, the excellent veteran New Orleans clarinetist, did much research and arranging of piano rags for jazz groups; Ralph Sutton, a young Missouri pianist, went to his roots in ragtime for solo playing and work with the ragtime ensemble of Mutt Carey; oldtime composer-pianists like Charles Thompson, Brun Campbell, Dink Johnson, and Joseph Lamb were interviewed and recorded playing their own works; and by 1959, a thoroughly authentic ragtime ensemble, the Love-Giles Ragtime Orchestra, could be assembled for a series of concerts and recorded to preserve the sound of the "Red-Backed Book of Rags."

Interest in ragtime spread in many directions. In 1951, the New York City Ballet presented a work entitled *Cakewalk,* with a score by Hershey Kay, adapted from the music of Louis Moreau Gottschalk, flavored strongly with ragtime and vaudeville music and recalling the golden years of ragtime on the stage. Many European jazz revival bands, such as those of Ken Colyer and Chris Barber, played and recorded instrumental ragtime in many forms. The music of Charles Ives, formed and influenced heavily by ragtime and once as neglected as the works of Scott Joplin, was beginning to be studied and played widely. Many musicians and listeners moved very logically from an interest in Ives's work to an interest in all the folk musics which inspired him, and they found ragtime to be a main influence in American music and culture of the turn of the century.

Through the 1960's the movement to rediscover and disseminate ragtime gained momentum, leading to the New York Public Library's edition of Scott Joplin's collected works; to a full-scale production of *Treemonisha* in Atlanta, January, 1972; to many fine recordings of classic ragtime, played and recorded as carefully as any reading of Chopin or Bach. Among the current purveyors of excellent ragtime in all its shapes are: Max Morath, whose series of educational television programs on ragtime in the early 1960's ("The Ragtime Years") provided both scholarly information and exuberant performances of classic rags, rag songs, and all the musical spectrum connected with the rise of ragtime; Joshua Rifkin, whose fine concert-style recording of major Joplin rags was an icebreaker leading the audience for classical music to the majesty and strength of ragtime as a pianistic form; William Bolcom and William Albright, composers who both play and write ragtime in its clearest vein; Trebor Tichenor of St. Louis, who has kept classic ragtime alive and well on its native grounds for over a decade; the New Orleans Ragtime Orchestra, with Lars Edegran and William Russell guiding it to play instrumental ragtime in its best forms; Dick Zimmerman and Los Angeles' Maple Leaf Club, who provide a focus for West Coast pianists and for the instrumental work of the Dawn of the Century Ragtime Orchestra; the concerted efforts of pianist John Arpin and the Ragtime Society of Toronto, who promote and distribute much good ragtime in the original land of the maple leaf. In addition, there are many other fine players and scholars in the field, such as David A. Jason, who plays and broadcasts regularly on ragtime; Robert Darch, a pianist who has also become Joseph Lamb's musical executor and publisher; and Eubie Blake—the last man in the great line of original ragtimers, who after ninety years on this earth is as strong and gracious an artist as any man alive and who is a living exemplar of ragtime's nobility and gentility.

All these workers in ragtime, plus hundreds more, have contributed to a new national attention to the music; and all promise to go on playing, singing, and discussing ragtime until the nation wakes to its full meaning, until the public realizes the beauty, variety, and vitality of this great black American music form. More than a hundred years have passed since Scott Joplin was born, but it seems as if the King of Ragtime is coming into his own again, as we begin to discern the work of Joplin and all his peers and followers in the seedtime of black music in America. Whether the present rediscovery of ragtime endures or passes as a momentary interest of a distracted culture, ragtime itself will endure as long as people have the sensibilities to understand its beauty and its strength, as long as they can see how this most American of all native musics is sewn into the fabric of our lives.

The Image on the Cover

One curious subchapter in the story of ragtime is the history of the cover illustrations for the sheet music. Early nineteenth-century popular sheet music generally appeared in rather simple and severe letterpress covers, often captioned in a fluid, thin copperplate style; but some early scores were decorated with line engravings as cover illustrations, in the tradition of the eighteenth-century political cartoon or broadside caricature. However, not until after the middle of the century did multi-color designs of any complexity appear in quantity. By the 1890's, a sophisticated school of advertising design emerged, and sheet music covers became elaborate productions. They are odd, intriguing examples of popular culture, of the diffuse commercial influences on our daily lives which Sigfried Giedion has detailed as "anonymous history."[1]

Covers for "coon songs," cakewalks, and ragtime were designed to catch the busy consumer's eye and to sell him the product. Like all advertising, they appealed to the potential buyer through a variety of rhetorical means. The combination of title, subtitle, blurbs, or other verbal promotion with the visual elements of the design was often quite subtle, and the total effect of graphic and verbal materials can be complex. More than most advertising, these covers were geared to an ephemeral demand, the fad of a passing instant; thus, they dealt often in stark stereotypes, symbols, and an iconology of very simple and straightforward images, almost as stripped and hieratic as the imagery of a political cartoon. Like the titles and lyrics of popular songs, the covers must convey an instantly recognizable idea in a highly efficient manner. There can be no waste motion, no subtleties to distract the consumer from the

[1] Sigfried Giedion, *Mechanization Takes Command* (New York: Oxford University Press, 1948).

basic point. Yet there is also an aesthetic motivation beyond the rhetoric of sales, and the covers must make at least a covert appeal through their design.

The most convenient iconology connected with the new black musics of the 1890's was, obviously, racist symbolism. Since the mechanism of racism already existed as a common code-language, it was immediately adaptable to visual representation. Racist stereotypes were conveyed with varying degrees of skill and complexity in the thousands of sheet music covers of the era. The "coon song" craze of the middle nineties brought these stereotypes into full play, since the basic point of the "coon song" was a purely racist "description" of Negro life and psychology. The quantity of "coon songs" (Figure 1) brought a wild variety of images to be expressed as visual emblems, all vicious and debasing, though of different orders.

Some images—the "cute pickaninny," the Old Mammy (Figure 10), the super-talented "natural musician"—are intended, presumably, as benign caricatures. Others—the razor-wielding bully (Figures 2, 3, 5), the lazy rustic (Figures 8, 11), or the absurdly overdressed "swell" (Figures 4, 7)—express fear and contempt, revealing the familiar residue of unconscious white insecurity and guilt. Further, all the images employ a rough caricature style to distort and ridicule black physical features: eyes, noses, and lips are grotesquely enlarged and colored; gestures are exaggerated, even when the style attempts naturalism (Figures 7, 10). A complete folk mythology of racism is transmitted by these covers as effectively as by the lyrics or titles; commercial publishers found in the combination poster-cartoon style a highly efficient complement to the musical/literary mode of the songs themselves.

The basic genre of the sheet music covers of the nineties is a simplified version of the art nouveau poster, a recent and highly popular medium used by many respectable and accomplished artists—Toulouse-Lautrec, Walter Crane, Aubrey Beardsley, Maxfield Parrish, Alphonse Mucha, and others.[2]

[2] For a thorough history of the art nouveau poster, see Bevis Hillier, *Posters* (New York: Stein and Day, 1969).

The sheet music cover became a miniaturized and debased version of the lithographed poster. The cover designer's job was complicated by demands of advertising—the need to include a fairly large and complex mass of verbal information, a small format (about 11″ × 14″), limited color-printing capabilities, and the pressures of large-scale publication. The music was geared to sell in large quantities at low prices, and the cost of setting up music for printing made the cover the last luxury in the logistics of publication. Yet the problems of the cover designer paralleled those of the popular poster-maker. Both had to create a powerful image, to impress a brief statement on the public eye and mind as directly and economically as possible.

Some covers convey a strong and aesthetically sophisticated image, but most designers worked only for maximum emotional impact—i.e., they dealt baldly in simplistic racist emblems. This was, after all, precisely what the traditions of white minstrelsy and the "coon song" were about. An early work in this vein, Rosenfeld's "I'll Send You Down a Letter from de Sky" (Figure 2), is a Janus-faced design. Its awkward and grotesque semiscript title recalls the earlier copperplate-lettered music covers of the first half of the century, while the color-printed cartoon anticipates later work (although it is more finicking and literal than later styles). It asserts several stereotypical ideas through one compact image: the Negro victim is dressed in the tails, gaiters, and striped dress trousers of the "swell" or dandy; he wields an ominously enlarged razor; one stolen chicken is wedged in a pocket, while others scamper away; and a powerful jackass is giving him his (presumably) deserved comeuppance. This simultaneously conveys fear (the huge, menacing razor); a sense of social superiority (the overdressed darky, out stealing chickens in his "dress suit"!); a sense of moral superiority (he *is* a thief!); and a sense of self-righteous poetic justice (a donkey is giving him what-for—how appropriate!). The cryptic little figure nestled in the crook of the title's capital "I" seems to extend the same imagery—the jackass-as-darky-minstrel, having the last song (and last hee-haw). It suggests also Shakespeare's Bottom in *A Midsummer*

Night's Dream, the oafish "rude mechanical" who is "translated" into an ass for his impudence. For all its absurdity, this whole cover image is complex.

The covers accompanying the great "coon song" craze of the middle nineties were cruder or more overt in their symbolism, even if they approximated an art nouveau stylishness in layout. The design for Logan's "The Coon's Trademark" (Figure 3) is simply a literal translation of the title idea — a set of symbols dispersed around a pleasantly articulated art nouveau titleframe: the ubiquitous watermelon, razor, chicken, and "coon" caricature listed in the subtitle. Hogan's "All Coons Look Alike to Me" (Figure 4) attempts again to translate the title idea literally, with a crowd of darky caricatures, all intended to appear identical despite their eccentric dress styles. Neither cover is distinguished as a piece of design or draftsmanship. They both mark a minimal effort to execute a visually striking approximation of their contents. These titles work simply as visual puns, like crude rebuses or hieroglyphics.

Others at least groped for an imagery with some aesthetic significance. The hideous caricature for Trevathan's "Bully Song" (Figure 5), although it is outlandishly cruel and distorted, at least conveys a sense of style. It also incorporates in elaborate detail blatant racist elements: the razor again, the overornate dress (carefully depicted, from spats to boiled collar and cravat), the facial features now distorted not comically but fearfully, a gruesome simian cast to the whole figure. This bully figure conveys the fear and guilt which are less conspicuous in the usual comic cartoons. This creature boils up from white nightmares, not from the usual fantasies of power or sexuality; he is almost an apocalyptic symbol of retribution. It is hard to believe that anyone ever smiled or laughed at this horrific scrawl. The design for Jefferson and Friedman's "Coon, Coon, Coon" (Figure 6) also shows at least a rudimentary sense of aesthetics. The dotted "O's" in "coon" were evidently a source of amusement and a convenient glyph (see Figure 1 also); and this designer has made maximum use of a compressed image by building his caricature around the title itself, a sophisticated device for this genre. Again, the caricature itself is perfectly standardized — goggle eyes suggesting the visual pun, lips and noses exaggerated, a minstrel man's caricature of fine dress in the cravats and toppers.

As the "coon song" craze was overtaken by the cakewalk fad, in the late nineties, fashions in cover art shifted. Kerry Mills, the finest cakewalk writer, established a characteristic cover style that was not only carried consistently through his own publications but was also stolen by virtually all other publishers of cakewalks. The design for "At a Georgia Campmeeting" (Figure 7) features sharp and careful art nouveau grotesque lettering and a fussy but well-executed drawing subordinated to the message. The figures of the black cakewalkers are still in the rude caricature vein, closely resembling the mob of identical "coons" of Hogan's cover (Figure 4), but are given a modicum of dignity and individuality. Another Mills cover, for "Impecunious Davis" (Figure 8), emphasizes the same elements — large, poster lettering and a finely detailed drawing, this time of a single stock figure, the old rustic, the levee lounger of folklore. Again, the figure is a caricature, but it is neither so harsh nor so fearful as the earlier "coon song" scarecrows. The Mills covers are carefully conceived and executed, designed to emphasize the title, the author's name, and a distinct "darky image" without resorting to a complex apparatus of symbolism.

The effectiveness of the Mills cakewalk designs is indicated by their imitators. Figure 9 shows a typical example, for Haack's "The Rag-Time Sports." It adopts the sharp-cornered quasi-oriental style lettering of the Mills covers and uses the same subordinated line-drawing elements. Quite possibly the same designer made this and other cakewalk covers; if not, the imitation is clever and exact. At any rate, similar design elements exist, along with a slight but fairly gentle caricaturing. (The two "sports" on this cover are engaged in plugging the song, as the overhead caption makes clear — so they cannot be all bad.)

As the cakewalk boom in turn gave way before the new vogue

for ragtime, fashions again shifted slightly. The Mills-style cake-walk cover was adapted, as in Figure 10, for Epler's "Ash-Cake Shuffle," just as the music itself was often retitled and adapted to suit changing tastes. The cover advertises itself as "A Characteristic March and Two Step—Can Also Be Used as a Polka or Rag-Time Cake Walk," which about covers all bets. The design echoes the Mills covers in the jagged hand-lettering and the delicate line drawing; but here the drawing is emphasized more strongly. It is less a screen of arabesques and light-and-shade patterns, more a self-conscious genre piece. It portrays a (presumably) happy family scene full of instantly identifiable stock characters—the handkerchief-headed Mammy at the fire (surely the precursor of Aunt Jemima) making ash-cakes; boys and girls (a bit old to be considered pickaninnies, but still winsome); and even the adults cavorting in wild ecstacy as they contemplate the impending feast. The title itself is a punning compromise—not quite a cake*walk,* but a "shuffle," and not merely ordinary cakes but good old downhome *ash*-cakes. The publisher has gone all-out in verbal and visual terms alike to capitalize on any positive and folksy ideas inherent in the concept. While the figures are still blatant caricatures, they are no longer harsh or purely comic. A strong feeling of folk nostalgia—the Old South syndrome—resides in the style.

As ragtime became the dominant popular black music fashion, about 1900, cover art avoided open racist stereotyping and iconology, although it was never totally abandoned. A later cover for Robinson and Adams' "Hanky Pank" (Figure 11) drags out all the obvious old emblems once again—the gigantic watermelon and the raggedy rustic, drawn in a wildly exaggerated fashion. While publishers like John Stark of St. Louis, who had some genuine sympathy for and understanding of the music, were able to produce and sell (in large quantities) scores with dignified and excellently designed covers, much of the trade mined the same old vein of the 1890's. The trend moved toward a standardized cartoon style, as in Figure 11, less in the mode of the art nouveau poster and more closely akin to a newer popular medium, the funny papers. But the warehouse of racist materials was always unlocked and ready for use, and even through the 1920's the same standardized characterizations appear on popular song covers. A later trend toward a stickily "artsy" abstraction, drawn from Art Deco motifs, finally ended the general use of racist iconology.

What is to be learned from turning over this particular moldy stone on the broad path of popular culture? The covers, even more than the lyrics or the advertising blurbs, show how black music was regarded and how it was sold to the general public. As the long tradition of white minstrelsy closed out in the 1890's, it was not instantly supplanted by a tradition of black musicians and black music. During the heyday of the "coon song," black performers began to make some small headway in big-time vaudeville and with big publishers. Hence, excellent black showmen like Bert Williams and William Walker (Figure 3) had to perform noxious material in order to be accepted; they were billed as "Two Real Coons," and the appearance of black men in black roles was a distinct novelty. (Jelly Roll Morton, among others, recalled the curious custom of black men appearing in burnt cork, as if the makeup itself was an essential magic ingredient of show business illusionism.) Hence, a black composer of real merit, Ernest Hogan, could compose and sell the most noxious "coon song" of all (Figure 4). The black artist, struggling for any foothold in the commercial music world, took what he could get — which meant cooperating with the basic conventions of white racism in the 1890's.

Further, this episode in a minor subgenre of a minor genre of commercial art captures concisely the involuted mental imagery of racism and expresses the central superstitions about the Negro more compactly and directly than words. The fact that the designs were instruments of commerce is the central issue. Racism is good business; this conclusion is inescapable after an examination of these covers. The distorted and degrading images were, of course, aimed at the white buying public. No one bothered to consider black buyers; they could damn well take what was offered, and if it was blatant racism, they could buy it or leave it alone. This often-applauded "tough-minded" *laissez-faire* attitude accounts for the blunt hard-sell approach of the covers, but it does not account for their wild success; clearly the public responded sincerely to the simplistic caricatures of the "coon song," just as they responded to the covers themselves. The cakewalks and instrumental ragtime did not draw overtly on the racist materials of the "coon song," by and large, but the producers still sold the goods in the same old package. Racism on the cover was good business, even if it no longer accurately reflected the contents. The publishers shrewdly maintained the image of the old-time darky as symbolic of the whole spectrum of new black musics. Even though ragtime — especially black folk rags and classic ragtime — was miles, socially and aesthetically, from the "coon song" tradition of white minstrelsy, the covers drew them with the same old blunt burnt cork.

This accounts, in part, for the guilt by association sometimes contracted by ragtime, when it is indiscriminately lumped with some of its antecedents or described as "racist" in content ("that old Uncle Tom music"). Yet it is not enough simply to separate later ragtime from the "coon song" material. Even much of this material was essentially innocent of overt racism. The whole process of commercial production is at fault, ultimately; like most phases of popular culture, the music business of 1890–1900 was geared to detect and utilize every shift in public taste and interest. The industry comprised a giant mechanism for producing standardized material for standardized minds, and one of the simplest blocs of raw material to use was the stereotypical mythology of racism. It could be triggered by so simple a word as "coon," an epithet that goes a long way back in frontier dialect and humor as a friendly or at least neutral nickname; or it could be triggered by a rough cartoon of a bug-eyed, rubber-lipped, razor-waving chicken thief.

The American tendency to accept utilitarian concepts, to applaud any obvious success ("If it works, it's good!") is a root motive in the dispersal and efficacy of racism like that of the sheet music covers. Clearly, most white Americans were ready to accept the stereotypes of the Negro which the covers perpetuated. Clearly, the publishers were not designing "hate art" as an end in itself; but the covers, like purposeful propaganda posters, were instrumental in maintaining century-old clichés of white minstrelsy. Only the appearance of black performers of great skill and sensitivity was able to divert and finally vanquish such sick and hostile projections of the white mind. In this revolution of cultural practices and values, ragtime was the first spearhead thrust of new black music which demonstrated the individuality and genius of black artists.

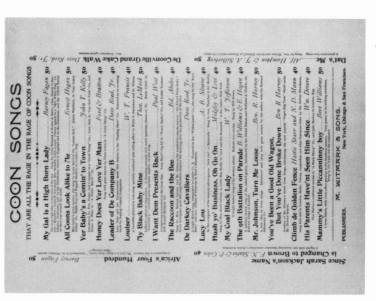

Figure 1. List of titles from the height of the "coon song" craze, *ca.* 1897.

Figure 2. An early (1884) stereotyping cover. Note iconology of chickens, razor, jackasses, and the curious minstrelform (Bottom?) at the upper left.

Figure 4. Ernest Hogan's great hit, the apogee of the "coon" song" craze (1896).

Figure 3. The complete iconology in a simple catalog form (1897).

Figure 6. Form follows function?—the quasi-art-nouveau design makes stereotyping a subsidiary of pure design.

Figure 5. May Irwin's greatest vehicle, another landmark in the "coon song" craze (1896).

Figure 8. Note continuity of cover styles in Mills's work—this became a clearly defined style used rather exclusively for cakewalks.

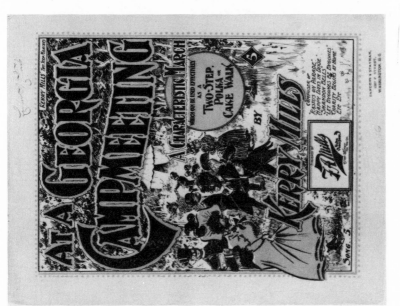

Figure 7. The archetypal cakewalk (1897), in the poster-style art nouveau which became the mode for cakewalk art.

Figure 10. An extension of the typical "cakewalk cover" poster style. Note the cover-all subtitling as ragtime supplanted the cakewalk in popularity (1899).

Figure 9. An imitation of the Mills covers. Note the Amos 'n' Andy or Moran and Mack stereotyped figures.

Figure 11. The stereotypes persisted unabated with rag-time (1914).

APPENDIX **II**

Ragtime Versus Jazz
Piano Styles

Is ragtime a sin or a misfortune? Is it a moral offence or just too much of a good thing? Is it permanent or a mere passing fancy like ping-pong? — The Musical Monitor, *1919*

A persistent problem with contemporary recognition of ragtime as an independent musical form is its confusion with later modes of jazz piano. Most listeners have heard various versions of pseudo-ragtime ("honky-tonk piano") or have heard jazz stylists casually essaying ragtime; but relatively few people have heard ragtime played "straight" from the score. Yet basic and significant differences in approach distinguish classic ragtime from all later improvisational jazz styles. Examples of ragtime and of jazz styles derived from ragtime reveal important distinctions between the genre of ragtime and the style of jazz.

Earliest examples of primitive ragtime show the folk roots of ragtime as both style and genre. D. Emerson's early "Kullud Koons' Kake Walk" (1892) is one interesting specimen of the immediate progenitors of classic ragtime (Figure 12). Written as a display or virtuoso piece by a banjo soloist, this simple cakewalk is a hybrid of folk rhythms and melodic motives without the complex "folded" structure of ragtime and with only rudimentary syncopations. It seems a peculiar synthesis of Irish jig and march-cakewalk styles, which recalls that one of the earliest common terms for ragtime piano playing was "jig-piano."[1] The piece, available as a banjo solo, piano solo, or banjo-piano duet, is obviously designed as an exhibition piece for banjo virtuoso; and even in the piano version it retains the sound of the plucked instrument. This suggests some classic

[1] For the influence of jig-dancing on early black dance styles of minstrelsy, see Marshall and Jean Stearns, *Jazz Dance* (New York: Macmillan, 1968), Chapter 6.

rags, especially those like James Scott's "The Ragtime Oriole" which have a strong guitar-banjo plectrum sound. At this point in ragtime's pre-history, we can see the folk style passing from the minstrel-show banjo mode to a piano style based on this staccato, percussive sound.

"Kullud Koons' Kake Walk" does not anticipate later jazz styles but harks back to minstrel music and folk tunes. Unsophisticated and direct, its analogues are not with jazz styles which arose in the next generation but with the continuing stream of folk ragtime which developed into popular country music — the work of string bands, southern songsters, and hokum bands of the 1920's. The style is reminiscent of the jug band music of Gus Cannon and vividly represents folk traditions in ragtime.

As ragtime became a nationwide vogue around 1900, one immediate response was to promote it as a style rather than a genre. Entrepreneurs like "Professor" Axel Christenson made a profitable business of purveying ragtime lessons. The process of "ragging" a tune (*i.e.,* applying simple and conventionalized syncopations and bass patterns) was touted as the substance of the new music. Most early "ragtime instructors" used this approach in their printed lessons and exercises — giving students examples of common hymns, folk songs, popular tunes, then printing the same work with ragtime syncopations. The basic process was to incorporate a standard ragtime boom-chick bass and to insert regular right-hand syncopations. This approximated the *sound,* not the form, of classic ragtime; and it was certainly the basic method of the ear-trained pianists (like Ben Harney) of minstrelsy and vaudeville. The result was a lively, bouncy music that most people would identify casually as ragtime.

A good early specimen of this popular method of "ragging" appears in Malcolm Williams' "My Ann Elizer (The Rag-Time Girl)," a rag song of 1898 (Figure 13). Its cover advertises an "Extra Chorus (Written in Rag-time)." The score includes a "straight" chorus, marked "Marcia," and an alternate chorus with the treble line rewritten to include consistent running sixteenth notes and syncopations in the very simplest ragtime formula. Since the song was already organized in the semimarch vein of most cakewalks and ragtime songs, the changes are slight. This illustration typifies the earliest approach to ragtime as a piano style. This differs from Emerson's original composition of a folk virtuoso piece. Williams' song treats ragtime as a "method," a set of piano techniques, as a universal *style* which can be imposed on sundry materials, while Emerson begins with the style and invents an appropriate composition to utilize it. The idea of "ragging" was current even while Joplin's classic rags made their first impact on the public, and there was never a clear distinction between the formal principles which Joplin represented and this concept of a flexible folk-ragtime style.

The distinction between ragtime and those later styles derived from it is perhaps clearer. Most early jazz pianists were trained on ragtime and knew it well, both in folk versions and through the formalized works of Joplin and his followers. An excellent jazz reconstruction of ragtime occurs in Jelly Roll Morton's personalized version of Joplin's first published rag, "Original Rags." Jelly Roll's "transformation" of Joplin's music was consciously and carefully developed. In his Library of Congress interviews with Alan Lomax, Morton discussed early ragtime stylists and writers, and he described his own departure from principles of ragtime as a process of creative exploration. To demonstrate, he played "Maple Leaf Rag" —first a fairly strict version of Joplin's written score, then his own free adaptation, in "Jelly Roll style." After this demonstration, he went on to record "Original Rags" in the same kind of free transformation (Figure 14). Morton's close friend and backer, Roy Carew, a long-time ragtime historian, urged him to continue his work with ragtime. At the time of his death, Jelly Roll was contemplating a "transformation" of Tom Turpin's highly inventive "A Ragtime Nightmare" (1900).[2]

[2] Richard B. Allen and William Russell, notes to "The New Orleans Ragtime Orchestra," Vol. 2, Pearl PLP-8.

Jelly Roll's version of "Original Rags," here transcribed from the 1939 recording, can be compared with Joplin's score (Figure 15) to elucidate Morton's basic method of transformation, a more sophisticated musical process than the early "ragging" idea or the later popular practice of "swinging" the classics. Morton alters the boom-chick bass line of Joplin's composition and uses a freer left hand, which is often syncopated more than ragtime usually allows. Morton gives himself the liberty of adding syncopations to Joplin's treble line also, a process of "jazzing" that can destroy the coherence of ragtime melody and rhythm unless used with Morton's selectivity and restraint. This becomes what Morton commonly called "stomp" piano, a propulsive two-handed improvisatory style that departs from ragtime's classical restraints but retains its form. An example like this transcription of "Original Rags" stands between classic ragtime and Morton's later original ragtime-jazz works such as "Perfect Rag," "Frogimore Rag," "Bert Williams" (originally titled "Pacific Rag"). Morton never traveled far from his early ragtime discipline, and this example, when compared with Joplin's score, shows in detail his debts to ragtime.

If Morton was a more than capable ragtime-trained stylist (he won ragtime contests and even defeated the legendary Tony Jackson and downed St. Louis' best players, *ca.* 1910), other jazz pianists also adapted ragtime in various ways. An example of casual ragtime transformation is Cow Cow Davenport's early 1920's recording called "Atlanta Rag," transcribed here (Figure 16). This tune, on inspection, turns out to be a slightly truncated and altered version of Carey Morgan's "Trilby Rag" (1915), also reproduced (Figure 17). Davenport's playing is less polished and imaginative than Morton's, and his "transformation" of the Morgan rag is probably as much a product of faulty memory and fingering as conscious intent. Yet it is interesting to see how Davenport, a blues pianist and vaudevillian, uses the materials of the Morgan rag and how he alters them. Basically, Davenport's "Atlanta Rag" is in the vein of pastiche ragtime (like that of Brun Campbell), in which the performer assembles strains or phrases from various ragtime works, pasted together with a self-consistent pianistic style.

Comparison of Davenport's free version of "Trilby Rag" with the original score shows how Davenport frequently alters the bass line into a freely flowing blues-fashion pattern. There are passages of fumbling, where he inserts blues-style figures to bridge the strains of Morgan's rag. On the recording, Davenport plays at a very bright tempo, clearly taxing his technical abilities to the limits. Also, like Morton, he often adds syncopation to already-syncopated phrases. His alterations are rarely as effective and as restrained as Morton's, however, and the total effect of "Atlanta Rag" verges on incoherence or disintegration. It does show a clear link between written ragtime and the developing style of improvisational jazz. Davenport's example typifies the playing of most ragtime-trained jazzmen of his generation. As they learned a basic jazz style, they naturally adapted ragtime materials they had known to this new improvisational approach. The results, when pushed further than Davenport and Morton go, created the so-called "novelty rag" style of the 1920's and led to such variations on early jazz styles as Earl Hines's or Teddy Weatherford's "trumpet-piano" ideas and the standard swing styles of Duke Ellington, Teddy Wilson, Jess Stacy, and others.

By the time Morton, Davenport, and other jazz piano pioneers were transforming classic ragtime into classic jazz, ragtime composition had virtually ceased. The idea of written-and-read compositions was vanquished by the universal practice of "faking" or improvisation, the basis of jazz style. This was a little more complex than the old practice of "ragging," but its roots lay there, in the first "jig-piano" conceptions of the 1890's.[3]

[3] It is interesting to note that the most successful popularizer of do-it-yourself home instruction ragtime courses, Axel Christenson, was careful to distinguish between the practice of "ragging" popular music and the playing of classic ragtime. He concludes his course of instruction with an admonition: "After finishing this book the pupil will take up popular songs to be converted into ragtime, or real ragtime pieces to be played as written." Axel W. Christenson, *Christenson's Rag-Time Instruction Book for Piano* (6th ed.; Chicago: Axel W. Christenson, 1909), 36.

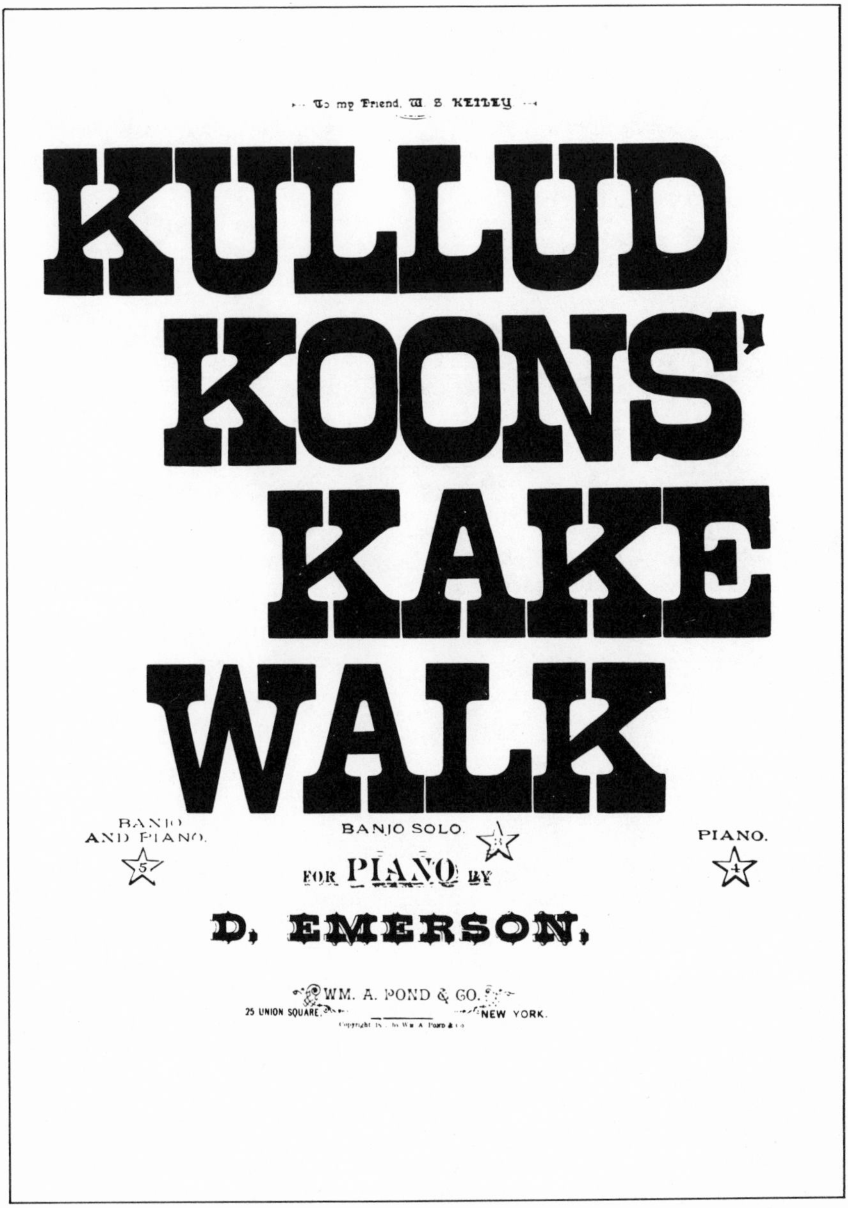
To my Friend, W. S. KELLEY
KULLUD KOONS' KAKE WALK
BANJO AND PIANO. 5
BANJO SOLO. 3
PIANO. 4
FOR PIANO BY
D. EMERSON,
WM. A. POND & CO.
25 UNION SQUARE. NEW YORK.

Figure 12.

KULLUD KOONS KAKE WALK

Bass to B

D. Emerson

CHOICE BANJO SELECTIONS

COMPOSED AND ARRANGED BY

D. EMERSON.

Pieces marked * are arranged for two Banjos, but are bright and effective when played as Solos.

*Barbecue Reel	25	*Monroe Jig	25
*Blue Bird Waltz	25	*Meteor Mazurka	25
*Brigand's Waltz	25	*Mazurka Mexicana	20
Blanche Polka	15		
		Netherwood Polka	20
*Crescent Clog	25	*Norine Waltz	35
*Carnival Folka	30		
*Cappa's March	50	*Pansy Schottische	25
		*Princess Waltz	30
Duchess Waltz	35	Premier Waltz	20
*Elite Polka	25	Royal Schottische	30
*Emerson's Favorite Clog	25	*Rita Polka	30
*Emerson's Favorite Song & Dance	35		
Elfin Polka	20	Serenade	20
		*Scratch Gravel Galop	30
*Fairy Schottische	30	*Souvenir Waltz	20
Fan Tan Polka	20	Star Waltz	15
*Fawn Mazurka	25	*Silver Bells Gavotte	40
*Favorite Schottische	20		
Forest and Stream Polka	15	*Twinkling Star Schottische	15
*Gracie Waltz	25		
*Grand Parade March	35	*Vesper Schottische	25
Gem Polka	15	Violet Waltz	15
*Grand Review March	35		
		*Will o' the Wisp Polka	25
Halcyon Polka	20	Wild West Galop Banjo and Piano	50
Kelpie Polka Mazurka	15	*Zephyr Galop	25
Kullud Koons Kake Waltz	30		

NEW YORK

Published by WM. A. POND & CO., 25 Union Square.

Figure 13.

Extra Chorus *(Written in Rag-time)*

D.S.

Scott Joplin's
ORIGINAL RAGS
as played by
Jelly Roll Morton

Transcribed by
Richard Thompson

Figure 14.

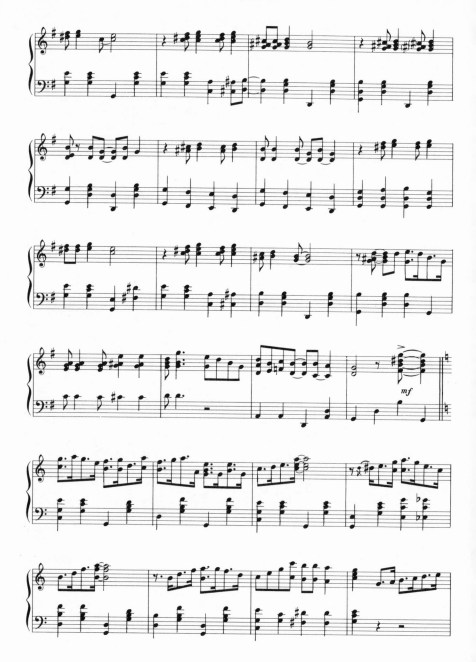

ORIGINAL RAGS

Picked by
Scott Joplin

Arranged by
Chas. N. Daniels

Copyright 1899 by Carl Hoffman

Figure 15.

ATLANTA RAG

Cow Cow Davenport

Transcribed by
Michael Polad

TRILBY RAG

Carey Morgan
arr. by D Onivas

Figure 17.

Trio D.S. ⅜ al 𝄐

Scott Joplin's *Treemonisha*

STRUCTURE AND MEANING IN *Treemonisha*

Treemonisha is the first demonstrably great American opera, for it speaks a genuine American musical idiom within the conventional forms of Western opera—forms such as the overture, the aria, the arioso, the recitative, the chorus, and the ballet. Joplin wrote his work long before George Gershwin conceived *Porgy and Bess* (1935). Like *Porgy and Bess, Treemonisha* consists of three acts, uses an instrumental language based on popular music of the time and contains vocal numbers likewise derived from the musical protoplasm and heartbeat of the land. *Treemonisha* does not suffer from the imitativeness that plagued earlier operatic attempts by American composers, as in Fry's *Leonora* (1845), Bristow's *Rip Van Winkle* (1855), Walter Damrosch's *The Scarlet Letter* (1896), and Horatio Parker's *Mona* (1912). These operas were written under the mesmerizing influence of Beethoven and Wagner.

It is the first great American opera in which a composer was his own librettist and choreographer. Integration of music, drama, and dance gives this opera its obvious quality of Americanness, since it borrows this concept of integration of the arts from the world of American minstrelsy and vaudeville, not from the *Gesamtkunstwerk*. Joplin's basic pragmatic borrowing from popular culture puts him at once in the tradition of American popular music and in the tradition of European grand opera, as he understood it. Specific choreographic directions are indicated in the ring play of "We're Goin' Around" (No. 4), the "Frolic of the Bears" (No. 13), and "A Real Slow Drag" (No. 27). The latter moves through the slow drag, the dude walk, the schottische, all popular dance forms of the ragtime era. Joplin clearly was as concerned with the verbal text and the balletic motion of the work as with the vocal and instrumental musical passages.

It is also the first great American opera in which the chorus, not the solo parts, predominates. Soloists are presented in constant interaction with the chorus—the individual with the group, the people, a community of black people. A musical democracy is established by this balance of group against solo voices. The soloist's voice is enhanced by the voices and noises of the choruses and vice versa. A close, fraternal, "soul" relationship exists between solo and chorus parts, between Monisha, Treemonisha, and the corn-huskers, cotton-pickers, and visitors. Of the twenty-seven numbers of the opera, nineteen contain choral participation. Sometimes it is the chorus of corn-huskers, singing in the distance (No. 3), or the same chorus performing a ring-play dance (No. 4); sometimes the choral singing is distributed between a leader and a six-part chorus (No. 9); sometimes the eight-part chorus participates directly in the action through reiterated questions aimed at a protagonist (No. 10). Usually the chorus interacts with the soloist(s) within a number. Only a few numbers are exclusively choral—the surprising male quartet "We Will Rest Awhile" (No. 16) and the marvelous worksong of the cotton-pickers "Aunt Dinah Has Blowed de Horn" (No. 18).

Treemonisha is Joplin's greatest accomplishment as a composer. In this work he synthesizes all his musical styles of ragtime, but throughout, the ragtime is applied in a sophisticated, subtle, and covert way and is fully integrated within the action of the opera. Listeners must study the score to discover the ragtime mannerisms which constitute the musical lifeline of the work, but we can excerpt some ragtime elements in detail.

There is first the Treemonisha strain-motif at the beginning of the overture. Its three figures show many similarities with rag melodies or figures used by Joplin and also by Kerry Mills, the most popular cakewalk composer. The whole concept of the Treemonisha motif appears in the melodic outline of Kerry Mills's "characteristic two-step march," "Happy Days in Dixie" (1896):

TREEMONISHA MOTIF
Overture, ms. 3–4

KERRY MILLS'S HAPPY DAYS IN DIXIE
Trio ms. 1–4

Also, the beautiful dude walk melody from the last number of the opera, "A Real Slow Drag," shows melodic similarities with the vocal part of the same two-step march by Mills:

A REAL SLOW DRAG
ms. 21–24

March-ing on-ward, march-ing on-ward, march-ing to___ that love-ly tune;

MILLS'S HAPPY DAYS IN DIXIE
Vocal line (as sung, one octave lower)

Ban- jos ring- in' Dark - ies sing - in' Ma- king mu- sic sweet and grand

A similar melodic activity appears in the beginning of the B strain of Joplin's "Afro-American Intermezzo," "The Chrysanthemum" (1904):

JOPLIN: CHRYSANTHEMUM
B strain, ms. 1–4 (an octave lower)

Similarities in mood and content are also apparent. The *larghetto* melody of "A Real Slow Drag," featured earlier in the overture, has a quality of nostalgia and sentiment similar to that found in the *dolce* part (C strain) of Joplin's "The Chrysanthemum":

A REAL SLOW DRAG
Theme

JOPLIN: CHRYSANTHEMUM
C strain, ms. 1–4

In "Something Doing" (1903), Joplin used a similar ascending and descending figure (A strain):

JOPLIN: SOMETHING DOING
A strain, ms. 1–2

The dotted rhythm pattern in the C strain of Joplin's "Eugenia" (1906) recurs in a superb and more sophisticated version in the prelude to Act III of *Treemonisha:*

JOPLIN: EUGENIA
C strain, ms. 1–3

TREEMONISHA, PRELUDE TO ACT III
Ms. 17–19

Similarities go as far as individual figures of a theme. Thus the first figure of the Treemonisha motif had an ancestor in the descending tetrachord figure from the introduction to Mills's two-step march, "Whistlin' Rufus" (1899):

MILLS: WHISTLIN' RUFUS
Intro, ms. 1

The octave leap of the second figure from the Treemonisha motif can be found in the first strain of Joplin's "Eugenia":

JOPLIN: EUGENIA
A strain, ms. 7

The descending lilt of the third figure from this motif can be detected in the first strain of the ragtime two-step, "The Favorite" (1904), also by Joplin:

JOPLIN: THE FAVORITE
A strain, ms. 1

Many more motivic similarities between well-known ragtime compositions and Joplin's *Treemonisha* could be found in a more thorough study. We can indicate just one more motivic relationship—the similarity between the chromatic figure in the introduction of "The Chrysanthemum" and the chromatic figure which appears shortly after the beginning of the opera overture:

JOPLIN: CHRYSANTHEMUM
Intro, ms. 1–2

TREEMONISHA, OVERTURE
Ms. 25–26

Obviously, the motivic-thematic musical material of the opera is closely related to the ragtime style of Joplin and other rag composers. From the musical vocabulary of ragtime, Joplin creates the most remarkable and impressive themes and songs of the opera: the Treemonisha theme stated at the beginning, "Aunt Dinah Has Blowed de Horn" and "A Real Slow Drag."

Other connections between ragtime music and this opera exist in the basic structure of the opera itself. The opera begins with an extensive overture which exposes three themes. The first theme is the Treemonisha theme or motif, which in addition to its many occurrences in the overture reappears at the end of No. 8 of Act I, at the beginning of No. 15 from Act II, and at the end of No. 21 in Act III. The second theme, in the *Largo con espressione* section of the overture, is stated in the same key in "The Wasp Nest" (No. 14) in Act II. The third theme, in a *larghetto* part of the overture, introduces the theme of "A Real Slow Drag," from the final, climactic number of Act III. By presenting these three prominent themes in the overture, Joplin uses the structure of the potpourri—or more accurately, the medley—overture.

In addition to the use of these three very distinct themes, the flavor of the medley becomes apparent through the many braking motions in the form of *ritardandi, dimenuendi,* and *fermatas,* indicating changes from one section to another by a decrease in tempo:

OVERTURE
Ms. 46

Other braking devices can be found — the repetition of the same tone or of its corresponding octave, or an extended *arpeggio:*

OVERTURE
Ms. 66–68

OVERTURE
Ms. 108

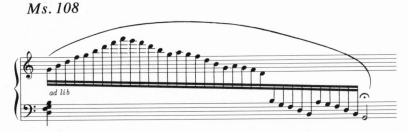

The medley is connected closely with the history of other forms popular during the ragtime era, especially the quadrille.

The debts of classic ragtime to a medley/potpourri form have been discussed earlier. Rag medleys were also popular, as in the "Rag Medley" by Max Hoffman or Blind Boone's two rag medleys. Clearly, Joplin adapted the basic "open-ended" or free form of the medley in his operatic construction.

Smaller ragtime devices occur frequently in *Treemonisha,* touches which echo the most basic idioms of piano ragtime. The prelude to Act III reveals the upbeat interval of the fourth which is so prominent in Joplin's "Maple Leaf Rag":

PRELUDE TO ACT III
Ms. 1

A few measures later in the same prelude, Joplin uses another idiomatic rag figure:

PRELUDE TO ACT III
Ms. 7–8

The "raggy" structure of the opera is also revealed in its construction as a number opera. The first act consists of ten, the second act of eight, the third act of nine separate numbers. As in a concert of ragtime, each number does not take too much time to perform; the various numbers do not have Wagnerian proportions, and, in fact, some are quite short. Each number, like a ragtime piece, is headed by an introduction of two, three, or four measures; and as in ragtime compositions, the introductory figures are often repeated within the numbers themselves (see No. 1, No. 4, No. 6). The whole structure is akin to a vaudeville show or olio or the impromptu organization of short skits and sketches in a minstrel show. The most obvious reminder of the ragtime quality of the opera is that it begins and ends with ragtime music — the Treemonisha theme and "A Real Slow Drag," respectively.

The music of *Treemonisha* is unique in its Americanness and calls for a brief account of most of its melodies. "The Bag of Luck" (No. 2) is a very strong, complex piece, with touches of beautiful *cavatina* and recitative writing. According to its frequent changes of mood, it moves through the keys of G major, E♭ major, d minor, B♭ major, C major, A♭ major, and C major. The music is set to black language, idioms, and abbreviations. The *cavatina* (*Andante assai*) uses the interval of the sixth of the Treemonisha motif:

"THE BAG OF LUCK"
Ms. 68–69

The "Hello" chorus of "The Corn-Huskers" (No. 3), with its stoptime accompaniment (one of Joplin's favorite rhythmic devices, adopted from vaudeville dance practices), leads to the first dance number of the opera — the ring-play chorus number, "We're Goin' Around" (No. 4), with its call-and-response pattern, ragtime accompaniment, and typically black melodic inflections. The through-composed "The Wreath" (No. 5) is remarkable for its soaring melodic outburst at the words "there are pretty leaves on this tree." Monisha's ballad-aria "The Sacred Tree" (No. 6) is an expressive stylization of black

American ballads and spirituals. The musical narration of
"Treemonisha's Bringing Up" (No. 8) shows Joplin's handling
of conventional English by means of recitative style. "Good
Advice" (No. 9) is a combination of Parson Alltalk's arioso-
like black sermonette and a call-and-response black spiritual
with the chorus' hummed "Un-n-n-n" following at times the
statement "O, my neighbors, you must be good." In "Confusion" (No. 10), Joplin dramatically uses the device of choral
Sprechstimme, to "speak in crying tones . . . not in strict time."

In Act II, the initial choral "Superstition" (No. 11) and the
ensemble number "Treemonisha in Peril" (No. 12) are absolute contrasts to the "Frolic of the Bears" (No. 13) and "The
Wasp Nest" (No. 14). Number 13 is a nostalgic ragtime waltz
in e minor, and its sequal is the literal transfer of the *Largo con
espressione* section of the medley overture. In both numbers,
the instrumental part is more important than the vocal part.
Even in "The Rescue" (No. 15), the instrumental part is still
of great significance, since it shows at its beginning a literal
quotation of the Treemonisha motif with its characteristic
introduction and accompaniment. To emphasize still more the
significance of the use of vocal versus instrumental sounds in
this act, Joplin concludes it with two beautiful choral numbers.
"We Will Rest Awhile" (No. 16) is a male quartet in the best
American barbershop tradition. The composer uses this sound
for the effect of dignity and need for rest, as many years later
Gian Carlo Menotti has the three wise men sing "How Far
Away We Come" in his *Amahl and the Night Visitors* (1951).
"Aunt Dinah Has Blowed de Horn" (No. 18) is one of the most
powerful choral numbers of the entire opera, with its ragtime
rhythm associated with the black laborers and its theme related
to the Treemonisha motif:

"AUNT DINAH HAS BLOWED DE HORN"
Ms. 4–6

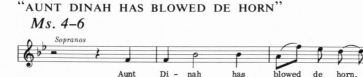

After the prelude to Act III, "I Want to See My Child" (No. 20) is a beautiful song and duet in the style of America's genteel tradition. The Treemonisha motif of the medley overture and the initial motif of the prelude to this act permeate the rather complex "Treemonisha's Return" (No. 21). In Remus' lecture, "Wrong Is Never Right" (No. 22), the sentimental quality of the mother-child parlor song (like No. 20) is expanded into a "good advice" gospel song. It culminates with an octet chorus, which with its ". . . do right and happy you will be" stresses still more the moral lesson to be learned. In Ned's aria, "When Villains Ramble Far and Near" (No. 24), Joplin, using the bass voice to sing out the message of good over evil, has created one of the finest solo arias of American operatic literature. Treemonisha's aria in "We Will Trust You as Our Leader" (No. 26) expresses a people's yearning for freedom and leadership, a moving away from "feeling blue." The ingenious eight-part chorus breathes a feeling of love, trust, and mutual understanding within the community. Finally, "A Real Slow Drag" (No. 27), with its very minute and detailed instructions on how to dance to this ragtime tune, is a beautiful realization and celebration of "soul-rhythm" at its best.

Treemonisha is America's first great opera, because it strikes a balance between the essential nonrealism of the opera form and the demands of an American audience for an entertainment which is concrete and not fantastic. The nonrealistic "wasp-nest" and "frolic of the bears" passages are set within the real world of rural black American workers somewhere in the state of Arkansas. Realism is sought in the vernacular dialogue of the soloists and chorus through the use of the language of southern blacks, musical styles known to American audiences, and a direct and comprehensible plot. Joplin tried to accomplish with his democratic realism what Twain, Howells, and Crane sought in American literature—a vernacular language which is truly American, non-European, useful, and thus beautiful. Joplin succeeded in *Treemonisha* in creating a musical and dramatic idiom appropriate both to black American language and to the black American scene.

Treemonisha AS SOCIAL MYTHOLOGY

The saddest chapter in Scott Joplin's life was his labor of (unrequited) love in his last venture into "classical" music, the composition of his opera *Treemonisha*. From the beginning of his career as a composer, Joplin worked with various musical genres which he considered art forms—including his development of the formalized piano rag. His earliest published works ("A Picture of Her Face" and "Please Say You Will," 1895), cast in the "respectable" genteel vein of the sentimental parlor song, were undistinguished examples of one such genre. As early as 1899 Joplin experimented with extended versions of the "new" ragtime music he was forming, as he developed the long version of *The Ragtime Dance* (performed in 1899, published in 1902). This song-rag-ballet suite was an ambitious attempt to illustrate the dance origins and functions of ragtime; and it apparently pushed Joplin on to another long work, his lost first opera *A Guest of Honor* (1903). At the time when "Maple Leaf Rag" had made him undisputed king of ragtime, when he was publishing a stream of distinguished and widely varied piano rags, Joplin also drove himself to invent larger musical forms.

The culmination of this direction in Joplin's creative energies was *Treemonisha,* which occupied the last decade of his life; it was published in 1911 and given one semipublic performance in 1915. While only vague legends of Joplin's first opera are left, we have scores for *The Ragtime Dance* and *Treemonisha* to show the direction his imagination took.[1] His resentment of the "low-class" implications of the term "ragtime," which he declared "scurrilous," apparently moved him to develop new and larger variants of the small syncopated tunes he first wrote and which made his reputation. Joplin seemed driven to prove himself through the production of larger works, explorations of extended forms, and through musical forms immediately

---

[1]The score, a facsimile of the 1911 edition, appears in Volume II of Vera Brodsky Lawrence (ed.), *The Collected Works of Scott Joplin* (New York: The New York Public Library, 1971).

acceptable as "genteel" idioms. What could be more natural, then, than to choose the most "high-toned" and upper class of musical forms, the elegant and sumptuous form of grand opera? Yet he continued to draw on folk tunes and vernacular syncopations of Missouri ragtime in all his works. He was caught in a paradoxical situation: the very material he knew best, his unique contribution to American music, was intrinsically "unrespectable," blindly identified as "sinful" or "low-down" by insensitive listeners. Joplin's apprenticeship as an itinerant barroom-bordello "professor" undoubtedly left him with a drive for musical respectability and acceptance. Yet Joplin had the intuitive sense not to abandon his origins, to turn from the pianistic form he had discovered in the playing of Louis Chauvin, Scott Hayden, Arthur Marshall, Tom Turpin, and other Sedalia–St. Louis folk masters.

In *The Ragtime Dance,* Joplin combined the characteristic folk dancing and accompanying ragtime music of the Missouri tradition and wrote them into an elaborately wrought ballet suite, with dance figures identified and "called" as they were to be executed. He produced the piece as an ensemble work, orchestrated for a production in 1899 in Sedalia.[2] It was never as successful as Joplin had anticipated, although John Stark published both the original version and a condensed version (1906) of the dance themes. In this work, Joplin played with the "multimedia" possibilities of narration/singing, ballet, and ragtime music, exploring all avenues of art and vernacular music as they seemed conjoined in his new musical forms. (The work is analogous to one of Stravinsky's later experiments also in part based on ragtime, his *Soldier's Tale* of 1918.) The next logical step in Joplin's progression toward scope and grandeur of form was to full-scale operatic work, which integrates singing, dancing, dramatic narrative, and instrumental music. We can assume that *A Guest of Honor* was a respectable journeyman experiment with the form, in the same manner as

[2] Rudi Blesh, "Scott Joplin: Black-American Classicist," in Lawrence (ed.), *The Collected Works of Scott Joplin,* II, xxiii.

The Ragtime Dance. Although this opera was produced at least once, in rough form, in St. Louis, it also was (apparently) not as successful as Joplin had hoped. It has been lost, and speculation on its form is fruitless.

But we have Joplin's complete piano-conductor's score for *Treemonisha,* his last foray into the extended form he sought, although its original orchestrations are lost. By 1911, Joplin had finished his composition and published the piano-accompaniment version (at his own expense, since commercial music publishers were not interested in such an idiosyncratic large-scale experiment). With *Treemonisha,* several intensely interesting aspects of Joplin's sensibility and genius become apparent.

Treemonisha is a wholly original and highly curious work. It is not precisely a "ragtime opera," as is sometimes said (and as the lost *A Guest of Honor* was explicitly labeled). It contains little "straight" ragtime — nothing like a whole and discrete piano rag — although passages in the piano accompaniment reflect the style of Joplin's most characteristic rags. And it is not even an "opera" in any conventional sense; instead, it is something much more interesting: *it is what Joplin conceived an opera as being.*[3] This shows us a great deal about Joplin's individual genius and about his milieu, for the music recalls many strong musical influences of the turn of the century — Gilbert and Sullivan, typical sentimental show music of the era, spirituals and "plantation songs" performed by black choral groups, sentimental parlor tunes, brass band marches, barbershop harmony, as well as commercial ragtime songs and classic piano ragtime. It contains densely integrated sequences of choruses, solo songs, and dance turns almost in the manner of

[3] This is not to deny the operatic structure which Joplin developed: "Black elements not withstanding, *Treemonisha* is an opera. It has three full acts, an overture to the first act, and introductions to the other two acts; the words are all set to music. It features arias, recitatives, choruses, ensembles, dance, chills and spills brought to you courtesy of the diminished-seventh chord, an implausible story, and a libretto which at its best is only serviceable and to-the-point." Carman Moore, "Notes on Treemonisha," in Lawrence (ed.), *The Collected Works of Scott Joplin,* II, xliii.

a minstrel-style olio. It does not approximate the "advanced" operatic music of the day — Richard Strauss, Puccini, Debussy — but is instead closer to kinds of music Joplin was more likely to hear, to veins of popular and semipopular music usually dubbed "light classics" or some such quasi-respectable term. Joplin undoubtedly hoped the work would be widely popular with a "mass" audience, not necessarily lauded as the successor to Wagner's music-drama. It was, clearly, a work of art in Joplin's imagination, but the art-form he invented was much different from anything before or since, a prophetic form of opera not explored successfully until the Brecht-Weill collaborations of the 1920's.

The libretto of *Treemonisha* is also curious and throws further light on Joplin's imaginative processes. In outline, it is the story of the birth and career of a black leader, a contemplation of the same problem which drove Ralph Ellison to write *Invisible Man* a half-century later — the question of black life, self-determination, and leadership, the quest for self-understanding and self-government for black people in America.[4] Cast in a semimythic or fairytale form, it is both an analogue to black history and a strangely reshaped version of Scott Joplin's own life.

Consider the parallels: Scott Joplin was born near Texarkana, Texas, in 1868, became a musical prodigy, learning classical piano techniques from a local white (German) teacher. He left home quite early, *ca.* 1885, to become an itinerant musician, wandering the South and Southwest, arriving in Missouri at a time when folk piano styles were coalescing into what was first called "jig piano" and would soon be known as ragtime. In his travels, Joplin played in bars and brothels and dreamed of acceptance as a skilled, well-trained artist, imagined himself a famous and respected black composer. One dream, evidently,

[4] In a *Paris Review* interview — *Writers at Work* (New York: Viking Press, 1965) — Ralph Ellison described the genesis of his novel in this way: "I was reading *The Hero* by Lord Raglan and speculating on the nature of Negro leadership in the U.S., I wrote the first paragraph of *Invisible Man,* and was soon involved in the struggle of creating the novel" (p. 328).

was to demonstrate that a black man could, only two decades after emancipation, be considered a great artist, creating music which was genuinely black but clearly a form of art comparable to the best white music. Compare this rough outline of Joplin's youth with its dream-reflection in his own opera libretto.

Treemonisha describes the genesis and life of a black leader, a female (following the matriarchal form of some black communities at that date?) who is found (magically) under a tree just after the Civil War—an emblematic representation of the "new" Negro of freedom, a parentless and newly born heir of a dawning age. The child is called Tree-Monisha, after her adoptive mother (Monisha) and after the tree with which she displays a mystical kinship, a bond something like little Pearl's intuitive connection with nature in *The Scarlet Letter*. Treemonisha, educated by a white woman, is the only literate black person in the locality (near Texarkana, Joplin's birthplace). The prehistory, which Joplin detailed explicitly in a preface to the opera, runs from 1866 to 1884, when the present action of the work commences. This is closely analogous to Joplin's own youth and experience as a child prodigy and his (rare) musical education. Clearly much of Joplin exists in Treemonisha, the child born just after the darkness of slavery, given a chance at education, preparing to lead his race, *ca.* 1885. One powerful vein in the opera is an expression of Joplin's dream-version of his own career.

The story reads like a simple folktale or myth, with Treemonisha growing up to do battle with three folk-sorcerers, conjure-men who hold the black community in superstitious bondage. She defeats them and prepares to lead her people to education, self-advancement, and social improvement through civilized, rational life. As social philosophy or analysis, this is painfully naïve and simpleminded, but as a powerful mythic form, it expresses what must have been Joplin's basic concept of himself and his artistic role. The form of the story is what Freud called the "family romance" myth—the familiar tale of the mysterious, semidivine foundling adopted by mortals (usu-

ally lower-class people of good instincts), who grows up to endure ritual trials and battles and becomes the king or leader of
his people. The root formula for all heroic tales, as Lord Raglan
and Joseph Campbell have catalogued them,[5] it is also a familiar
fantasy of many sensitive children, who suspect that they are of
"secret" royal birth, that their "real" parents are the king and
queen, that the mere mortals who feed and shelter them are base
foster parents. It is most familiar through many fairytales of the
Grimm Brothers or Hans Christian Anderson. In *Treemonisha,*
Joplin used this family romance myth to build an epic picture of
black leadership, as Ellison used the same root myth later in
Invisible Man. It is a basic means of describing imaginatively
the process of heroic leadership.[6]

If the heroine, Treemonisha, is in part Joplin's projection of
himself, she most clearly expresses his sensitivity and his
frustrations with the hard world in which he found himself
trapped. Joplin, like Treemonisha, wanted to lead his people
from ignorance and superstition—to escape from the categoriz-
ing that sneeringly called his music "ragtime" and relegated it
to bordellos. He longed to demonstrate that a black musician
could compose totally new and completely respectable music,
something more than ephemeral ditties or popular musichall
successes. In effect, *Treemonisha* is a self-descriptive, self-
reflective work, and its central story mirrors in only slightly
disguised form Joplin's struggle with its composition and production. Unfortunately, its triumphant conclusion was not
prophetic—Joplin could not, like his heroine, lead his people
off to a New Eden in a stately dance of triumph. But the opera
reflects his deep desire that this occur, his need to serve his
people through his music. Treemonisha's conquest of the three
voodoo men is a fantasy enactment of Joplin's need to conquer

[5] See Lord Raglan, *The Hero* (New York: Oxford University Press, 1937), and Joseph
Campbell, *The Hero with a Thousand Faces* (New York: Pantheon, 1949).
[6] For a fuller description of Ellison's use of the mythological development of the
epic hero, see: William J. Schafer, "Ralph Ellison and the Birth of the Anti-Hero,"
Critique, X (1968), 81–93.

the musical and social establishments which frustrated his drive toward respectability and acceptance as a serious artist.

Further, the myth underlying *Treemonisha* reflects Joplin's sense of black culture and history. Like many black leaders of his era (Booker T. Washington, W. E. B. DuBois), Joplin saw that white aid in education and social advancement was initially indispensable; but his vision of a utopian emancipation and self-advancement was magically quick — one generation (or less), the span of maturity of one young woman. And in a sense *Treemonisha* is a "historical" opera, since it is set some twenty-five years before its composition. Joplin seems to say that black emancipation and self-government was by 1911 an established fact, that men and women of his generation were in fact as free to be rational, responsible leaders as Treemonisha, a parentless young woman from the canebrake country of Arkansas. This basic belief of Joplin's must have been sorely frustrated in his various thwarted schemes to bring his music to serious recognition. The naive optimism of Joplin's feeling in *Treemonisha* is touching, but it is easy to understand why this fairytale did not appeal to the sophisticated black community of Harlem in 1915. It must have seemed a peculiar throwback to the downhome folk literature of an earlier generation, the sort of bucolic folk-fable as dead as the hopes of Reconstruction.

Though its story is a simple fairytale, *Treemonisha's* aesthetic is sophisticated and complex. The root musical style is that of musical comedy or light opera, an amalgam of choral and dance themes scored for eleven voices. The music is not especially difficult, but it demands a feeling for precise timing and rhythm, a deep understanding of black musical idiom, like Joplin's piano rags. The opera depends on a series of scenes or segments loosely organized around Treemonisha's story and the Arkansas backwoods setting, but it is more like a revue or pageant than a music-drama in modern (*i.e.,* nineteenth-century post-Wagner) terms. The feeling is akin to that of Mozart's *The Magic Flute,* in which a naïve mythic/allegoric story is exploited for tone and image rather than for consecutive dramatic narration. Joplin's tale is not nearly as arcane or involuted as Schikaneder's book for Mozart's work, but parallels exist in the "magic" qualities of both operas. More important, Joplin's revue-organization—a series of song/dance set pieces —like Mozart's, frees the music of any heavy dramatic-narrative interest. The plot is bare and translucent as that of most musical comedies or operettas, and the music itself is thus emphasized.

Joplin's vocal idiom in *Treemonisha* is not that of ragtime so much as of pre-ragtime black folksong—choral and solo "plantation" songs, simple dance forms. It is lyrical in feeling, with a strong dance-like quality to instrumental passages as well as in such deliberate balletic pieces as "A Real Slow Drag" (which closes the work) or the "Frolic of the Bears." In this respect, *Treemonisha* is a development of *The Ragtime Dance,* an investigation of the "multimedia" synthesis of drama, singing, narration, and dance in one integral sensuous structure. Like *The Magic Flute,* it depends less on an intellectual apprehension of the "story" (although it is certainly a highly didactic work) than an aesthetic absorption in the *process* of playing, singing, and dancing. This marks *Treemonisha* as a profoundly black work, light-years distant from Wagner's highly intellectualized music-dramas or the stock melodramas of Puccini or Verdi. Dramatic spectacle and apparatus are abandoned for a purely audio-visual appreciation of virtuoso singers and dancers performing. This, too, is close to the basic motivation of vaudeville, minstrelsy, or the revue, where drama is apt to be naïve or rustic, because the audience is not interested in subtlety of literary plot but in style of performance. The aspect of stylization is a very modern attribute of *Treemonisha,* looking forward to the expressionistic opera of, say, Alban Berg or Carl Orff rather than back to the music-theater of the nineteenth century. Like all great black composers, Joplin here put his aesthetic emphasis on the creative personality of his performers, on their ability to express themselves through his score. This is clearly why he fused song and dance elements in the work, why the expression comes as much through the solo and group dances as through formalized arias or virtuoso song passages. Joplin envisioned a cast for the opera capable of total participation—the song-and-dance capabilities of the great vaudeville artists of his day, like Bert Williams or Ernest Hogan.

Another parallel with *Treemonisha* might be the English pantomime stage tradition, which (like *The Magic Flute*) illustrated fairytale stories in loose song-and-dance formats. Or, even earlier, the ballad-opera tradition of the eighteenth century (now known best through John Gay's *The Beggar's Opera,* with music scored by Pepusch) established a form much like that which Joplin re-invented. It is doubtful if Joplin knew about such analogues to his work. Rather, he worked in a direction musically parallel with these genres and rediscovered their basic principles, because he sought the same effects they established—simplicity, a direct charm, lyricism, a folk-level communication of ideas in musical idioms which could readily be absorbed. As the ballad-opera composers worked from common musical fonts, most frequently using extant folk tunes and airs, so Joplin drew on folk idioms of Missouri's black culture (the same source for his version of piano ragtime) as a musical foundation. As the pantomime-writers used simple folktales and fables for vehicles for song and dance, so Joplin erected a revue on a very slender tale of magic, heroism, and tribal celebration.

A social and historical principle seems to dictate that cultures losing track of their real needs and desires get precisely what they deserve. It is not surprising that America was not prepared to listen to *Treemonisha* in 1911. After decades of unparalleled crassness, vulgarity, and social retrogression—the "Gilded Age" and collapse of Radical Reconstruction in the late nineteenth century—America was hardly prepared for a naive, delicate, and almost translucently gentle operatic style. It was not interested in black social or aesthetic advances, and it had no curiosity about Scott Joplin, once his phenomenal success with "Maple Leaf Rag" faded from the popular mind. While black people were vitally interested in questions of social and political progress, as mirrored in statements by W. E. B. DuBois, Booker T. Washington, and other figures of the day, they were not especially attracted to a modest folktale set to lyrical, unpretentious music. *Treemonisha* failed to capture the imagination of its age.

What is more puzzling is the obscurity in which the opera has languished since Joplin published it out of his own pocket in 1911. While it has been mentioned as a curiosity in books and articles on jazz, ragtime, and American music in general, it waited nearly sixty years for a second production after the initial rehearsal which Joplin gave it in New York in 1915. Produced by a brilliant troupe in Atlanta early in 1972, it was well received by audience and critics and may find a place in the small pantheon of respected and performed American operas. One of the first — and finest — examples of opera in a truly American idiom, it is a thoroughly original, imaginative, and enjoyable work of music. It is a bitter irony of history, one of which Joplin was all too aware, that *Treemonisha* could only be produced and appreciated when it had become an exhibit in a museum, safely aged and softened by time.[7]

[7] The question of a demand for a black opera may arise, but there is evidence of an interest in opera in New York City's black community at the time Joplin conceived and wrote *Treemonisha*. Black musicians were breaking into the opera world, and one black singer, Theodore Drury, formed a black troupe that beginning in 1903 "annually performed grand operas, such as 'Carmen,' 'Faust,' and 'Aida' at the Lexington Avenue Opera House in New York City" (Orrin Clayton Suthern II, "Minstrelsy and Popular Culture," in *Remus, Rastus, Revolution*, edited by Marshall Fishwick [Bowling Green, Ohio: Bowling Green University Popular Press, n.d.], 70).

APPENDIX **IV**

Bibliography of Ragtime

The following listing is suggestive rather than exhaustive. In it are listed materials of all sorts which may prove useful to the student or performer of ragtime. Thanks are due to Paul G. Kaatrud, who did the principal work in locating and assembling the information here. The bibliography is organized as follows:

BOOKS

MUSIC
  Collections
  Instruction Books

PERIODICALS
  General
  Individual Musicians
    Eubie Blake
    Scott Joplin
    Joseph Lamb
    James Scott

  Book Reviews
  Record Reviews
  Fiction and Poetry
  Discography and Rollography

NEWSPAPERS
  Ragtime Newsletters
  Articles in Newspapers

RECORD LINER NOTES

BOOKS

Blesh, Rudi. *Combo U.S.A.: Eight Lives in Jazz*. Philadelphia: Chilton Book Co., 1971. Chapter, "Little Eubie (Eubie Blake)," 187–217.

Blesh, Rudi, and Harriet Janis. *They All Played Ragtime: The True Story of an American Music*. 4th ed. New York: Oak Publications, 1971.

Brown, Sterling. "Negro Producers of Ragtime." Pp. 49–50 in *The Negro in Music and Art,* edited by Lindsay Patterson. International Library of Negro Life and History, Vol. XVI. New York: Publishers Co., 1967.

Charters, Samuel B., and Leonard Kunstadt. *Jazz: A History of the New York Scene.* Garden City, N.Y.: Doubleday and Co., 1962. Chapter 3, "Treemonisha," 42–50.

Chase, Gilbert. *America's Music from the Pilgrims to the Present.* New York: McGraw-Hill, 1955. Chapter 21, "The Rise of Ragtime," 433–51.

Fletcher, Tom. *100 Years of the Negro in Show Business.* New York: Burdge and Co., Ltd., 1954.

Goffin, Robert. *Jazz from the Congo to the Metropolitan.* Garden City, N.Y.: Doubleday, Doran and Co., 1944. Pp. 22–42.

Gold, Robert S. *A Jazz Lexicon.* New York: Alfred A. Knopf, 1964. Pp. 243–45.

Goldberg, Isaac. *Tin Pan Alley: A Chronicle of the American Popular Music Racket.* New York: John Day Co., 1930. Pp. 139–77.

Grossman, Stefan. *Ragtime Blues Guitarists.* New York: Oak Publications, 1965.

Harris, Rex. *The Story of Jazz.* Edited by Thomas K. Sherman. New York: Grosset and Dunlap, 1960. Pp. 28–30.

Hitchcock, H. Wiley. *Music in the United States: A Historical Introduction.* Englewood Cliffs, N.J.: Prentice-Hall, 1969. Pp. 119–25.

Hofmann, Heinz Peter, and Peter Czerny. *Der Schlager: Ein Panorama der leichten Musik. Band I.* Berlin: VEB Lied der Zeit, 1968. Pp. 227–34. (Section on the cakewalk and ragtime as predecessors of the new social dances.)

Howard, Laura Pratt. "Ragtime," M.M. thesis in theory. Eastman School of Music, University of Rochester, 1942.

Johnson, James Weldon. *Autobiography of an Ex-Colored Man.* New York: Hill and Wang, 1960.

———. "Preface," *The Book of American Negro Poetry,* edited by James Weldon Johnson. New York: Harcourt, Brace, 1931. Pp. 10–17.

Kaufman, Helen L. *From Jehovah to Jazz.* New York: Dodd-Mead, 1937. Pp. 240–54.

Lange, Horst H. *Jazz in Deutschland: Die deutsche Jazz-Chronik, 1900–1960.* Berlin: Colloquium Verlag, 1966. Pp. 7–14.

List, George, and Juan Orrego-Salas, eds. *Music in the Americas.* Bloomington, Ind.: Indiana University Publications, 1967. Essay, "Hot Rhythm in Ragtime," by Frank Gillis, 91–104.

Locke, Alain. *The Negro and His Music.* "Negro Culture and History." Port Washington, N.Y.: Kennikat Press, 1968. (Originally published by Associates in Negro Folk Education, 1936.) Also published with the author's *Negro Art: Past and Present* in the series "American Negro: His History and Literature," New York: Arno Press, 1969.

Mellers, Wilfred. *Music in a New Found Land: Themes and Developments in the History of American Music.* London: Barrie and Rockliff, 1964. Pp. 276–80.

Sargeant, Winthrop. *Jazz: Hot and Hybrid.* 2nd ed. New York: E. P. Dutton and Co., 1946. Pp. 131–46.

Schwerke, Irving. *Kings David and Jazz.* Paris: privately printed for the author, 1927. Pp. 31–39.

Southern, Eileen. *The Music of Black Americans: A History.* New York: W. W. Norton, 1971. Pp. 310–39.

Stearns, Marshall. *The Story of Jazz.* New York: Oxford University Press, 1956. Pp. 140–49.

Waterman, Guy. "A Survey of Ragtime" and "Joplin's Late Rags." Pp. 11–31 in *The Art of Jazz,* edited by Martin T. Williams. New York: Oxford University Press, 1959. (Mr. Waterman has informed us that his musical examples are incorrectly reproduced in this volume, although the texts of the essays are correct. See the original appearances of these essays, listed below under the Periodicals heading.)

————. "Ragtime." Pp. 45–57 in *Jazz,* edited by Nat Henthoff and Albert J. McCarthy. New York: Rinehart and Co., 1959.

————. *Jelly Roll Morton.* New York: A. S. Barnes and Co., 1963. Pp. 34–44.

Witmark, Isadore. *The Story of the House of Witmark: From Ragtime to Swing Time.* New York: L. Furman, 1939.

MUSIC

COLLECTIONS

Charters, Ann, ed. *The Ragtime Songbook.* New York: Oak Publications, 1965.

Lawrence, Vera Brodsky, ed. *The Collected Works of Scott Joplin.* 2 vols. New York: New York Public Library, 1971.

Morath, Max, ed. *Guide to Ragtime: A Collection of Ragtime Songs and Piano Solos.* New York: Hollis, 1964.

————, ed. *One Hundred Ragtime Classics.* Denver: Donn Printing, 1963.

INSTRUCTION BOOKS

Harney, Benjamin Robertson. *Ben Harney's Rag Time Instructor.* New York: M. Witmark and Sons; Chicago: Sol Bloom, 1897.
Joplin, Scott. *The School of Ragtime.* Sedalia, Mo.: John Stark and Son, 1908. (Also available in *The Collected Works of Scott Joplin,* edited by Vera Brodksy Lawrence. 2 vols.; New York: New York Public Library, 1971.)

PERIODICALS

GENERAL

Affeldt, Paul. "Editorial," *Jazz Report,* I (January, 1961), 20–21. (Discusses interest in ragtime and efforts to preserve it.)
"America's Best Writers and Composers (of Ragtime)," *Tuneful Yankee,* I (January, 1917), 37 f.
Anderson, J. L. "Evolution of Jazz," *Down Beat,* XVI (September 9, 1949), 14; (September 23, 1949), 10.
Autolycus. " 'Rag-Time' on Parnassus," *Musical Opinion,* XXXVI (February, 1913), 328–29.
Bickford, Myron A. "Something About Ragtime," *Cadenza,* XX (September, 1913), 13; (November, 1913), 10–11.
Blesh, Rudi. "Ragtime Revaluated," *Playback,* II (May, 1949), 5–6.
Borneman, E. "One Night Stand: Early American Piano Music," *Melody Maker,* XXVII (March 17, 1951), 2.
Bowman, James C. "Anti-Ragtime," *New Republic,* V (November 6, 1915), 19.
"Brings Back Ragtime, Gordon Leader of the Band," *Billboard,* LXXVI (July 18, 1964), 10.
Buchanan, Charles L. "Ragtime and American Music," *Opera Magazine,* III (February, 1916), 17–19 ff.
———. "Two Views of Ragtime. II. Ragtime and American Music," *Seven Arts,* II (July, 1917), 376–83.
Burk, John N. "Ragtime Has Its Possibilities," *Opera Magazine,* II (January, 1914), 11–13.
Cadman, Charles W. "Rag-Time," *Musical Courier,* LXIX (August 12, 1914), 31.
Campbell, S. Brunson. "Early Great White Ragtime Composers and Pianists," *Jazz Journal,* II (May, 1949), 11–12.
———. "More on Ragtime," *Jazz Journal,* IV (May, 1951), 4.
———. "Ragtime," *Jazz Journal,* II (April, 1949), 9–10.
———. "Ragtime Begins," *Record Changer,* VII (March, 1948), 8 ff.

Carew, Roy J. "Assorted Rags," *Record Changer,* VIII (February, 1948), 6.

———. "Those Days Are Not Gone Forever," *Playback,* II (July, 1949), 6 ff.

———. "Hodge Podge," *Jazz Report,* II (September, 1961), 3–5.

Cassidy, R., and T. Tichenor. "Are We Ready for an International Ragtime Fraternity?" *Jazz Report,* I (April, 1961), 11–12.

Charters, A. R. Danberg. "Negro Folk Elements in Classic Ragtime," *Ethnomusicology,* V (1961), 174–83.

"Concerning Ragtime," *Musical Monitor,* VIII (September, 1919), 619.

"Concert in Ragtime," *Variety,* CCXXVI (May 16, 1962), 60.

Cook, Will Marion. "Clorindy, the Origin of the Cakewalk," *Theatre Arts,* XXXI (September, 1947), 61.

Converse, C. Crozat. "Rag-Time Music," *Etude,* XVII (June, 1899), 185; (August, 1899), 256.

Damon, S. Foster, "American Influence on Modern French Music," *Dial,* LXV (August 15, 1918), 93–95.

Davin, T. "Conversations with James P. Johnson," *Jazz Review,* II (June, 1959), 14–17.

Downes, Olin. "An American Composer," *Musical Quarterly,* IV (January, 1918), 23–36.

"Ducasse Uses Ragtime in New Tone Poem," *Musical America,* XXXVII (March 10, 1923), 15.

"The Ethics of Ragtime," *Jacobs' Orchestra Monthly,* III (August, 1912), 27–29.

Farjeon, Harry. "Rag-Time," *Musical Times,* LXV (September, 1924), 795–97.

———. "Rag-Time," *New Music Review and Church Music Review,* XXIII (November, 1924), 513–15.

Featherstone, J. G. "Ragtime: A Comment," *Storyville,* No. 11 (June–July, 1967), 29–30.

"Flays Rag-Time As Not Reflecting Americanism," *Musical America,* XXVIII (July 20, 1918), 22.

Gates, W. F. "Ethiopian Syncopation—The Decline of Ragtime," *Musician,* VII (October, 1902), 341.

Godwin, H. E. "The Sixth Annual St. Louis Ragtime Festival," *Second Line,* XXIII (July–August, 1970), 352 ff.

Goodrich, A. J. "Syncopated Rhythm vs. 'Rag-Time,'" *Musician,* VI (November, 1901), 336.

"Great American Composer—Will He Speak in the Accent of Broadway?" *Current Opinion,* LXIII (November, 1917), 316–17.

Hazeldine, M. "Ragtime: A Further Comment," *Storyville,* No. 12 (August–September, 1967), 4–5.

Henderson, W. J. "Ragtime, Jazz, and High Art," *Scribner's,* LXXVII (February, 1925), 200–203.

"Hot Plunk from a Pub," *Life,* XXXV (December 14, 1953), 89–90.

Hubbard, W. L. "Hopeful View of the Ragtime Roll," *Musician,* XXV (August, 1920), 6.

Hubbs, Harold. "What Is Ragtime?" *Outlook,* CXVIII (February 27, 1918), 345.

Hughes, Rupert. "A Eulogy of Ragtime," *Musical Record,* 447 (April, 1918), 157–59.

———. "Will Ragtime Turn to Symphonic Poems?" *Etude,* XXXVIII (May, 1920), 305.

"The International Ragtime Society on Launching Pad," *Jazz Report,* II (November, 1961), 22.

Jason, D. A. "Ragtime: A Re-evaluation," *Jazz Journal* (April, 1968), 22–23; also, *Ragtimer* (Weston, Ontario), VI (1967), 26–28.

"Jazz and Ragtime Are the Preludes to a Great American Music," *Current Opinion,* LXIX (August, 1920), 199–201.

"Jazz? Swing? It's Ragtime," *Time,* XLVI (November 5, 1945), 62–63.

Judson, Arthur L. "Works of American Composers Reveal Relation of Ragtime to Art-Song," *Musical America,* XV (December 2, 1911), 29.

Kaufmann, H. L. "From Ragtime to Swing: Short History of Popular Music," *Scholastic,* XXXII (April 30, 1938), 29–30 ff.

Kay, G. W. "Basin Street Stroller: New Orleans and Tony Jackson," *Jazz Journal,* IV (June, 1951), 1–3.

———. "Ragged But Right," *Record Changer,* IX (March, 1950), 5 ff.

———. "Reminiscing in Ragtime: Recollections of Roy J. Carew," *Jazz Journal,* XVII (November, 1964), 8–9.

Kramer, A. Walter. "Extols Ragtime Article," *New Republic,* V (December 4, 1915), 122.

Laurie, J., Jr. "The Ragtime Kids," *Variety,* CLXXIX (August 9, 1950), 51 f.

Liebling, Leonard. "The Crime of Ragtime," *Musical Courier,* LXXII (1916), 21–22.

Lucas, J. "Lucas Hails Dixie Uprising," *Down Beat,* XVII (November 3, 1950), 5.

———. "Ragtime Revival," *Record Changer,* VII (December, 1948), 8.

McCarthy, A. "Early Piano Jazz and Ragtime Played on Piano Rolls," *Jazz Monthly*, No. 185 (July, 1970), 20.

Mason, Daniel Gregory. "Concerning Ragtime," *New Music Review and Church Music Review*, XVII (March, 1918), 112–16.

––––––. "Folk Song and American Music," *Musical Quarterly*, IV (July, 1918), 323–32.

––––––. "Prefers Demonstration to Cheers (H. K. Moderwell's argument in favor of ragtime)," *New Republic*, IV (December 4, 1915), 122.

Mitchell, B. "Those Ragtime Years (television program)," *Jazz Report*, I (June, 1961), 7–8.

Moderwell, Hiram K. "American Ragtime," *New Republic*, IV (October 16, 1915), 284–86.

––––––. "Two Views of Ragtime. I. A Modest Proposal," *Seven Arts*, II (July, 1917), 368–76.

––––––. "Ragtime and Its Possibilities," *Opera Magazine*, II (June, 1915), 24.

Morath, Max. "Any Rags Today?" *Music Journal*, XVIII (October, 1960), 76–77.

––––––. "First There Was Ragtime," *Jazz Report*, II (January, 1962), 8–9. (Reprinted from *Music Journal*.)

––––––. "Ragtime – Folk Music of the City," *Music Journal*, XXII (November, 1964), 29–30 f.

Morgan, William J. "A Defense of Jazz and Ragtime," *Melody*, VI (September, 1922), 5.

Moynahan, James H. S. "Ragtime to Swing," *Saturday Evening Post*, CCIX (February 13, 1937), 14–15 ff.

Narodny, Ivan. "The Birth Processes of Ragtime," *Musical America*, XVII (March 29, 1913), 27.

"Negro's Contribution to American Art," *Literary Digest*, LV (October 20, 1917), 26–27.

Nelson, Stanley. "A Jubilee of Jazz, 1910–1935," *London Dancing Times*, new series, CCCI (October, 1935), 71.

Norris, J. "They Still Play Ragtime," *Down Beat*, XXXV (October 17, 1968), 14 f.

Oehlmer, Leo. "Ragtime," *Musical Observer*, XI (September, 1914), 14–15.

"Old Ragtimer," *Time*, XXVI (August 5, 1935), 54.

"Origin of Rag-Time," *Brainard's Musical*, I (Autumn, 1899), 6.

"Origin of Rag-Time," *Metronome*, XVII (August, 1901), 7.

Ostransky, L. "A Short Course in the History of Jazz," *Educational Music Magazine*, XXXIV (November–December, 1954), 16–17.

Pease, Sharon A. "Ragtime Ash, Busy with TV, Niteries, Radio," *Down Beat,* XVII (June 2, 1950), 18.

"Questions and Answers," *Etude,* XVI (October, 1898), 285; (December, 1898), 349; XVIII (February, 1900), 52.

"Rag-Time," *Musician,* V (March, 1900), 83.

"Ragtime," *Jazz Forum,* No. 4 (April, 1947), 5–7.

"Ragtime," *Record Changer,* X (July–August, 1951), 12–13.

"Rag Time and Program Making," *American Musician,* XXVIII (August 10, 1912), 10.

"Ragtime as a Source of National Music," *Musical America,* XVII (February 15, 1913), 37.

"Ragtime Game," *New Yorker,* XXXVI (July 2, 1960), 20–21.

"Rag Time, Old and New," *Brainard's Musical,* I (Autumn, 1899), 2.

"Ragtime Wrangling," *Literary Digest,* LII (January 8, 1916), 68–70.

"Remarks on Rag-Time," *Musical Courier,* LXVI (May 28, 1913), 22–23.

"Report on Ragtime," *Jazz Monthly,* IX (April, 1963), 7–8.

Robertson, C. A. "Knocky Parker: Old Rags," *Audio,* XLII (February, 1958), 44.

Rogers, Charles Payne. "Ragtime," *Jazz,* I (June, 1942), 10–12.

Rust, Brian. "Ragtime su dischi; prima che ci fosse il jazz," *Musica Jazz,* XX (August–September, 1964), 28–29.

———. "Ragtime on Records," *Storyville,* No. 27 (February–March, 1970), 110–13.

Sachs-Herbert, Hirsch. "Dangers That Lie in Ragtime," *Musical America,* XVI (September 21, 1912), 8.

Saenger, Gustav. "The Musical Possibilities of Rag-Time," *Metronome,* XIX (March, 1903), 11; (April, 1903), 8.

Scoggins, Charles H. "The Ragtime Menace," *Musical Progress,* II (April, 1913), 3–4.

"Sedalia, Missouri Stakes Claim as Birthplace of Ragtime: Pitches for Historical Status," *Variety,* CCXL (November 10, 1965), 1 ff.

Shapiro, E. "Ragtime, U.S.A.," *Notes,* VIII (June, 1951), 457–70.

Shaw, J. L. "First Recordings of Jazz, Spelled 'Jass,' " *Variety,* CLXXXVIII (October 1, 1952), 95.

Sherlock, Charles Reginald. "From Breakdown to Rag-Time," *Cosmopolitan,* XXXI (October, 1901), 631–39.

Simms, B. D., and Ernest Borneman. "Ragtime, History and Analysis," *Record Changer,* IV (October, 1945), 8.

Smith, C. E. "The Chicken and the Egg," *Record Changer,* VIII (August, 1949), 7 ff; (September, 1949), 13–14 ff. (Part II entitled "From Jelly Roll to Bop.")

Spottswood, R., and D. A. Jason. "Discoveries Concerning Recorded Ragtime," *Jazz Journal,* XXI (February, 1968), 7.

Stewart-Baxter, D. "Preachin' the Blues," *Jazz Journal,* IV (December, 1951), 5–6 f.

"Syncopated Melody Not Negro Music," *Music Trade Review,* XLVIII (February 20, 1909), 15.

"Syncopation," *Brainard's Musical,* I (Autumn, 1899), 27.

Thompson, K. C. "More on Ragtime," *Record Changer,* VIII (October, 1949), 9–10 f.

––––––. "Ragtime vs. the Blues," *Jazz Journal,* III (November, 1950), 1–3.

––––––. "Ragtime and Jelly Roll," *Record Changer,* VIII (April, 1949), 8 ff.

––––––. "Reminiscing in Ragtime: An Interview with Brun Campbell," *Jazz Journal,* III (April, 1950), 4–5.

"'To Jazz' or 'To Rag,'" *Literary Digest,* LXXIII (May 6, 1922), 37.

Toye, Francis. "Ragtime: The New Tarantism," *English Review,* XIII (March, 1913), 654–58.

Traill, S. "Jig-Piano or Ragtime – It Still Has a Beat," *Melody Maker,* XXVI (December 23, 1950), 654–58.

W. H. A. "Rag-Time," *Metronome,* XV (May, 1899), 4.

Walker, E. S. "Early Jazz/Ragtime," *Jazz Monthly,* No. 186 (August, 1970), 28.

"War on Ragtime," *American Musician,* V (July, 1901), 4.

Waterman, Guy. "Ragtime: Piano Roll Classics," *Jazz Review,* I (December, 1958), 42.

––––––. "A Survey of Ragtime," *Record Changer,* XIV (1955), 7–9.

"Where It Was! 1970 Edition (Los Angeles, Calif.)," *Jazz Report,* VII (1970), 3–4.

Wilford, C. "Collector's Corner (Review of Recordings of Ragtime Piano Rolls, Vols. I and II)," *Melody Maker,* XXX (October 23, 1954), 13.

"Will Ragtime Save the Soul of the Native American Composer?" *Current Opinion,* LIX (December, 1917), 406–407.

Winn, Edward R. "Ragtime Piano Playing," *Cadenza,* XXI (March, 1915), 6–7; (April, 1915), 4–6; (May, 1915), 2–4; (June, 1915), 3–4; XXII (July, 1915), 2–4; (August, 1915), 3–5; (September, 1915), 3–4; (October, 1915), 3–4; (November, 1915), 3–4; (December, 1915), 2–5; (January, 1916), 2–3; (February, 1916), 2–3; (March, 1916), 3–4; (April, 1916), 3; (May, 1916), 3; (June, 1916), 3; XIII (July, 1916), 3–4; (August, 1916), 3; (September, 1916), 3–4; (October, 1916), 3–4.

ON INDIVIDUAL MUSICIANS

Eubie Blake

Ackerman, P. "Eubie Blake Takes a Session at Studio in Stride," *Billboard*, LXXXI (February 22, 1969), 6 f.

Bellantonio, D. D. "Eubie Blake," *Jazz and Pop*, VIII (March, 1969), 24–26.

Davies, J. R. "Eubie Blake, His Life and Times," *Storyville*, No. 6 (August, 1966), 19–20; No. 7 (October, 1966), 12–13 f.

"Eubie Blake Celebrates His Eighty-Second Birthday," *Second Line*, XVI (January–February, 1965), 23.

"Eubie Blake Honored," *Variety*, CCLIX (June 17, 1970), 47.

"Eubie Blake Honored (recipient of first James P. Johnson Award)," *International Musician*, LXIX (August, 1970), 13.

"Yale University Band Recruits Ted Lewis, Sissle and Blake As Honorary Members," *Variety*, CCLVIII (April 29, 1970), 13.

Scott Joplin

Campbell, S. Brunson. "From Rags to Ragtime," *Jazz Report*, V (1967), 5–6.

_____. "The Ragtime Kid (An Autobiography)," *Jazz Report*, VI (1967), 9–14; (November, 1967), 7–12.

Charters, Ann. "The First Negro Folk Opera! 'Treemonisha,'" *Jazz Monthly*, VIII (August, 1962), 6–11.

Hoefer, G. "Missouri Group Honors Memory of Scott Joplin," *Down Beat*, XIX (January 25, 1952), 9.

"King of the Ragtimers," *Time*, LVI (October 30, 1950), 48.

Testoni, G. "Gli autori dei temi," *Musica Jazz*, XV (December, 1959), 37.

Thompson, Kay C. "Lottie Joplin," *Record Changer*, IX (October, 1950), 8 f.

Waterman, Guy. "Joplin's Late Rags: An Analysis," *Record Changer*, XIV (1956), 5–8.

Joseph Lamb

Cassidy, R. "Joseph Lamb—Last of the Ragtime Composers," *Jazz Monthly*, VII (August, 1961), 4–7; (October, 1961), 12–15; (November, 1961), 9–10; (January, 1962), 1–6; (February, 1962), 1–4; (March, 1962), 1–3; (April, 1962), 7–8.

"Inside Stuff—Music," *Variety,* CCXVI (October 7, 1959), 65.
"Joseph Francis Lamb Dies," *Second Line,* No. 3–4 (1961), 15.
Montgomery, M. "Joseph F. Lamb—A Ragtime Paradox, 1887–1960," *Second Line,* No. 3–4 (1961), 17–18.
(Obituary), *Jazz Monthly,* VI (December, 1960), 16; *Jazz Report,* I (October, 1960), 12; *Variety,* CCXX (September 28, 1960), 79.
Tichenor, T. J. "The World of Joseph Lamb: An Exploration," *Jazz Monthly,* VII (August, 1961), 7–9; (October, 1961), 15–17; (November, 1961), 10–11; (December, 1961), 16–17. Also, *Jazz Report,* I (January, 1961), 7–10; (February, 1961), 4–6; (March, 1961), 5–6; (April, 1961), 9–10; (August, 1961), 7–9; (October, 1961), 15–17; (November, 1961), 10–11; (December, 1961), 16–17.

James Scott

Affeldt, P. "James Scott, 'Crown Prince of Ragtime,'" *Jazz Report,* I (October, 1960), 7–9.

BOOK REVIEWS

Guide to Ragtime, by Max Morath, reviewed in *Second Line,* XV (1964), 28; and *Sing Out,* XV (1965), 55–56.
One Hundred Ragtime Classics, by Max Morath, reviewed in *Ethnomusicology,* VIII (1964), 371 f.
The Ragtime Songbook, edited by Ann Charters, reviewed in *Jazz Journal,* XVIII (August, 1965), 13 f; and *Notes,* XXII (1966), 1312–13.
They All Played Ragtime, by Rudi Blesh and Harriet Janis, reviewed in: *Saturday Review of Literature,* XXXIII (November 25, 1950), 30; *Jazz Journal,* IV (February, 1951), 235; *Musical America,* LXXI (July, 1951), 36; *Melody Maker,* XXXIII (May 10, 1958), 6; *Gramophone,* XXXVI (September, 1958), 181; *Jazz Journal,* XIV (July, 1961), 36; *Jazz Monthly,* VII (October, 1961), 30; *Music Educators Journal,* LIII (October, 1966), 14; *Down Beat,* XXXIII (November 17, 1966), 42; *Second Line,* XVII (November–December, 1966), 160–61; and *Jazz Report,* V (1966), 4.

RECORD REVIEWS

Mitchell, B. E. Review of "Max Morath Plays The Entertainer and Other Rag Classics, with Jim Tyler," *Jazz Report,* VI (1967), 5–6.
———. Review of "Golden Treasury of Ragtime," *Jazz Report,* V (1966), 3–4.

Review of "Joseph Lamb—A Study in Classic Ragtime," *Jazz Report*, I (January, 1961), 23–24.
Winner, L. Review of "The Eighty-Six Years of Eubie Blake," *Rolling Stone*, LIV (March 19, 1970), 50.

FICTION AND POETRY

Frankau, G. "Rag-Time Hero (Story)," *Century*, XCIII (December, 1916), 290–96.
"Ragtime in the Trenches (Poem)," *Literary Digest*, LII (April 8, 1916), 997.
Von Hutten, Baroness. "Ragtime (Story)," *Putnam's Magazine*, VII (March, 1910), 690–93.

DISCOGRAPHY AND ROLLOGRAPHY

"Discographies of Ragtime Recordings," *Jazz Forum*, No. 4 (April, 1947), 7–8.
Montgomery, M. "Eubie Blake Rollography," *Record Research*, No. 27 (March–April, 1960), 19.
_____. "Revised Eubie Blake Rollography," *Record Research*, No. 33 (March, 1961), 16.
_____. "Scott Joplin Rollography," *Record Research*, No. 22 (April–May, 1959), 2.
Stanleigh, B. "Jazz (recordings)," *Audio*, LIV (February, 1970), 76.

NEWSPAPERS

RAGTIME NEWSLETTERS

Rag Times. Newsletter of The Maple Leaf Club, Los Angeles, California.
The Ragtimer. Newsletter of The Ragtime Society, Weston, Ontario, Canada.
Ragtime Review. Chicago, I–IV, No. 7 (December 1914–January, 1918). Vols. I–II, No. 5 (1914–April, 1916), issued as *Christensen's Ragtime Review*.

ARTICLES IN NEWSPAPERS

"Musical Gossip," New York *Daily Tribune*, April 15, 1900, III, 8:1.

"The Origin of Ragtime," New York *Times,* March 23, 1924, IX, 2:8.

"Ragtime," London *Times,* February 8, 1913, 11:3–4.

Record Liner Notes

Affeldt, Paul. Notes on "The Professors: Brun Campbell and Dink Johnson," Euphonic ESR 1201 and 2102.

Allen, Richard B., and William Russell. Notes on "The New Orleans Ragtime Orchestra," Pearl PLP 7 and 8.

Blesh, Rudi. Notes on "They All Play Ragtime," Jazzology JCE 52.

————. Notes on "William Bolcom: Heliotrope Bouquet; Piano Rags, 1900–1970," Nonesuch H–71257.

Bolcom, William. Notes on "William Bolcom: Heliotrope Bouquet; Piano Rags, 1900–1970," Nonesuch H–71257.

Bourne, David E. Notes on "Dawn of the Century Ragtime Orchestra," Arcane 1.

Charters, Samuel B. Notes on "Ann Charters: A Joplin Bouquet," Portents 1.

————. Notes on "Ann Charters: Essay in Ragtime," Folkways FG 5363.

————. Notes on "Joseph Lamb: A Study in Classic Ragtime," Folkways FG 3562.

————. Notes on "The New Ragtime Guitar," Asch AHS–3528.

————. Notes on "Ragtime 1, The City: Banjos, Brass Bands, and Nickel Pianos," Record, Book, and Film Sales, RBF 17.

————. Notes on "Ragtime 2, The Country: Mandolins, Fiddles, and Guitars," Record, Book, and Film Sales, RBF 18.

Grinstead, Dan. Notes on "Louis Delano: The Music of Joe Jordan," Arpeggio ARP 1205S.

Hoefer, George. Notes on "Hank Jones: This is Ragtime Now!" ABC-Paramount 496.

Kimball, Robert E. Notes on "The Eighty-Six Years of Eubie Blake," Columbia C2S–847.

Notes on "Knocky Parker: The Complete Piano Works of James Scott," Audiophile AP 76–77.

Notes on "Knocky Parker: The Complete Works of Scott Joplin," Audiophile AP 71–72.

Koenig, Lester. Notes on "Wally Rose: Ragtime Classics," Good Time Jazz S-10034.

Montgomery, Michael. Notes on "Scott Joplin—1916: Classic Solos Played by the King of Ragtime Writers and Others from Rare Piano Rolls," Biograph BLP 1006Q.

Raichelson, Dick. Notes on "Ragged Piano Classics," Origin Jazz Library OJL 15.
Rifkin, Joshua. Notes on "Piano Rags by Scott Joplin," Nonesuch H-71248 and H-71264.
Rust, Brian. Notes on "I'll Dance Till the Dawn Breaks Through: Ragtime, Cakewalks, and Stomps," Vol. II, Saydisc SDL 210.
Tichenor, T. J. Notes on "The Piano Roll Ragtime and Other Piano Rolls," Record, Book, and Film Sales, RBF 7.

Index